THE ANALYSIS OF
PUBLIC POLICY

THE ANALYSIS OF PUBLIC POLICY

A Bibliography of Dissertations, 1977-1982

Compiled by
John S. Robey

Greenwood Press
Westport, Connecticut • London, England

627/20

Ref

H
97
· R619
1984

Library of Congress Cataloging in Publication Data

Robey, John S.
   The analysis of public policy.

   Bibliography: p.
   Includes index.
   1. Policy sciences—Bibliography. 2. Dissertations,
Academic—Bibliography. I. Title.
Z7161.R587 1984 [H97] 016.35'007'2   83-22556
ISBN 0-313-23957-6 (lib. bdg.)

Library of Congress Catalog Card Number: 83-22556
ISBN: 0-313-23957-6

First published in 1984

Greenwood Press
A division of Congressional Information Service, Inc.
88 Post Road West, Westport, Connecticut 06881

Printed in the United States of America

10 9 8 7 6 5 4 3 2 1

Contents

Introduction

Review of the Literature

Public policy analysis has been defined as a discipline that attempts to determine what governments do, why they do it, and what difference it makes. Policy analysis has a strong interdisciplinary flavor to it--traditional policy analysts could easily fit into history, sociology, or philosophy departments. Since the emergence of the behavioral "revolution" in the thirties, however, policy analysis has expanded into even more disciplines such as political science, public administration, and economics. The emergence of the scientific analysis of public policy has resulted in a discipline that is not only inter- disciplinary but one that is committed to objective, value-free inquiry. The objective of this approach is to reduce unexplained variation in the policies being examined. For example, if Aid to Families with Dependent Children (AFDC) varies from $100 a month in Mississippi to $300 a month in Connecticut, the policy analyst attempts to answer why that variation exists.

The policy scientists are not as interested in persuading others that a policy is "good" or "bad" as they are in explaining what variables might associate at statistically significant levels. This interest leads the value-free scientist to avoid using prescriptive terminology (that is, good, bad, ought, should) in favor of quantitative techniques which are objective. Interest in quantification of data has led the policy analyst to develop statistical and computer skills.

The early attempts at explaining (not merely describing) policy variables led political scientists to assert the centrality of political variables. This early work by V. O. Key, Duane Lockard, and John Fenton resulted in much emphasis being placed on measures of political participation and competition.[1] In the early sixties, however, Richard Dawson and James Robinson found that nine measures of welfare variation were more significantly associated with measures of a state's economic characteristics than political participation or competition.[2] In the mid-sixties, Thomas Dye published his classic Politics, Economics, and the Public, which found that not only welfare policy, but a great many of the states' policy enactments were more closely associated with economic rather than political variables.[3] This finding was disconcerting to a great number of political scientists, especially those who were heavily committed to pluralist values.

In the late sixties and early seventies, Ira Sharkansky and Richard Hofferbert attempted to use more sophisticated statistical techniques; additional policy variables other than public expenditures were examined by Brian Fry and Richard Winters; Virginia Gray examined policy variation over time; Charles Cnudde and Donald McCrone introduced causal modeling; and Jack Walker systematically examined policy innovation.[4] Much of this research was directed toward reestablishing the importance of political determinants. Dye was labeled an "economic determinist" in an attempt to show that somehow in a pluralist democracy "politics counts." However, recent attempts using path analysis to examine the causes of social security spending in sixty countries led Harold Wilensky to conclude that "economic growth makes countries with contrasting cultural and political traditions more alike in their strategy for constructing the floor below which no one sinks."[5] In other words, presumably the social security effort of the economically developed, democratic United States is more similar to the social security effort of the economically developed, authoritarian USSR than it is to democratic but economically undeveloped Costa Rica.

The difficult task of constructing causal models that illuminate sequential and developmental stages of how political as well as economic variables interact with public policies is an attempt to go beyond the use of statistical tests of association (that is, correlation and regression). Perhaps the most sophisticated analysis of the causal implications of the determinants of state policies has been conducted by Michael Lewis-Beck.[6] In a recent essay, he maintains that one cannot at the same time maintain that both the economic model and the political competition-participation model are valid. He rejects the use of both partial correlation coefficients and standardized beta regression coefficients in favor of a three-variable recursive system and a path analytic test using "effects" coefficients. The use of effects coefficients to determine the relationship of economic affluence, competition-participation, and welfare and educational policies was an advancement in methodological sophistication because it examined both direct and indirect effects of causal variables. Lewis-Beck's findings confirmed the original groundbreaking work of Dye. Lewis-Beck writes: "When the effects coefficients for a common model of welfare policy are estimated in a data-based example, socioeconomic variables are found to be considerably more important than political variables."

In sum, it would seem that the recent methodological innovations of path analysis, causal modeling, and the use of effects coefficients have strengthened the case of the economic determinists. Of course, we have not yet heard the final word. The staggering growth of policy science in the past decade is likely to continue (unlike most other subfields of political science and public administration), and one will see further methodological innovations as well as the publication of further research findings. Certainly the breadth of interests of those involved in policy analysis has increased in recent years. This field of academic inquiry has already matured to the point where some of the leading universities in the nation (for example, Florida State University, University of California at Berkeley, and Harvard) are now offering

doctoral programs in policy analysis. The reference volume on doctoral
dissertations in the policy sciences submitted here is one small
testimony to that healthy trend.

Scope

      This volume offers the only systematic and thorough guide to the
research findings of over one thousand recent English language dissertations. Most were submitted at universities in the United States, but
institutions in Canada are also represented. They were selected from
those reported in Dissertation Abstracts International in dozens of
specific policy areas. Disregarding areas of relatively minor concern,
sixteen fields of concentration were chosen on the basis of the amount
and scope of work being done, and serve as chapter headings, as follows:

      1. Policy Analysis
      2. Policy Making at the State Level
      3. Policy Making at the Local Level
      4. Public Administration and the Making of Public Policy
      5. Agricultural Policy
      6. Civil Rights and the Status of Women
      7. Domestic Taxing and Economic Policy
      8. Educational Policy
      9. U.S. Foreign Policy
     10. Governmental Regulation of Morality: Sex, Drugs, and Abortion
     11. Housing Policy
     12. Energy and the Environment
     13. International Trade and Economics
     14. Judicial Policy Making
     15. Military Policy
     16. Social, Health, and Welfare Policy

Arrangement within each chapter is alphabetical by author, and entries
are numbered sequentially throughout the volume. Each entry states the
author and title of the dissertation, the institution at which it was
accepted, and the year of acceptance. Annotations are based on the
candidates' own abstracts as printed in Dissertation Abstracts
International. Volume and page references to that publication are
supplied to assist readers in locating the text of the full abstract as
well as ordering information.

      Readers should view the volume's topical organization as its main
reference system. The subject index offers more detailed access and
helps to locate entries that fit more than one chapter. An author
index completes the volume. All index references are to entry, not page
numbers.

      Policy studies is a rapidly growing academic discipline. The
present volume hopes to be of service to the scholars and students
engaged in advancing its findings and furthering its contributions.

Notes

1. V. O. Key, Jr., *American State Politics* (New York: Knopf, 1956);
    Duane Lockard, *The Politics of State and Local Government* (New York:
    Macmillan, 1963); John H. Fenton, *People and Parties in Politics*
    (New York: Scott, Foresman, 1966).

2. Richard E. Dawson and James E. Robinson, "Inter-Party Competition, Economic Variables, and Welfare Policies in the American States," *Journal of Politics* 25 (May 1963):265-89. See also Richard I. Hofferbert, "The Relation between Public and Some Structural and Environmental Variables in the American States," *American Political Science Review* 60 (March 1966):73-82. Hofferbert examined the relationship of the same welfare policies that were used by Dawson and Robinson with environmental variables, malapportionment, and party competition. He concludes that there is a relationship between his environmental variables and public policies but that his measures of the nature of party systems do not result in any significant explanatory power.

3. Thomas R. Dye, *Politics, Economics, and the Public: Policy Outcomes in the American States* (Chicago: Rand McNally, 1966).

4. Ira Sharkansky and Richard Hofferbert, "Dimensions of State Politics, Economics and Public Policy," *American Political Science Review* 63 (September 1969); Brian R. Fry and Richard F. Winters, "The Politics of Redistribution," *American Political Science Review* 64 (June 1970); Virginia Gray, "Models of Comparative State Politics: A Comparison of Cross-Sectional and Time Series Analyses," *American Journal of Political Science* 20 (May 1976); Charles F. Cnudde and Donald J. McCrone, "Party Competition and Welfare Policies in the American States," *American Political Science Review* 62 (December 1968); Jack Walker, "The Diffusion of Innovation among the American States," *American Political Science Review* 63 (September 1969).

5. Harold L. Wilensky, *The Welfare State and Equality* (Berkeley: University of California Press, 1975); in Thomas R. Dye and Virginia Gray, *The Determinants of Public Policy* (Lexington: D. C. Heath and Co., 1980) p. 12.

6. Michael Lewis-Beck, "The Relative Importance of Socioeconomic and Political Variables in Public Policy," *American Political Science Review* 71 (June 1977):559-5660.

THE ANALYSIS OF
PUBLIC POLICY

Policy Analysis

1. Abrams, Richard K. "Monetary Policy Reaction Functions Using a Random Coefficient Regression Model." The University of North Carolina at Chapel Hill, 1978, 40:356-A.

    This dissertation is a study of the short-run monetary policy reaction functions of the United States and Canada. The research tests the response of the monetary authorities to forecasted macro aggregate targets, and places special emphasis on the stability of that response both across time and between varying exchange rate regimes.

2. Acay, Gerardo M. "The Maximin Criterion of Distributive Equity: Implications for Public Policy." University of Missouri-Columbia, 1981, 42:4140-A.

    The maximin equity criterion states that a decision maker ought to choose the set of rules that maximizes the highest welfare or utility for the worst-off member/social group of society. This is a choice criterion. The criterion applies mainly to the basic structure of society.

3. Amy, Douglas J. "Policy Analysis as a Political Activity." University of Massachusetts, 1981, 42:3747-A.

    Traditionally, the methods of public policy analysis have been thought to be neutral and apolitical. This dissertation demonstrates that policy analysis can often be politically biased.

4. Bradsher-Fredrick, Howard R. "Gaming-Simulation: A Mode for Communicating the Research Embodied in the Mesarovic-Pestel World Model to Policy-Makers." The University of Michigan, 1980, 41:2324-A.

    Explores the use of gaming-simulation as a communication mode, and advances the argument that gaming-simulation is particularly effective in communicating social science research aimed at understanding complex problems.

5. Bremer, Frederick C. "An Economic Approach to the Measurement of Income Inequality for Public Policy Analysis." Columbia University, 1981, 42:2780-A.

The primary goal is to develop a new methodology based on economic
theory, and use it to assess the change in the level of income inequality in the United States during the 1967-75 period.

6. Brewton, Audie R. "A Simulation Model for Examining the Effect of
University Policy on Faculty Structure." The University of Utah, 1980,
41:4793-A.

Predicting the response of the internal organization of universities
to external disturbances has been imprecise. This research attempts
to develop a mathematical model which realistically depicts faculty
structure.

7. Curry, William F. "The Use of Field Tests in the Making of Public
Policy: Comparative Case Studies." West Virginia University, 1981, 42:
4576-A.

Concerns the use made of field tests in the making of public policy.
Specifically, does a field test make a difference in the policy-
making process and if so under what conditions?

8. Euell, Julian T. "An Epistemology for Social Policy Analysis."
Cornell University, 1980, 41:4194-A.

The objective is to develop an epistemology for producing descrip-
tions and analyses of the relationships created during the implementation of social plans to enable planners to be reflective about how
plans integrate people into communities.

9. Fischer, Frank. "Political Evaluation in Public Policy Analysis: A
Methodology for Integrating Empirical and Normative Judgments." New York
University, 1978, 39:3822-A.

The purpose is to develop a methodology for political evaluation which
can be employed in the analysis of public policy.

10. Franke, James L. "Comparative Research as an Aid to Policy Analysis." Northern Illinois University, 1979, 40:5988-A.

This presentation's objective is to evaluate the utility of the comparative state approach for the expanding political science subfield
of public policy research. Extant research in the comparative state
area is evaluated in terms of both theory and method.

11. Franks, Robert G. "Postsecondary Student Consumerism: A National
Delphi Forecast of Developments and Articulation of Policy Options."
Oregon State University, 1979, 40:695-A.

The purpose of this research, expressed in two coequal parts, is: to
establish a forecast of developments and an articulation of policy
options vis-a-vis postsecondary student consumerism; and to determine
if interest groups of experts differ significantly in their evaluations of the aforementioned developments and policy options.

12. Grossman, Naava B. "Policy Formation and Coalition Governments: A
Game Theoretic Approach." The University of Chicago, 1977, 38:5059-A.

A new game theoretic model of political coalition formation is developed. The model is designed for and used in the prediction of the party composition of European coalition governments.

13. Hart, Aileen F. "The Policy Sciences, Social Work, and the Analysis of Social Policy." Columbia University, 1978, 39:2549-A.

Addresses two issues: (1) the means by which particular policy science concepts and technologies inform social workers functioning as analysts of social policy; and (2) the caveat of social work regarding the analysis and development of social policy.

14. Hill, Joseph G. "The Public Interest and the Evaluation of Public Policy." University of Washington, 1981, 42:2835-A.

The purpose of this essay is to critically examine some of the standards and methods by which public policies are currently evaluated, and to outline alternative criteria and methods for making judgments about public policy.

15. Ho, Lok Sang. "Value Capture: Analysis of Policy Instruments." University of Toronto (Canada), 1981, 42:4521-A.

While the need for additional revenues is probably responsible for the recent revival of interest in value capture among policy makers, the economic justifications are improved efficiency and equity. This thesis analyzes the efficiency and equity implications of value capture policy instruments.

16. Knerr, Charles R. "Confidentiality of Social Science Research Sources and Data: Analysis of a Public Policy Problem." Syracuse University, 1977, 38:5042-A.

Specific research questions include: 1. What are the various kinds or types of difficulties which may arise in establishing and maintaining a confidential research relationship? 2. What variables associated with scholarly inquiry processes may serve to enhance or reduce the occurrence of these problems? 3. What conflicts of interest are identifiable from these issues?

17. Krieger, Sandra C. "Tests for the Misspecification of the Role of Policy Variables in Money Market Models: An Application of the Lagrange Multiplier Test for Weak Exogeneity." University of California, San Diego, 1981, 42:3700-A.

Presents and demonstrates a statistical test of the weak exogeneity assumptions in the context of a model that has been estimated conditional on the values of the policy variable.

18. Krueger, Richard A. "The Development of a Dynamic Simulation Model Used as a Tool in Policy Analysis in the Expanded Food and Nutrition Education Program." University of Minnesota, 1979, 40:3148-A.

Investigates the use of dynamic computer simulation and its relationship to the management of an educational delivery system. The system studied is the Expanded Food and Nutrition Education Program in an urban environment.

19. McWilliams, Robert N. "A Bayesian Model for the Prediction of Local
Policy Outputs in California Public Sector Labor Relations." University
of Southern California, 1979, 40:4223-A.

A Bayesian model for the prediction of secondary public policy outputs is developed and tested for the Meyers-Milias-Brown Act of California. The model should be applicable to a wide range of topics
within the policy field where legislation is permissive and secondary
outputs are not set forth.

20. Mandell, Marvin G. "The Development and Field Testing of a Framework
for Improving the Effectiveness of Policy Analysis." Northwestern University, 1979, 40:5627-A.

A major premise of this study is that strategic aspects of policy
analysis--specifically, various aspects of the analyst-client rela-
tionship--represent an important focus for increasing the effectiveness of policy analysis.

21. Michalski, Raphael J. "An Application of Consistent Statistical
Estimation to a Nonlinear Macroeconomic Policy Model." Iowa State University, 1977, 38:6832-A.

Applies economic and statistical theory to (1) specify the structural
equations and identities of a medium size (30 equations) nonlinear
macroeconomic model of the U.S. economy....

22. Milward, Hendree B., Jr. "The Policy System Approach to Public
Organizations." The Ohio State University, 1978, 39:6326-A.

Examines how policy systems, or what are commonly called policy or
political subsystems, affect governmental decision making and choice
activities in a federal system. This general problem is factored into
two major subproblems--one theoretical and one empirical.

23. Reilly, George M. "The Use of the Delphi and Cross Impact Matrix
Techniques in Educational Policy Planning." Columbia University, 1978,
39:7098-A.

Assesses the utility of the Delphi and Cross Impact Matrix techniques
in clarifying alternative future policy options available to a suburban school system. Results of these processes are compared with
actual decision-making processes observed in the district.

24. Rogers, James M. "Policy Analysis and Governing: The Impact of Impact Analysis." The Pennsylvania State University, 1981, 42:4581-A.

Develops an explanation of the impact of social policy analysis in
advanced capitalist societies at the national level, which accounts
for variations in impact across social contexts.

25. Rosenthal, Debra C. "The Concept of Rationality in the Policy Sciences." State University of New York at Binghamton, 1981, 42:838-A.

Examines the concept of rationality in the theoretical writings of
students of public policy and decision making.

26.   Rowe, Brenda J.   "The Organizational Structure and Functioning of the Evaluation of a National Field Demonstration Project: Implications for the Development of Public Policy via Social Field Experimentation." University of Maryland, 1981, 42:4143-A.

Employing the qualitative field study method of undisclosed partici-pant-observation for one year (March, 1980 through March, 1981), this study examines the structure and functioning of the collaborative ap-paratus constructed for the evaluation of a national welfare reform field experiment.

27.   Scarpino, Georgine M.   "The Shaping of a Problem: The Influence of Conceptual Models on Policy Formation."   University of Pittsburgh, 1978, 40:1110-A.

The shaping of a policy problem is a process of transforming situa-tional dissatisfactions into implementable courses of action.   Since conceptualization is viewed as the key component in such transforma-tions, this study examines the role of conceptual models in the pol-icy formation process.

28.   Thai, Khi V.   "Public Policy as a Self-Conscious Area of Study." Syracuse University, 1978, 39:6327-A.

The purpose of this dissertation is to examine three questions: 1. Do contemporary public policy studies now have a strong intellectual foundation?   2. Do contemporary public policy studies reach a degree of institutionalization?   3. Do contemporary public policy studies have a distinctive scope and methodology?

29.   Wagner, Mary M.   "The Policy Analyst as an Independent Variable in the Policy Implementation Process."   The University of North Carolina at Chapel Hill, 1980, 41:1765-A.

Examines the implementation of policy change within public organiza-tions.   A case study research design and participant-observation data collection methods are used to explore the role of the policy analyst in increasing the effectiveness of the policy implementation process.

30.   Weinberg, Hillel.   "Policy Analysis: Its Impact on Congressional Policy-Making."   Yale University, 1981, 42:5233-A.

While Congressmen may be presumed to be interested in the effects of the laws they make, the actual impact on Congress of scientific anal-yses and evaluations of the effects and costs of the laws it passes has been a matter of speculation.

31.   White, Jay D.   "Public Policy Analysis: Reason, Method, and Praxis." The George Washington University, 1982, 42:545-A.

Examines three problems in the theory of public policy analysis: (1) the narrow and distorted view of the nature of reasoned thought and action in the practice of policy analysis; (2) the inability of the instrumental method of scientific explanation to comprehend ade-quately the normative, ethical, aesthetic, historical, and crisis dimensions of our social existence; and (3) the mainstream policy

analysts' philosophically naive and scientistic attitude toward praxis, the relationship between theory and practice.

32. Wong, Shek-Ho. "Determinants of Satisfaction with Management Information Systems among Executives: Implications for Policy Decisions."
Harvard University, 1981, 42:2763-A.

   The purposes of this study are: (1) to ascertain the degree of satisfaction with management information systems (MIS) among executives;
   (2) to examine the factors affecting the degree of satisfaction with
   MIS expressed by executives at various levels; (3) to analyze the
   relative importance executives attribute to each of the components of
   satisfaction; and (4) to investigate the relationships between the
   components of satisfaction, the institutional environment and some
   characteristics of the MIS.

33. Yarusso, Lowell C. "Implications of the Youth Employment and Demonstration Projects Act, PL 95-93: An Application of Policy Analysis Techniques." Virginia Polytechnic Institute and State University, 1979, 40:
4844-A.

   The purpose of this study is to determine whether or not empirical
   analysis of policy questions could be profitably integrated with
   formal conceptual analysis of the assumptions underlying the response
   to the problem. To this end, the Youth Employment and Demonstration
   Projects Act, an amendment to the Comprehensive Employment and Training Act, was chosen for study.

Policy Making at the State Level

34. Andeen, Gerhardt K. "Resolution of Interinstitutional 'Turf' Issues in State Higher Education Agency Policy for New Program Approval." The Ohio State University, 1980, 41:4301-A.

 Surveys state higher education agency policies regarding review and approval of new academic programs.

35. Appelgate, William K. "State-Based Public Policy, Regulation, and Financial Support for Resident Proprietary Education in the United States." Southern Illinois University at Carbondale, 1978, 39:5967-A.

 Attempts to determine what the states have done in the areas of planning, regulation, and cooperation in postsecondary vocational education that involved resident proprietary education.

36. Badarak, Gary Wayne. "Educational Policy Formation and the Work Orientations of State Legislative Staff." University of California, Riverside, 1982, 42:1357-A.

 The research is a secondary analysis of data reported in *Shaping Legislative Decisions: Educational Policy and the Social Sciences* (Mitchell, 1981). Analysis is made of responses by leadership, committee, personal, and chamber staff to the Legislative Decision-Making Resource Rating Scale.

37. Bainbridge, Linda M. "A Comparative Policy Development Analysis of Educational Accountability Legislation in Three States: Colorado, Michigan and Ohio." The Ohio State University, 1980, 41:2843-A.

 The primary purpose of the research is to determine the policy process used to enact educational accountability legislation in the three states, and, through a comparative analysis, to describe and draw conclusions about the educational policy process.

38. Baird, Lawrence M. "The Use of Scientific and Technical Information and Advice by the California Legislature: A Survey of Current Policies and Proposals for Improvement." University of Southern California, 1979, 40:1046-A.

Describes the information network used by legislative staff to obtain scientific and technical knowledge and advice in their role as advisors to California legislators and assesses the utility of mechanisms proposed by the author to improve the scientific and technical capacity of the staff.

39. Barone, Vincent T. "Industrialization and Public Policy: A Study of Industry Employment Shares and Their Impact on Migration and Labor Force Participation in Nonmetropolitan State Economic Areas, 1960-70." Syracuse University, 1979, 40:4667-A.

Deals with the policy relevance of changes in industry employment shares and their impact on Migration Rates and Labor Force Participation Rates in nonmetropolitan areas.

40. Block, William J., Jr. "State Legislation, Educational Reform, and Fiscal Policy in New Jersey." Rutgers University, 1980, 41:1394-A.

The purpose of the investigation is to answer the following question: Has the New Jersey Cap Law, after three years of implementation, equalized spending between high, medium and low expenditure districts in New Jersey?

41. Boese, Sally K. "The Shaping of Political Behavior: A Study of Policy Determinants in the Virginia Legislature." Virginia Polytechnic Institute and State University, 1979, 40:4815-A.

Concerns the development of a framework that could be used to guide the examination of policy determinants. Specifically, the research problem seeks to identify environmental factors that are operative in shaping the perceptions of Virginia legislators on education issues and to assess the perceived relative influence of the factors identified.

42. Crane, Stephen C. "The Legislative Marketplace: A Model of Political Exchange to Explain State Health Regulatory Policy." The University of Michigan, 1981, 42:2851-A.

Proposes a theoretical framework for the analysis of state health policy decisions based on the concept of political exchange.

43. Crawford, Chase W. "A Planning System for Producing Useful Information for Policymakers to Judge Alternatives about a State Educational Finance System." The Ohio State University, 1979, 40:3647-A.

The study's primary purposes are to develop and to test a planning system for producing useful information for policymakers to judge alternatives about a state educational finance system. Because this planning system functions in a political environment, a policy formation system is also developed as a context for the study.

44. Deans, John W. "The Restoration of State Aid to New York State Community Colleges for Fiscal Year 1976-77: A Study of Higher Educational Policy Making." State University of New York at Albany, 1980, 41:1422-A.

Describes and analyzes the state level policy-making process by which a decision to restore the state aid formula to community colleges was made.

45. Dickenson, Martha K. "The Impact of Federal Policy on State Policy Innovations." The University of Nebraska-Lincoln, 1978, 39:4466-A.

The central focus is to measure the federal impact on state policy adoptions and to identify socioeconomic demographic and political variables associated with innovation. Two other areas of focus are the investigation of the differences between innovative and laggard states as defined by their relative speed of adoptions of policies across time and the analysis of the regional variation in adoption rates according to policy types.

46. Dillard, Jan E. "Determinants of State Land Use Policies: A Comparative State Policy Study." Emory University, 1982, 42:1277-A.

Attempts to determine why some state governments have become more involved in adopting land use policies. It also attempts to further clarify the on-going debate regarding the relative importance of socioeconomic variables and political variables in determining policy adoption.

47. Entman, Robert M. "The Psychology of Legislative Behavior: Ideology, Personality, Power, and Policy." Yale University, 1977, 39:1804-A.

Legislative decisions are often ascribed to the power of other actors. This study suggests that legislators' own ideologies and personalities shape their decisions by affecting their responses to others' power and preferences.

48. Felzenberg, Alvin S. "The Impact of Gubernatorial Style on Policy Outcomes: An In Depth Study of Three New Jersey Governors." Princeton University, 1978, 39:2509-A.

Focuses on the impact three successive governors have had on policy outcomes in a single state. Its purpose is to direct the attention of scholars to a most understudied office, the governorship and to suggest methods of measuring the contributions specific governors have made to major policy developments.

49. First, Patricia F. "A Study of a State Board of Education Policy Development Process." Illinois State University, 1979, 40:574-A.

Attempts to describe, validate, and evaluate the formal process used by the Illinois State Board of Education to develop education policy: the EVES/CAPERS Long-Range Planning Model is used as the instrument of validation and evaluation.

50. Grasso, Patrick G. "State Policy and Economic Growth: The Centralization-Concentration-Regressivity Syndrome." The University of Wisconsin-Madison, 1977, 38:6307-A.

An attempt is made to test some of Sharkansky's propositions. Specifically, cross-sectional analyses are made to determine whether less-developed states exhibit the theorized syndrome, the extent to which conformity to the syndrome is related to economic growth, and whether economic growth is related to income redistribution.

51. Hamm, Keith E. "The Effects of Organized Demand Patterns on State Legislative Policy Making: The Case of Wisconsin." The University of Wisconsin-Milwaukee, 1977, 38:6287-A.

This research is a theoretical and empirical attempt to answer two questions about state legislative policy making: what factors account for legislative success, and what factors account for conflict in the legislature over proposed legislation. The major focus examines the relationships between organized demand patterns external to the legis- lature and legislative success and conflict.

52. Hess, Paula K. "An Analysis of the Influence of the Pennsylvania State Education Association within the State Legislative Policy Process." The Pennsylvania State University, 1980, 41:3805-A.

Seeks to identify and analyze the role and influence of the Pennsyl- vania State Education Association within the process of legislative policy formulation for education in the state of Pennsylvania.

53. Igoe, Dennis P. "The Centralization of State Policy Control and Its Relationship to Indicators of Educational Attainment." State University of New York at Buffalo, 1981, 42:481-A.

Seeks to answer the question whether or not the extent of state con- trol or local control of school policy makes a significant difference in educational attainment.

54. Johnson, Ralph W. "Effect of a Federal Law on State Policy Process and on Local Implementation." Virginia Polytechnic Institute and State University, 1981, 42:4228-A.

Describes the state policy-making process as it was affected by the impact of the 1976 Federal Vocational Amendments.

55. Jones, Walter J. "On the Basis of Knowledge: The Use of Program Evaluations in Federal Compensatory Education Policymaking." The Univer- sity of Wisconsin-Madison, 1980, 41:5239-A.

Attempts, through questionnaires from and interviews with executive and legislative branch implementors, to determine whether Title I program evaluations are in fact useful in policy making. More gener- ally, an effort is made to uncover the dynamics of evaluation produc- tion and utilization.

56. Kisteneff, Alexis P. "The New Federalism of Richard Nixon as Counter- Revolution to the American Liberal State: A Study in Political Theory and Public Policy." Brown University, 1977, 38:6288-A.

The thesis is that initiatives, variously subsumed under the rubric of the New Federalism, amounted to a counter-revolutionary assault on the American liberal state, one which was designed to alter the *modus operandi* of its power, while preserving its ethos.

Policy Making at the State Level 13

57. Klass, Gary M. "The Dynamics of Politics and Policy in American States and Canadian Provinces." State University of New York at Binghamton, 1980, 41:2750-A.

The premise is the proposition that a governmental system consists of a pattern of causal interaction among political and policy-making behavior.

58. Krysiak, Barbara H. "The Administrator's Role: Implementing the Massachusetts' Basic Skills Improvement Policy and Improving Basic Skills in Writing and Writing Instruction through In-Service Education in Holistic Scoring." Northeastern University, 1981, 42:1407-A.

Establishes for administrators an initial systematic in-service approach to the improvement of instruction in writing and to the assessment of writing through holistic scoring.

59. Lennertz, James E. "The Policy Consequences of State Legislative Apportionment." University of Pennsylvania, 1980, 41:3245-A.

Develops a linkage model which reformulates the role of political institutions: variation in political structure systematically affects the fidelity of transmission of citizen demands by the political process. More particularly, it is asserted that the distribution of the net benefits of state policy varies systematically with the distribution of representational strength.

60. Longshore, Richard H. "The Power Authority of the State of New York: Accountability and Public Policy." Syracuse University, 1981, 42:2853-A.

This case study examines the extent to which the Authority has fulfilled expressions of the public interest.

61. Lyell, Edward H. "The Cost Structure of Higher Education: Implications for Governmental Policy in Steady State." University of Colorado at Boulder, 1977, 38:3944-A.

A computer based model of higher education institutional cost is developed which separates costs into fixed and variable groups. Policy alternatives at one institution, the University of Colorado, Boulder are examined to determine the sensitivity of the institution to changes in student enrollment.

62. McAllister, John E. "The Political Model of University Governance and Relations between State-Related Institutions and the State Government in Pennsylvania: View of Policymakers." University of Pittsburgh, 1980, 41:961-A.

Assesses the usefulness of the extended intra-institutional Baldridge "political system" governance model to explain the extent of relationships in the higher education external policy-making structure in Pennsylvania.

63. McCarthy, Eileen F. "Policy Considerations for State Special Education Funding Systems." Syracuse University, 1980, 41:3988-A.

Legal and philosophical support for special education has changed and developed dramatically in the past decade. Special education requires a focus on individual pupil needs, for which general fiscal systems, based on average group needs, are insufficiently flexible.

64. McMahon, Linda R. "Independent College Interest Groups' Influence on State Policy." The George Washington University, 1981, 41:4997-A.

Examines the remarkable increase in state aid to independent colleges and the doubling of interest groups representing independent colleges in the states and tests the proposition that the two are more than coincidentally related.

65. Mohan, William J. "Rawlsian Perspectives on Health Care Policy." State University of New York at Binghamton, 1980, 40:4629-A.

The objective is to develop a soundly Rawlsian perspective on a principle of access to health care services, and to deduce from this perspective certain significant implications for health care policy.

66. Murray, Jeanne M. "Development and Application of a Methodology for Policy Design: New Directions for the Role of Governmental Regulation in University Affairs." The American University, 1980, 41:5239-A.

Includes the development and application of a futures methodology for capturing and using information from experts to create scenarios for desirable futures for policy problem areas.

67. Parkinson, Geoffrey W. "Policy-Making at the State Level for K-12 Education." The Ohio State University, 1980, 40:49-A.

The purpose of this study is to devise an "ideal" system for policy making at the state level for K-12 education.

68. Petrock, Edith M. "The Policy-Making Process of the Education Commission of the States: The Adaptation and Application of an Optimal Process Model." The University of Wisconsin-Madison, 1978, 39:4636-A.

Attempts to determine whether or not the Education Commission of the States, in the development of policy, followed an accepted norm for policy formulation as expressed in theory.

69. Schilling, Ronald G. "An Analysis of the Policy-Making Process of the Interstate Distributive Education Curriculum Consortium." The Ohio State University, 1981, 42:4239-A.

Is an attempt to examine in detail the policy process as it relates to the development of curriculum materials within one vocational education consortium. The consortium studied is the Interstate Distributive Education Curriculum Consortium located at Columbus, Ohio.

70. Smith, Russell L. "Policy Innovativeness of the American States: A Policy Dimension Focus." The University of Tennessee, 1977, 38:7535-A.

Ascertains which characteristics of state socioeconomic and political environments are related to state policy actions and how these determinants vary across "dimensions" of public policy.

71. Stark, Bennett S. "The Political Economy of State Public Finance:
A Model of the Determinants of Revenue Policy: The Illinois Case 1850-
1970." The University of Wisconsin-Madison, 1982, 42:1269-A.

   While the dissertation focuses on Illinois during the 1850-1970 period, it does so within the comparative context. Included among the
   variables are: (1) political power of contesting interest groups;
   (2) the management of cultural cleavages; (3) political actors' organizations; (4) economic conditions; (5) underassessment practice; (6)
   campaign finance legislation; and (7) per capita revenue receipts.

72. Tompkins, Mark E. "The Impact of Politics on State's Policy Adoptions: Tests of a Contingency Theory and Alternative Models." University
of Minnesota, 1981, 42:370-A.

   Examines the role played by political factors in determining public
   policy adoptions.

73. Wilson, Samuel P., Jr. "The Politics of Funding State Senior Higher
Education in Texas: An Analysis of the Pressure Group-Policy Process."
North Texas State University, 1980, 41:1756-A.

   The purpose of this study is to provide research on the funding of
   state senior higher education in Texas. The focus of this work is
   on the pressure group-policy process.

74. Ziter, Mary L. "Social Policy Practice in State and Local Govern-
ment: A Study of Tasks, Skills, and Job Related Opinions of Researchers,
Evaluators and Designers in the Executive Branch." The University of
Utah, 1980, 41:4841-A.

   The study's purpose is to facilitate effective social work education
   in policy practice by providing baseline data on selected practitioners and their work in research, design, and evaluation in state
   and local government.

Policy Making at the
Local Level

75. Berg, Bruce F. "Explaining Policy Activity in Metropolitan Councils
of Governments." The American University, 1978, 39:1827-A.

   Three theories are used to examine differences in the level of policy
   activity among sixty-five metropolitan councils of governments.

76. Bowman, Ann O. "Policy Innovation in Local Government." The University of Florida, 1979, 40:5164-A.

   Explores the adoption of policy innovations by municipalities, and is
   a study of new policies rather than new technologies. The research
   is fueled by a central question: in terms of adopting new policies,
   why are some cities more innovative than other cities?

77. Bradley, Robert B. "City Councils and Public Policy." The University of Florida, 1977, 39:440-A.

   City councils are breakwaters for public policy. There is a strong
   link between the political features of councils and their communities
   and the types of policies which they pursue. So argues this dissertation as it examines city councils and their handling of public policy
   in cities throughout Florida.

78. Burnell, Barbara S. "Central City Fiscal Policy and the Intrametro-
politan Distribution of Income." University of Illinois at Urbana-Champaign, 1977, 38:6241-A.

   In an attempt to understand the nature and causes of central city
   fiscal problems, this study examines the extent to which central city
   fiscal policies alter the distribution of income within metropolitan
   areas in the direction of more high-income households residing in
   suburban jurisdictions and more low-income households residing in the
   central city.

79. Curry, Monika P. "Optimal Policy for a Circular City with Public
and Private Transportation." University of Kansas, 1980, 41:2214-A.

   Investigates optimal settlement and transportation patterns in a circular city. Control theory is used to derive conditions for optimum

city size, city population, land value gradients, and allocation of
land between housing and transportation.

80.   Davis, Margaret C.   "A Survey of Community Services Policies, Procedures, and Practices in Institutions of Higher Education in Georgia."
University of Georgia, 1981, 42:3455-A.

The purpose of the study is to determine the capability and commitment of Georgia colleges to respond to community educational needs
and expectations.

81.   Deknatel, Charles Y.   "Land Ownership: An Assessment of the Institution with Reference to Land Use Planning and Policy and the Attitudes of
Land Owners."   The University of Wisconsin-Madison, 1978, 39:5762-A.

Addresses the problem of the lack of a contemporary assessment of the
institutional status and public policy significance of land ownership
in the United States.   This problem is related to a perceived gap between land use planning and policy and the attitudes and behavior of
those affected.

82.   Diggins, William F.   "Local Elites and Natural Disaster Risk Mitigation Policy: Politics and Policy."   University of Massachusetts, 1979,
40:4752-A.

The effects of three community environments (contextual, problem, and
political), along with individual biographical characteristics, on
local elected officials' (chief executives and legislators) natural
hazard risk mitigation policy preferences are examined.

83.   Dolak, Mirko J.   "Toward the Development of a Policy Typology and
Policy Implementation Model: The Case of School Desegregation in the Los
Angeles Unified School District, 1977-1980."   University of Southern Cali-
fornia, 1980, 41:3704-A.

Examines and critiques the traditional pluralist orientation in policy
sciences and focuses on the development and application of a new policy typology and policy implementation model which offers a more useful approach to implementation analysis.

84.   Erickson, Robert L.   "Social Policy Planning, Networks, and Exchange
in Ten Low-Income Tenement Block Neighborhoods."   Cornell University,
1978, 39:4547-A.

The functioning of social policy programs in ten low-income tenement
block neighborhoods of New York City are examined in this study from
the perspective of network analysis, exchange theory, the ecological
model, social policy analysis, and analysis of the constraints imposed by social class.

85.   Feinberg, Lotte E.   "Analysis of the Planning Function in the Administration of a Municipal Service-Delivery Agency: Case Study, the Office of Programs and Policies in the New York City Police Department."
New York University, 1977, 38:7548-A.

This two-fold study is first an empirical investigation into formal centralized planning activities and processes of one municipal agency, the New York City Police Department, and second, an analysis of the relationship between these activities and selected theoretical models of organizations and planning.

86. Fraser, Craig B. "Urban Political Culture and Policy in Ten American Cities." Purdue University, 1981, 42:4918-A.

American urban political culture is defined in this study as the patterns of orientation of city residents toward the political objects and processes in the cities in which they live. The study constructs measures of political culture, by factor analysis, from sample survey data gathered in each of ten cities by the National League of Cities in 1970.

87. Gabris, Gerald T. "Federal Aid Decentralization and Local Policy Outcomes: Emerging Community Development Block Grant Trends in Small to Medium Size Missouri Cities." University of Missouri-Columbia, 1977, 38:5040-A.

Analyzes how form of municipal government, local bureaucratic orientations, socioeconomic conditions, and local political culture influence the acquisition and implementation of the Community Development Block Grant in several small to medium size Missouri cities.

88. Gallagher, David R. "Price and Investment Policies for Urban Water Supply Enterprises." University of New South Wales (Australia), 1980, 42:1732-A.

This study is concerned with the integrated problems of pricing outputs and of setting the timing and scale of supply capacity investment, urban water supply enterprises have to deal with. The focus is the headworks storage component of water supply systems.

89. Gardner, Brian M. "Intergovernmental Fiscal Relations and Local Government Policy: A Study of Federal Wastewater Treatment Grants in Maryland." University of Maryland, 1981, 42:918-A.

Studies the effects of federal wastewater treatment grants on municipal government policy in Maryland, and involves analyzing wastewater treatment grants to determine if the type of federal assistance impact on a lower level of government depends on the goals and objectives, as well as the specific conditions tied to a particular grant.

90. Glacel, Barbara P. "A Policy Analysis of Regional Transit Authorities in Massachusetts." The University of Oklahoma, 1978, 39:4543-A.

Examines the regional transit authorities in Massachusetts as examples of several trends of governmental policy as well as innovative public institutions.

91. Griffin, Jerry M. "A Study of Policymaking Processes in Local School Divisions in Virginia." Virginia Polytechnic Institute and State University, 1980, 41:868-A.

Investigates and describes current practice and ascertains desirable practices for developing educational policy as perceived by policy-makers in local school divisions in Virginia.

92. Haggett, William F. "An Analysis of the Policy Implementation Process: P.L. 94-142 in Philadelphia." Temple University, 1980, 41:2376-A.

Using a previously developed model of policy implementation, this study describes and analyzes the implementation of the Education for All Handicapped Children Act of 1975 (P.L. 94-142) in the School District of Philadelphia during the period from September 1977 through August 1979.

93. Haupt, Roy C., Jr. "The Power to Promote Growth: Business and the Making of Local Economic Development Policy." Cornell University, 1981, 41:5247-A.

The dissertation is a study of local economic development policy--what it is, and how it gets to be that way.

94. Johnston, George M. "The Impact of Local Government Policies on Land Values and Appreciation." Michigan State University, 1980, 41:3198-A.

Specifically the question is whether differences in site prices and appreciation across metropolitan areas can be explained by zoning, sewer provision and pricing, and property tax policies.

95. Kenny, Gerard J. "California City Managers: Policy Leaders or Political Dinosaurs." Claremont Graduate School, 1981, 42:3296-A.

Assesses the policy and political role of the city manager as it pertains to the enigma of council-manager relationship, manager-community involvement, manager role perception, and the viability of council-manager government in today's complex society.

96. Khan, Muhammed A. "Policy Prioritization and Critical Choices for Fiscally Distressed Cities: A Hierarchical Search." University of Pittsburgh, 1982, 42:949-A.

The study objectives are: (1) to analyze the urban fiscal problem in an integrative manner by systematically considering the interactions of the various attributes which have an impact on the problem, and (2) to suggest a set of policy choices capable of redressing the fiscal problem.

97. Kincaid, John. "Political Success and Policy Failure: The Persistence of Machine Politics in Jersey City." Temple University, 1981, 42:837-A.

Seeks to explain the persistence of machine politics in Jersey City, New Jersey, between 1887 and 1977.

98. Klein, Arlette D. "The Massachusetts Department of Youth Services, 1969-1974: Strategies of Policy Implementation under Varying Conditions of Change." Bryn Mawr College, 1978, 40:2881-A.

This thesis is a case study of the process of change and the strategies that were used to introduce changes and reform the juvenile correctional system in Massachusetts.

99. Ladewig, Howard W. "Community Satisfaction and Public Policy: Theory and Measurement." North Carolina State University at Raleigh, 1977, 38: 4387-A.

Seeks to determine the magnitude of the direct and indirect effects of objective conditions and subjective experiences on one's satisfaction with his residential environment.

100. Latanich, Gary A. "Federal Water and Sewage Grants: The Implied Urban Policy." The University of Nebraska-Lincoln, 1978, 39:4380-A.

The study is designed to examine certain government grants-in-aid programs to see if they reflect a commitment to an implied urban policy. In the broadest sense the study is aimed at investigating the pattern of federal grants-in-aid and comparing these grants with several theoretical "norms."

101. Lee, Gun Young. "Policy Evaluation of Value Capture Strategies for Urban Rapid Transit: An Empirical Case Study of Chicago's Southwest Corridor." Northwestern University, 1981, 42:4179-A.

Studies the impacts of transit policy on housing rents, household welfare and commuting mode split to explore the key questions regarding the value capture potential of urban rapid transit.

102. Lesher, William G. "An Analysis of Northeastern Rural Land Use Policies." Cornell University, 1977, 38:4278-A.

Inventories and analyzes the state and local rural land use policies of the urbanized Northeast to find out if there are discernible trends or valuable lessons that could be gleaned from their "experiments" in institutional change.

103. Lindsey, Eddie T. "Analysis of a Selected Negotiated Contract as Related to Educational Personnel Policies in Georgia." Auburn University, 1978, 39:1231-A.

Analyzes components of a selected negotiated teachers contract, existing statutory requirements, State Board of Education regulations and local policy manuals to determine commonalities, contrasts and the potential impact on educational policy development in the State of Georgia.

104. Marshment, Richard S. "Urban Region Transportation Policy Development and Conflicts: 1960 to 1980." University of Washington, 1981, 42: 2900-A.

The problem is to inventory the content of federal urban transportation policy, determine how the policy affects urban area planning and decision-making practices, and provide recommendations on how federal policy can be better structured to achieve its stated objectives.

105. Martinez Cruz, Americo. "The Birth, Development, and Survival of
Demonstration Programs and Their Impact on and Implications for Public
Policy, Specifically Using Model Cities as a Prime Example." New York
University, 1978, 40:2883-A.

   Prior to the mid-Sixties, urban programs concentrated on the visible
   and immediate. With the "discovery" of poverty and a national awareness of racial discrimination, public policy underwent a marked change.

106. Mercer, Leslie K. "Urban School Policy Making: The Saint Paul
School Board, 1951-1978." University of Minnesota, 1981, 42:4234-A.

   Concerns the policy-making processes of the St. Paul (Minnesota)
   School Board over time. Focuses on three research questions in determining the changes in school board membership, meetings and relationships from 1951 to 1978.

107. Myers, Joanne. "Urban Communication: Public Policy Implementation
Awareness." Rensselaer Polytechnic Institute, 1980, 41:4532-A.

   Explores the various communication channels used and available, by
   empirically measuring citizens' awareness of public policy implementation information (specifically, the Housing and Community Development
   Act), and the citizens' modes of information access--interpersonal and
   media, both print and electronic.

108. O'Mara, Allyn H. "Design with Climate: The Importance of Climate
Analysis in Urban Policy and Planning." University of Southern California, 1978, 38:6358-A.

   The dissertation is both heuristic and normative. The first half
   describes the known effects of urbanization on climate, and connects
   these effects to several urban problem areas. The second half suggests several approaches to forming policies that encourage or even
   require that climatological analysis be brought into urban planning
   and decisions.

109. Phillips, Bruce A. "A Decade of Change: Municipal Budgetary Policy
during the 1960's." The University of Chicago, 1978, 39:6342-A.

   Examines the financial policies of American municipalities and the
   ways in which those policies changed during the 1960's.

110. Pizor, Peter J. "Growth Management as Public Policy: A Study in
Community Building." Rutgers University, 1979, 40:4212-A.

   Investigates the relationships between public participation and growth
   managements. Recent developments in public participation are discussed, and the political context of land use decisions is analyzed.

111. Powers, Judith L. "The Absence of Conspiracy: The Effects of Urban
Technology on Public Policy in Los Angeles, 1850-1930." University of
California, Los Angeles, 1981, 42:2290-A.

   Los Angeles has received as much abuse as praise for its solution to
   the problems created by its rapid growth. To understand the causes

of its development, this study offers an historical analysis of the
uses of urban technology within the city's political and economic
framework.

112. Quinn, Sandra L. "Time and Geography: As Additional Variables on
Municipal Policy Development." Claremont Graduate School, 1978, 39:5182-A.

The context of this dissertation is the consideration that the importance of time and geographical reference, and the developments from
such considerations, have been overlooked in other considerations of
the development of the city.

113. Rashid Farokhi, Nasrolah. "The Influence of Nongovernmental, Business, and Interest Group Organizations on Urban Politics and Policy Making: A Case Study of the Leadership Role and Influence of the Atlanta
Chamber of Commerce, 1960-1978." Atlanta University, 1979, 40:5991-A.

Examines the numerous power structure studies that have been conducted
throughout the United States as well as Atlanta, over the past three
decades. These investigations basically reveal that the businessmen
within the community most often wield the power or influence within
the respective cities under study.

114. Reader, Jonathan W. "The Social, Economic and Political Determinants of Town Fiscal Policies." Cornell University, 1981, 42:3778-A.

The purpose of this dissertation is to engage in a preliminary analysis of the determinants of town fiscal policies.

115. Rice, Robert M. "An Introduction to Public Policy toward the American Family." State University of New York at Buffalo, 1977, 38:4375-A.

Analyzes possibilities for family policy development by assessing the
functioning of families in modern United States society. It also
examines the environment for family policy making. It concludes with
initial proposals for policy and program explication.

116. Robertson, Kent A. "The Redevelopment of the American Central Business District: An Examination of the State of Knowledge, Policy Dilemmas,
and Recent Retail Trends." University of Delaware, 1981, 42:4954-A.

The present state of knowledge regarding the structure and functions
of central business districts (CBDs) and the effects of public policy
is insufficiently developed, thereby hindering the ability of policymakers and planners to adequately address policy dilemmas and to effectuate future change. In response to this problem, this dissertation attempts to further our understanding of activity mixes and
levels in large American CBDs over the past thirty years.

117. Rodgers, Robert C. "Public Policy and the Duration of Public Employee Strike Activity." Michigan State University, 1981, 42:5243-A.

The determinants of the duration of all nonrecognition strikes occur-
ring in local government bargaining units in the United States between
January, 1977 and October, 1978 are examined in this study.

118.   Santiago Santiago, Isaura. *"Aspira v. Board of Education of the City of New York*: A History and Policy Analysis." Fordham University, 1978, 38:7199-A.

Analyzes the impact on policy of the consent decree which was the outcome of this suit. The process and substance of policy reform and policy accommodation in five areas is described and analyzed: minimum educational standards, parental rights, assessment, personnel, and finance.

119.   Scott, Jim A. "The Role of the City Manager and Matrix Management in Formulation of an Infilling Policy in Colorado Springs." University of Colorado at Denver, 1981, 42:5243-A.

Describes the role and management style of the City Manager of Colorado Springs in establishing a new land use policy. The formulation of this policy prefaced the Colorado Springs City Council adoption of an Urban Infill Resolution which encourages the development of vacant, bypassed land within the city.

120.   Shapiro, Judith N. "Implementing Public Policy: The 'Fogo Process' and Community Action." Princeton University, 1978, 39:2539-A.

Criticizes the conventional political science and public administration approaches to analyzing the implementing of public policy in the United States.

121.   Singerman, Phillip A. "Politics, Bureaucracy and Public Policy: The Case of Urban Renewal in New Haven." Yale University, 1980, 41: 2286-A.

The central theme of this study is that the political conditions necessary for the existence of a pluralist democracy in New Haven were weakened during the 1960s and a competitive political system transformed into a monopolistic one.

122.   Sjogren, Jane O. "Federal Aid to Education: Local Response to Federal Policy." Stanford University, 1982, 42:4719-A.

Investigates how different forms of federal grant-in-aid policies affect school district use of federal funds and, ultimately, the realization of federal educational goals.

123.   Smith, Elton C. "Executive Policy Roles in the Urban County." The University of Florida, 1978, 39:4490-A.

Utilizes a systems perspective of urban county government, to assess the effect of metropolitan reform on the roles which urban county chief executives play in the policy process.

124.   Sullivan, Arthur M. "Public Policy in an Urban Economy: A General-Equilibrium Approach." Princeton University, 1981, 42:1249-A.

Analyzes the effects of public policy on the structure and efficiency of an urban economy. The focus is on externalities that are spatial in character, and on public policies designed to correct such externalities.

125. Tran, Thanh K. "An Urban Transportation Policy Planning Methodology: System Dynamics Approach." Virginia Polytechnic Institute and
State University, 1979, 40:5625-A.

Develops a computer model, using the methodology of System Dynamics,
to enable transportation planners, engineers, and other decision
makers to plan and evaluate a variety of transportation policies.

126. Turnage, Martha A. "Consortium for Continuing Higher Education in
Northern Virginia: Public Policy in Action." Virginia Polytechnic Institute and State University, 1978, 39:3296-A.

Pursues concerns of the forces that created the Consortium and altered
its operation; the goals established for it by the General Assembly,
the State Council of Higher Education and the Statement of Agreement
drawn up by the Governing Board; and the impact of Consortium policies
on its operation.

127. Visser, James A. "The Potential for Policy Role Conflict: Policy
Role Attitudes of Officials in Council-Manager Governments." The University of Oklahoma, 1978, 39:2541-A.

Analyzes the key policy-making role attitudes of three hundred officials in fifty-six council-manager municipalities in Kansas, Oklahoma
and Texas. Examines the attitudes of council members, city managers
and selected department heads toward the roles they, their colleagues
and community interest groups should perform in shaping, deciding and
implementing public policy.

128. Ward, Sally K. "The Impact of Community Characteristics on Local
Social Programs and Policies: A Comparative Analysis of American Cities."
Brown University, 1977, 38:5064-A.

Studies of community power structures have evolved during the past
twenty years from case studies designed to uncover a particular community's power structure to large-scale comparative studies. This
study departs from much of the previous work in the field by examining
the effect of relationships among communities on both the structure of
power or influence and on the level and type of outputs within communities.

129. Whitney, Rodger F. "Public-Private Planning and Policy-Making in
the Development of a Mixed-Use Urban Community: An Evaluative Study and
Experience in Decision-Making Regarding Public Approval of the Dallas
Homestead Project, 1977-78." Harvard University, 1978, 39:3321-A.

This final report/project serves as a case study-analysis of the
Homestead Planned Urban Development Community, specifically focusing
on the significant interactions and problems in policy-making efforts
between the public and private sectors in the controversy since 1969.

130. Yancy, Dorothy C. "The Spectre of Public Unionism from 1966 to
1976: A Critical Analysis of the Labor Policies of the City of Atlanta."
Atlanta University, 1978, 40:2263-A.

The dissertation is a descriptive and analytical study of the city

of Atlanta's labor relation policy from 1966 to 1976. It is composed
of two parts: part one provides the background and perspective for
viewing the city's labor policy; part two provides empirical data
which allows for the examination of the perceptions of the rank and
file toward the city's labor relation policy.

131.   Zuercher, Lawrence B. "An Analysis of the Impact of Growth Management Policies on the City of Petaluma, California." Texas Tech University, 1981, 42:1825-A.

Studies were conducted to determine if the impact of the growth management plan adopted by Petaluma, California in 1972 for a five-year
period, accomplished the goals and objectives established at the onset of the program.

Public Administration and the Making of Public Policy

132. Ahmad, Mohammad Q. "Development Theories and Administrative Policies: A Critique and a Search for an Alternative." University of Southern California, 1979, 40:5585-A.

The dissertation is a critique of development theories and a quest
for a better alternative. It explores the historical roots of development as a philosophy of history and as an ideology of social science, and outlines and critically analyzes the theories of development, discussing their assumptions, policy, implications, and inherent
limitations.

133. Al-Turki, Khalid A. "Decision-Making Strategy for Development:
Value-Weighted Utility Analysis and Its Application to the Formulation of
Public Policy in Developing Countries." University of Southern Califor-
nia, 1981, 42:3746-A.

Offers a decision-making strategy for use by developing countries in
the formulation of public policy for the many complex issues of economic and social development.

134. Avgar, Amos. "Post-Disaster Development: Implications for Public
Policy." Cornell University, 1978, 39:4535-A.

Examines the social processes underlying the long-range response of
communities to a natural disaster. An attempt is made to identify
the critical variables, both external and internal to the community,
that determine the pattern of recovery.

135. Bal Kumar, K.C. "The Spatial Diffusion of Public Policy Innovations
and the Role of Modernization in the United States, 1870-1970." The University of Texas at Austin, 1977, 38:5757-A.

Demonstrates the relationship between the spatial diffusion of public
policy innovations and the levels of modernization in the forty-eight
contiguous American states over the period 1870-1970. Evaluates the
relative importance of the dimensions of modernization in controlling
the adoption of innovations.

136. Bengston, William F. "The Relationship of Theory to Policy: A Case Study of the President's Commission on Law Enforcement and Administration of Justice." Fordham University, 1981, 41:5250-A.

Locates the problem of the relationship of social science knowledge to the development of social policy within the framework of the sociology of knowledge, and presents one of the few case studies which analyzes the detailed interplay between social science knowledge, an advisory commission, and the legislative attempts to carry out the recommendations of that commission.

137. Berg, Mark R. "The Use of Technology Assessment Studies in Policy-Making." The University of Michigan, 1978, 39:6321-A.

This dissertation and the NSF-funded project focused on three primary questions: (1) To what extent do factors identified in the literature as affecting the utilization of scientific knowledge and policy research apply to the specific context of technology assessment? (2) What are the major factors empirically associated with the utilization and nonutilization of technology assessments? And (3), in light of the insights provided by the literature, and the experience to date in producing and using technology assessments as documented by this research, what lessons can be learned to increase the utility and utilization of future technology assessment studies?

138. Bertozzi, Mark. "Oversight of the Executive Branch: A Policy Analysis of Federal Special Prosecutor Legislation." State University of New York at Albany, 1980, 41:2759-A.

Analyzes federal special prosecutor legislation and the special prosecutor provisions of the Ethics in Government Act.

139. Bewersdorf, Leonard L. "Perceptions of Superintendents and School Board Members in Rural and Urbanized School Settings with Respect to Policy-Making and Policy-Administering." Northern Illinois University, 1980, 41:860-A.

The problem investigated deals with the different perceptions that superintendents and board members in rural and urbanized school settings have about policy-making and policy-administering.

140. Bruce, James B. "The Politics of Soviet Policy Formation: Khrushchev's Innovative Policies in Education and Agriculture." University of Denver, 1977, 38:5693-A.

Examines the policy-making process in the Soviet Union. The primary concern is theoretical--an effort to build empirically testable generalizations from a systematic comparison of the political dynamics of two policy cases.

141. Bruder, Paul T. "A Study of the Policy Making Process: Lindblom's Theory of Partisan Mutual Adjustment in the Formulation and Implementation of the Uniformed Services Physicians' Variable Incentive Pay Legislation." The George Washington University, 1977, 38:4362-A.

Uses Charles Lindblom's theory of partisan mutual adjustment and at-

tempts to make it more explanatory. The objective is to see how the
theory can be made to work in a context of selected organizational
variables described by a case study.

142. Buri, James E. "The Role of the Regulations of the Securities and
Exchange Commission as a Means to Strengthen Federal Policy Regarding
Conglomerate Mergers." University of Notre Dame, 1979, 40:1599-A.

   Constructs a more serviceable federal policy regarding the emergence
   of conglomerate corporations. To this end, analysis is made of the
   regulations of the Securities and Exchange Commission as they apply
   to the growth behavior of conglomerates.

143. Calder, James D. "Presidents and Crime Control: Some Limitations
on Executive Policy Making." Claremont Graduate School, 1978, 39:3797-A.

   Collects and codifies much of the scattered literature that probes
   the ability of the President to be all things to all people in the
   crime control policy area.

144. Carr, T.R. "Government Reorganization for Economy and Efficiency:
The Impact of Government Reorganization on Public Policy." The University of Oklahoma, 1980, 41:4488-A.

   Investigates the non-efficiency outcomes of government reorganization
   to determine if government reorganization has an impact on public
   policy.

145. Carter, Ralph, III. "Beyond the Executive: Understanding Congressional Foreign Policy Behavior." The Ohio State University, 1980, 41:
4486-A.

   What factors produce congressional foreign policy behaviors? Which
   factors are more important than others? When do congressional foreign
   policy initiatives occur? What is the public's impact on this process? A conceptual framework is advanced to structure the search for
   answers to these questions.

146. Chappell, William L. "Technology Assessment in the American Policy
Process." The University of Alabama, 1977, 39:440-A.

   Examines policy making on technologically related matters in the
   United States. Emphasis is placed on technology assessment as an attempt to control societal change related to technology purposefully
   through applying expert knowledge.

147. Cline, Barry G. "The Area Agency on Aging Concept: Policy Implementation in Pennsylvania." The University of Wisconsin-Madison, 1980,
41:3254-A.

   The central objective is to analyze policy implementation as a distinctive phase in the larger sequence of political activity traditionally subsumed under the rubric of the policy-making process.

148. Colwell, Mary. "Philanthropic Foundations and Public Policy: The
Political Role of Foundations." University of California, Berkeley, 1980,
41:3271-A.

Demonstrates that philanthropic foundations influence public policy
through the nonprofit organizations they support and, increasingly,
through programs they initiate and develop.

149.   Conlan, Timothy J.   "Congressional Response to the New Federalism:
The Politics of Special Revenue Sharing and Its Implications for Public
Policy Making."   Harvard University, 1982, 42:1277-A.

Examines congressional responses to the Nixon Administration's Special
Revenue Sharing proposals in the early 1970's.

150.   Copeland, Gary W.   "The Effects of Congressional Campaign Expenditures on Voting Behavior: A Behavioral and Policy Analysis."   The University of Iowa, 1979, 40:6403-A.

Campaign spending in congressional elections is a significant determinant of voting behavior.   The research indicates that campaign
spending affects both outcomes at the congressional district level
and the behavior of individuals.

151.   Dilger, Robert J.   "The Northeast-Midwest Congressional Coalition:
Its Effect upon the Congress and the Federal Policy-Making Process."
Brandeis University, 1981, 42:834-A.

Much attention has been recently given to what has come to be known
as the Sunbelt/Snowbelt controversy.   This study examines in five
separate case studies the efforts of the northeastern representatives
to revise federal spending policies and the effect of their efforts
on the Congress and the federal policy-making process.

152.   Ellis, Larry V.   "Wealth, Government Debt and the Crowding Out of
Fiscal Policy Actions."   University of Missouri-Columbia, 1978, 39:5065-A.

Examines the nature of the crowding out that may occur when it is assumed that government bonds are not viewed as net wealth and to assess
the likelihood of such an occurrence.

153.   Fleming, Joseph L.   "Scientific Attitudes, Public Conceptions of
Science and Technology and Public Policy."   The University of Michigan,
1979, 40:2575-A.

The success of a high technology democracy appears to depend critically upon the ability of the public to participate in this process
in a knowing way.   It is suggested here that the development of scientific attitudes in citizens may be a key to this success.

154.   Greene, Wilhelmina S.   "The Dynamics of Reorganization within a
Microsystem, as Precipitated by Executive Succession, Policy Formulation,
and a Pluralistic Environment."   University of California, Riverside,
1978, 39:568-A.

Describes the process or dynamics of reorganization within the microsystem of the central office of a school district, when this process
is precipitated by executive succession, policy formulation, and a
pluralistic environment.

155. Gregorian, Hrach. "Congressional-Executive Relations and Foreign Policymaking in the Post-Vietnam Period: Case Studies of Congressional Influence." Brandeis University, 1981, 42:836-A.

The working hypothesis of the study is that the legislative branch was not as wholly ineffectual in foreign affairs as most commentaries would have us believe and that the changes wrought by Vietnam and Watergate, as well as certain historical shifts, rendered popular perceptions about congressional-executive relations anachronistic.

156. Harris, Brian F. "Shared Monopoly and Antitrust Policy: An Empirical Investigation of the Effects of the FTC's Restructuring Proposals for the Cereal Industry." Michigan State University, 1978, 39:4460-A.

The purpose of the study is twofold. First, the theoretical foundations of "shared monopoly" are investigated by examining relevant aspects of the theories of oligopoly and industrial organization. The second purpose is to empirically investigate the effects of the proposed remedies on cereal retail prices.

157. Hirsh, Richard F. "Science, Technology, and Public Policy: The Case of X-Ray Astronomy, 1959 to 1972." The University of Wisconsin-Madison, 1979, 40:4721-A.

Deals with the evolution of x-ray astronomy as a scientific specialty during the years from 1959 to 1972. The thesis focuses on the roles of technological innovation and American public policy.

158. Jennings, Jeanette. "American Value Orientation and Its Impact on Policy." The University of Michigan, 1980, 41:4165-A.

Analyzes black-white differences in the value orientation of Americans on two value pairs that are crucial to policy formulation: public versus private responsibility and adequacy versus equity of benefits.

159. Lawless, Michael W. "Toward a Theory of Policy Making for Directed Interorganizational Systems." University of California, Los Angeles, 1980, 41:5226-A.

An exploratory analysis is made of "directed interorganizational systems." These are systems of autonomous public agencies induced by a policy maker to interrelate for the purpose of addressing large, complex problems.

160. Light, Paul C. "The President's Agenda: Domestic Policy Choice from Kennedy to Carter." The University of Michigan, 1980, 41:2750-A.

This research rests on the analysis of the five administrations: Kennedy, Johnson, Nixon, Ford, and Carter. The study is restricted to the President's domestic agenda. The end aim of this research is to isolate those variables which can be said to have an impact on domestic choice.

161. Lowell, Harvey D. "Policy Implementation and Organizational Change: The Case of the Camp Hill Project." The Pennsylvania State University, 1980, 41:4190-A.

The paper is a case study of the processes by which externally mandated policy change was implemented in an organization, and the way
in which the new policy and the process by which it was implemented
culminated in effects on organizational operation.

162. McAfee, Randolph P. "Some Formal Methods in Policy Formation."
Purdue University, 1980, 41:3680-A.

Develops a mathematical theory of problem solving in a dynamic environment. An application of this theory to auditing policy, in particular to the Foreign Corrupt Practices Act of 1977, is developed and
the value of formal analysis demonstrated.

163. MacKuen, Michael B. "Social Communication and the Mass Policy
Agenda." The University of Michigan, 1979, 40:5576-A.

Examines the roots of short-term shifts in the public's agenda orientations for a period of fifteen years, paying particular attention to
the part played by the mass media.

164. Maggiotto, Michael A. "Senators, Constituencies, and Roll Calls:
Legislative Policy Making in the 92nd Senate." Indiana University, 1977,
38:6911-A.

Attempts to reevaluate the role of constituency influence on legislative policy making by looking at the linkage between the attitudes
and interests of constituencies and the roll call voting of U.S. senators.

165. Mangiameli, Paul M. "The Effects of Managerial Policies on Aggregate Plans, the Master Production Schedule, and Departmental Plans." The
Ohio State University, 1979, 40:2164-A.

Envisions a multistage, multiproduct manufacturing system as a sequential planning process with interrelated decisions being made at
the levels of aggregate planning, master production scheduling, and
departmental planning. A model of this process is presented as a
zero-one mixed integer program.

166. Moody, Robert J., III. "Impoundment Policy and Congressional Oversight: Bureaucratic Perversity and Congressional Impotence." The University of Texas at Austin, 1979, 41:3256-A.

Based on both extensive interviews in Washington, D.C. with congressional staff and Executive Branch specialists and on government documents, demonstrates that the Impoundment Control Act has failed and
that it has failed for institutional reasons.

167. Moran, Michael J. "The Formation of Monetary Policy." The Pennsylvania State University, 1980, 41:4104-A.

With the use of internal Federal Reserve documents, the thesis investigates the policy-making process of the Federal Reserve, and evaluates its policy performance in the early 1970's.

168. Morlock, Mark J., Jr. "Public Service Employment as Manpower Development Policy." Washington State University, 1978, 39:3052-A.

There has occurred a substantial increase in the size of federally
funded public employment programs operating in the United States.
This study is an empirical investigation into the contribution of
these programs to the manpower development of program participants.

169. Moskowitz, Eric S. "The Politics of Neighborhood Disinvestment: A
Study of U.S. Federal Policy-Making." Indiana University, 1979, 40:
2244-A.

This dissertation is an outgrowth of the pluralist/elitist debate and
explores an alternative framework premised on the notion that the
socioeconomic structure of society constrains the outputs of a multi-
group policy process.

170. Nagy, Charles J., Jr. "Political Parties and the Flexibility of
the Policy-Making Process." Fordham University, 1980, 40:6408-A.

Argues that the flexibility of a system depends on the ability of its
institutions, particularly its parties, to identify new demands as
they arise and develop policy responses to them.

171. Naveh, David. "The Political Role of the Professionals in the
Formation of National Policy: The Case of the President's Council of Economic Advisers." The University of Connecticut, 1978, 39:6942-A.

The creation of the President's Council of Economic Advisers was a
landmark in transforming the science of economics into a policy-making
tool. It was designed as an on-going institutional link between those
responsible for the promotion of "maximum employment, production and
purchasing power," mainly the President.

172. Nunes, Ralph. "Patterns of Congressional Change: Critical Realignment, Policy Clusters, and Party Voting in the House of Representatives."
Columbia University, 1978, 41:3246-A.

It is the thesis of this study that the effects of critical realignment can be measured in the institutions of government. Specifically,
in this case, political change fostered by realigning elections can be
noted in the legislative agendas, patterns of roll call voting and
norms of operation of the Congress.

173. Olufs, Dick W., III. "Decentralization and American Politics: Analyzing Theories and Policies." The Pennsylvania State University, 1979,
40:5586-A.

Presents a framework for the analysis of decentralization theories
and policies, and surveys seven major types of decentralization theories and policies.

174. Oneal, John R. "Creative Adaptation: Process and Potential for
Foreign Policy Making in Times of Crisis." Stanford University, 1979,
40:5176-A.

The primary purposes of the thesis are, first, to clarify the impact
of international crises on the structure, process, and content of
policy making in the fields of national security and foreign affairs
and, second, to identify means by which key decision-making functions
can be performed to increase the likelihood that an effective response
will be made when a severe environmental challenge does occur.

175. Parker, Mary H. "Organizing Domestic Policy for the President."
The Johns Hopkins University, 1978, 39:5719-A.

This thesis is an examination and analysis of the functioning of
domestic policy organizations which have served presidents from 1933
to 1976.

176. Perkins, Edward J. "The Priorities Policy Group: A Case Study of
the Institutionalization of a Policy Linkage and Resource Allocation
Mechanism in the Department of State." University of Southern California, 1978, 39:4489-A.

Examines the implementation of a policy linkage and resource allocation mechanism in the Department of State. This includes the conceptualization, implementation, and institutional processes of the
Priorities Policy Group during the period 1975-76.

177. Porto, Brian L. "The Policy Process in American Indian Affairs;
Patterns of Interaction between American Indian Interest Groups, the
Bureau of Indian Affairs, and the Indian Affairs Committees of the Cong-
ress." Miami University, 1979, 40:4213-A.

The novel character of this analytical perspective lies in its reli-
ance upon a factor external to a particular group, namely, the organization's capacity to wield influence in its relations with government
officials, in order to account for organizational survival. The
framework is applied to an examination of voluntary associations which
represent American Indians.

178. Radharao, Chaganti. "Use of Knowledge in Policy-Making: A Study of
the Use of Research, Planning and Management Studies in Local Government
Organizations." State University of New York at Buffalo, 1979, 40:957-A.

Examines the conditions which encourage the use of knowledge inputs
(in the form of one-time special studies) by city government agencies.

179. Redmon, Thomas E.R. "The Emergence of Policy as an Organizing Concept for Academic Planning and Governance." University of Georgia, 1978,
39:3408-A.

Through a systematic review of literature related to political science
and higher education administration, a conceptual analysis of policy
is performed. The primary context of the analysis is academic administration, although other areas of institutional governance are considered briefly.

180. Reinhard, David W. "The Republican Right: Leadership, Policies,
and Intra-Party Politics, 1945-1965." The Pennsylvania State University,
1981, 42:1764-A.

Investigates the Republican Right Wing as an intra-party political
movement from 1945 to 1965. Examines the general doctrine of the
Republican Right, and the Republican Right's successful and unsuccessful response to major post-World War II domestic and foreign policy
issues.

181. Renka, Russell D. "Kennedy, Johnson and the Congress: Serial Gaming
and Change in Legislative Policy Coalitions." The University of Texas at
Austin, 1979, 41:4826-A.

The coalition leadership of Presidents Kennedy and Johnson with the
Congresses of 1961 through 1968 is examined. Primary research materials are papers on file with the Lyndon Baines Johnson Presidential
Library generated by the principals of the White House Office of Congressional Relations.

182. Sanzone, John G. "The Impact of General Revenue Sharing on Federal
Policy-Making Authority." University of California, Riverside, 1978, 39:
6944-A.

The problem explored is what impact will general revenue sharing (and
the consolidation of categorical grants-in-aid) have on the federal
government's policy-making authority over subnational social programs,
once the programmatic authority of these programs is removed?

183. Shelley, Mack C., II. "The Conservative Coalition in the United
States Congress, 1933-1976: Time Series Analysis of a Policy Coalition."
The University of Wisconsin-Madison, 1977, 38:7534-A.

Analyzes the dynamics of the rates of appearance and success of the
conservative coalition in both the House and the Senate annually from
1933 to 1976, and examines the coalition's appearance and success
across seven issue dimensions, as well as the interaction between
presidential position taking and the activity of the coalition, the
relevance of the coalition to the American party system, and the relevance of traditional coalition theory to the study of this congressional coalition.

184. Smith, Jeffrey W. "A Positive Model of Leadership Provision: Implications for Policy and Leadership Outputs." University of Oregon,
1979, 40:3516-A.

Anthony Downs' positive model, *An Economic Theory of Democracy*, is
adapted to allow for voter consideration of both policies and personal
attributes offered by candidates.

185. Smith, Lance M. "Political Theory and Policy Research." The Ohio
State University, 1980, 41:1755-A.

Evaluates a Department of Labor on-the-job training program for vet-
erans, the Help through Industry Retaining [sic] and Employment Program. The theory held by policy makers in formulating this program
is identified.

186. Smith, Steven S. "Senate Policy Alignments, 1957-1976." University
of Minnesota, 1980, 41:1203-A.

Tests prevalent perspectives on the character of Senate voting alignments by examining four properties of voting patterns during the 1957-
1976 period.

187. Sorg, James D. "A Theory of Individual Behavior in the Implementation of Policy Innovations." The Ohio State University, 1978, 39:5140-A.

A theory intended to predict the behavioral response of implementors
to directives to carry out new policies is advanced. The research
question addressed is: How can the behavior of implementors in policy
implementation situations be predicted?

188. Spitzer, Robert J. "The Presidency and Public Policy: The Four
Arenas of Presidential Power." Cornell University, 1980, 40:398-A.

Represents an attempt to overcome many of the problems associated
with the study of the Presidency by analyzing the president as a
policy maker, and thus using policy as the unit of analysis. The
core of the argument is that the type of policy with which the president deals determines his ability to affect political processes and
outcomes.

189. Spohn, Cassia C. "The Role of Advisory Boards in the National
Policy-Making Process." The University of Nebraska-Lincoln, 1978, 38:
4476-A.

Attempts to broaden knowledge about advisory boards and to answer
some unanswered questions, focusing on the characteristics, attitudes,
and perceptions of 150 members of HEW advisory boards.

190. Staffaroni, Janice. "The Study of an Accountability Policy."
Columbia University, 1980, 40:491-A.

This is a study about administrator and teacher interpretation of
New Jersey's "Thorough and Efficient" accountability policy. It is
specifically focused on the link between policy initiative and interpretation.

191. Stenger, Thomas C. "Congressional Committee Staff Members: Policy
Advocates or Process Administrators?" Southern Illinois University at
Carbondale, 1978, 39:2521-A.

Examines the policy role orientations of congressional committee
staff members as they perform their duties in the hearings process.

192. Stewart, Patricia E. "The Pinocchio Effect: A Study of the Development of an Inservice Policy for Massachusetts." Harvard University, 1980,
40:6100-A.

In April 1978 the Massachusetts Board of Education adopted a policy
creating The Commonwealth Institute, a decentralized inservice network
designed to encourage and fund collaborative school-based staff development programs. The policy, like Pinocchio, changed considerably in
the process of coming alive. The author uses qualitative methodology
to attempt to describe and account for these changes.

193. Taylor, Marilyn L. "The Role of the Staff Specialist in the Policy Implementation Process." Harvard University, 1979, 40:1593-A.

This dissertation is exploratory in nature and focuses on the role of staff specialists who are responsible for coordinating the implementation of affirmative action.

194. Trauth, Eileen M. "An Adaptive Model of Information Policy." University of Pittsburgh, 1979, 41:2337-A.

Following an examination of three policy model configurations--maximization, optimization, and adaptive--the adaptive or cybernetic representation was chosen as the most appropriate way to represent the information policy-making process.

195. Turner, Michael. "Finding a Policy Role for the Vice President: The Case of Nelson A. Rockefeller." State University of New York at Binghamton, 1978, 39:1818-A.

The study is concerned with the extent to which Rockefeller was able, as Vice President, to play an active role as a developer and shaper of policy proposals and policy initiatives within the Ford administration.

196. Tutchings, Terrence R. "Public Policy-Making Models: A Test Using Data on Presidential Advisory Commissions." The University of Texas at Austin, 1977, 38:7575-A.

The Eastonian policy model and several variations of it are tested using data on Presidential advisory commissions. The sample consists of those commissions created between 1945 and 1973, a total of ninety-nine commissions. By means of content analysis of commission reports, a typology of commission recommendations is derived. This typology and secondary data are used to operationalize the policy models.

197. Wynn, Mark E. "The Political Agenda: Public Policy Issues in the United States." Northwestern University, 1977, 38:6917-A.

Investigates agenda setting in American domestic politics. Using Gallup Poll data from 1945 to 1975, public opinion about major political issues in this period is described.

198. Zimmermann, Erwin. "Interests and Control in Community Decision-Making, the Case of Federally Funded Redistributive Policy Outputs." The University of Chicago, 1979, 40:497-A.

The research presented is a comparative study of collective decision making concerning federally funded redistributive policy outputs. The study is limited to the consideration of federal allocations by the Office of Economic Opportunity to thirty middle-sized American cities during the years 1968 to 1970.

199. Zisser, Michael H. "The Design of a Public Policy: National Land Use Planning and Organizational Theory." University of Pennsylvania, 1979, 40:1719-A.

This dissertation is concerned with the design of public policies. Specifically, it considers two interrelated components of the design process. The first is the delineation of policy objectives, means for implementing the objectives, and expected linkages between the two, that, when taken together, comprise the theoretical construction of the policy. The second is the set of methodological questions that must be asked in determining what the objectives, means, and linkages are and what is to be done when they are neither clearly defined nor well integrated.

Agricultural Policy

200. Allen, Albert J. "An Economic Analysis of Optimal Grain Market
Structure and Grain Flow Patterns with Selected Policy and Technological
Changes in the Northeast, South, and Delta Areas within Mississippi,
1970." Mississippi State University, 1978, 39:1724-A.

  The purpose of this study is to determine an optimum number, size,
  and location of grain elevators, feed mills and soybean processors,
  and modes of transportation for handling specific grains in each of
  the three substate areas (Delta, Northeast, South) within Mississippi.

201. Banker, David E. "A Model for the Analysis of Alternative Pricing
Policies in Federal Milk Marketing Orders." Purdue University, 1977,
38:6230-A.

  Nearly 78 percent of the fluid milk consumed in the United States is
  priced under the provisions of one of forty-seven federal milk marketing orders. Under marketing order provisions, minimum prices are set
  which dairy processors must pay to the dairy farmers from which they
  acquire milk. An operational model is designed which projects the
  consequences of changes in order provisions for a future period of up
  to five years on a quarterly basis.

202. Baumes, Harry S., Jr. "A Partial Equilibrium Sector Model of U.S.
Agriculture Open to Trade: A Domestic Agricultural and Agricultural Trade
Policy Analysis." (Volumes I and II) Purdue University, 1978, 40:372-A.

  Develops an analytical tool which focuses on U.S. agriculture and its
  linkages to the nonagricultural sector and the foreign market. A
  secondary objective is to demonstrate the use of the model developed
  as a policy analysis tool.

203. Bedestenci, Halil C. "Foreign Market Demand for U.S. Soybeans and
Soybean Products: A Policy Approach." The Ohio State University, 1978,
39:3057-A.

  To understand trade policy effects, the U.S. export demand functions
  for soybeans and soybean products for five countries are estimated,
  and U.S. supply relationships are formulated and estimated for these
  commodities--namely, soybeans, soymeal and soyoil.

204. Campbell, Joseph C. "Agricultural Exports and Sediment Effluent:
Their Relationship, and the Economic and Environmental Impacts of National
Sediment Control Policies." Iowa State University, 1978, 39:5635-A.

   Investigates the national and regional changes in mainstream sediment,
   soil loss, cropping patterns, farm incomes, and consumer food prices
   under two agricultural export demand projections.

205. Curry, Dean C. "Foreign Policy in an Evolving Global System: Global
Transformation and Its Impact upon United States-European Community Relations with a Focus on Agriculture, 1958-1979." Claremont Graduate School,
1981, 42:1303-A.

   Demonstrates the increasingly important role which economic issues
   have come to play in foreign policy since the end of the Second World
   War.

206. de las Casas Moya, P. Lizardo. "A Theoretical and Applied Approach
towards the Formulation of Alternative Agricultural Sector Policies in
Support of the Peruvian Agricultural Planning Process." Iowa State University, 1977, 38:6841-A.

   Presents an effort to develop a system for agricultural policy analysis in support of the Peruvian agricultural planning process. Of
   primary emphasis is the specification of reaction functions of producers and consumers.

207. Doka, Yahaya. "Policy Objectives, Land Tenure, and Settlement Performance: Implications for Equity and Economic Efficiency in the Columbia
Basin Irrigation Project." Washington State University, 1979, 40:2182-A.

   The issues of control of land resources, farming efficiency, and the
   use of public funds for irrigation development make a study of land
   use, control, and land tenure in the Columbia Basin Project of utmost
   importance. The approach in this study is to examine reclamation policy in terms of its distributive impact and in terms of its effect on
   efficiency of resource allocation in agriculture.

208. Drabenstott, Mark R. "Capital and Credit Demands in U.S. Agriculture: Projections for Alternative Economic and Policy Environments."
Iowa State University, 1981, 42:1729-A.

   Capital and credit demands in U.S. agriculture are projected for alternative policy and economic environments. The primary objective is
   to incorporate a finance sector in a sequential, econometric simulation model of U.S. agricultural production.

209. Eckholm, David C. "Rural Agri-Social Systems: Policy Indicators
and System Response." University of Minnesota, 1981, 42:383-A.

   A methodology is developed for building conceptual models of specific
   social contexts from which indicators may be derived, and a preliminary conceptual model of the rural agri-social system is constructed.

210. Essel, Albert. "Estimated Impacts of a Land Set-Aside Policy on
United States Agriculture in 1985: A Quadratic Programming Analysis."
Iowa State University, 1980, 41:2699-A.

Agricultural policy makers in the United States have become increasingly concerned with several facets of economic and structural developments in American agriculture. This study is concerned with the analysis of a supply control policy using a mathematical programming approach.

211. Frank, Garry L. "U.S. Agricultural Policy and the Federal and State Commodity Check-Off Programs." The University of Nebraska-Lincoln, 1980, 41:5230-A.

The research question addressed is: Does a market philosophy necessitate that the "coercive" powers of government be used to instill a collective economic framework for agricultural producers similar to that which existed under a supply management approach?

212. Griffith, Garry R. "An Econometric Simulation of Alternative Domestic and Trade Policies in the World Markets for Rapeseed, Soybeans and Their Products." University of Guelph (Canada), 1980, 40:6366-A.

An econometric model of the world markets for rapeseed, soybeans and their products is used to evaluate the potential impacts on the Canadian rapeseed industry of alternative domestic and trade policies.

213. Gunjal, Kisan R. "Econometric Analysis of Farm Machinery Investment and Simulations under Alternative Energy, Price Support, and Export Policies." Iowa State University, 1981, 42:4880-A.

The historical trends in structure, extent, and intensity of agricultural mechanization are analyzed in this study.

214. Henningson, Berton E. "United States Agricultural Trade and Development Policy during World War II: The Role of the Office of Foreign Agricultural Relations." University of Arkansas, 1981, 42:2819-A.

In 1939, the Office of Foreign Agricultural Relations (OFAR) was established in the Department of Agriculture with Leslie A. Wheeler as Director. During World War II, OFAR participated in the most extensive effort the United States ever had undertaken to formulate an agricultural trade and development policy.

215. Hill, William T. "Food, Energy, and Population: Are They 'World' Problems? An Analysis of Policy Responses in Brazil, Tanzania, the United States, and Yugoslavia." University of Massachusetts, 1980, 40:6404-A.

The study is a comparative analysis of the policy responses of four developmentally diverse nations in the areas of food, energy, and population--three issues which have gained wide popular currency as "global" or "world" problems.

216. Hutchison, Jon K. "Urban Fringe Agriculture, Nonpoint Water Pollution and Policy Considerations." The University of Wisconsin-Madison, 1977, 39:509-A.

Agriculture on the urban fringe responds to the uncertain pace of urban development by relocating, removal of livestock, emphasis of cash grains and depreciation of fixed capital. Farm operations on

the urban fringe are typified by absolute and relative declines in
size, rising rates of agricultural land rental and withdrawal of traditionally accepted levels of soil and water conservation.

217. Hutton, Patricia A. "U.S. Dairy Policy: A Quantitative Analysis of
the Post World War II Period." The University of Wisconsin-Madison, 1980,
41:4109-A.

   Government dairy programs have been a central feature of the U.S.
   dairy economy for over forty years. Although the economic characteristics and performance of the dairy industry have changed drastically,
   the basic structure of these programs has remained largely unchanged.

218. Kezis, Alan S. "An Examination of Economies of Size and Net Revenues on Columbia Basin Farms: Implications for Acreage Limitation Policy."
Washington State University, 1978, 39:997-A.

   In the future, reclamation policy will probably undergo major revision. The task of this study is to provide some of the economic input necessary for the reformulation of the acreage limitation policy.

219. Kurian, N. John. "Behavior under Uncertainty and Public Policies
in Peasant Agriculture: Applications of Economic Theory of Uncertainty."
The University of Western Ontario (Canada), 1977, 38:5609-A.

   The thesis analyzes the implications of agricultural uncertainty on
   peasant decision making, investigates the impacts of various public
   policies on peasants' behavior, and suggests suitable modifications
   in the existing public policies and recommends new measures in the
   light of the theoretical results obtained.

220. Lamb, Fred M. "The Linkages of Continuing Education to the Formation of Forestry Policy in Virginia." The Pennsylvania State University,
1980, 41:4253-A.

   The objective is to explore the role of continuing education, especially Extension Forestry programming, in the formation of state
   forestry policy in Virginia.

221. Lamm, Ray M., Jr. "A Policy Analysis of the United States Vegetable
Oilseeds, Oils, and Oil Products Industry with Special Emphasis on Optimal
Control." Virginia Polytechnic Institute and State University, 1977, 38:
5609-A.

   The objectives are to develop a discrete dynamic model to explain the
   duality of supply flows from production and inventory stocks; to specify a monthly sectoral model of the United States vegetable oilseeds,
   oils, and oil products industry; to analyze policy alternatives using
   simulation; and to evaluate the potential of optimal control theory
   for stabilizing prices in the industry.

222. Leholm, Arlen G. "Potential Impact of Ground Water Policy Alternatives on Nebraska Agriculture, 1977-2020." The University of Nebraska-
Lincoln, 1981, 42:1730-A.

   Nine agricultural and related ground water policy scenarios are analyzed for Nebraska over the time period 1977-2020 to determine how they might influence returns to land and management, farm production and aquifer conditions.

223. Lopes, Mauro. "The Mobilization of Resources from Agriculture: A Policy Analysis for Brazil." Purdue University, 1977, 39:998-A.

Develops a theoretical analysis of the impact of alternative policies on the agricultural sector, estimates empirically the effect of these alternative policies on the agricultural sector, and draws policy implications from the empirical results obtained.

224. Macaulay, Thomas G. "A Recursive Spatial Equilibrium Model of the North American Beef Industry for Policy Analysis." University of Guelph (Canada), 1976, 38:4278-A.

With a recursive spatial equilibrium model of the North American beef industry alternative stabilization schemes for the Canadian beef industry are evaluated in the light of revisions to the Agricultural Stabilization Act.

225. McGregor, Andrew M. "The Lome Convention and the ACP Sugar Exporters: The Political Economy of Conflicting Policies." Cornell University, 1978, 39:2419-A.

Examines how the resolution of inconsistent external and internal policy objectives has led to the generation of a recurring EEC sugar surplus. The impact of these surpluses on the major ACP sugar exporters is explored in detail.

226. MacLennan, Carol A. "Plantation Capitalism and Social Policy in Hawaii." University of California, Berkeley, 1979, 40:306-A.

Describes a contemporary social policy in Hawaii designed to curb the effects of sugar and pineapple plantation closings on rural communities, and places the formation and failure of this policy in the context of plantation capitalism and the origin of modern class relations in the islands.

227. Meyers, James M. "Urban and Rural 4-H Programs: Research for Policy and Planning in Nonformal Education." Harvard University, 1980, 40:6093-A.

Provides a conceptual definition of the archetypical 4-H club, a systematic framework for program comparisons, and comparison between the traditional 4-H club model and a major urban alternative.

228. Moery, Phillip W. "An Economic Inquiry into the Costs and Benefits of the U.S. Agricultural Policy for Rice, 1955-1975." The George Washington University, 1980, 41:334-A.

Sets the political and economic framework in which the commodity program for rice and the related programs evolved, and examines the development of econometric commodity modeling and establishes the criteria for a statistical explanation of the U.S. rice market and the U.S. government intervention in that market.

229. Montgomery, Katherine R. "U.S. Policy in a Changing Global Food Regime." University of Pittsburgh, 1980, 41:5237-A.

   Examines the role of the United States in changing the global food regime.

230. Mortimer, John W. "Designing Government Policy for the Cotton Industry." University of Missouri-Columbia, 1979, 41:2225-A.

   To successfully achieve stabilization goals, policy makers need to consider the medium and long term effects of their policies, which in the past they have tended to neglect, due in part to the nature of the American political system and to the absence of a formalized structure for decision making. This study attempts to provide such a policy-making structure for the U.S. cotton industry.

231. Morton, Andrew S. "Potential Price Variability in the U.S. Grain and Livestock Sector in the 1980s under Alternative Policy Scenarios: An Econometric Approach." Iowa State University, 1982, 42:1621-A.

   Utilizes an annual structural econometric model of the U.S. grain and livestock sector to simulate market price instability resulting from potential fluctuations in domestic crop yields and demand for U.S. grain exports over 1981-90.

232. Nguyen, Hoang Dang. "World Food Projection Models and Short-Run World Trade and Reserve Policy Evaluations." University of Illinois at Urbana-Champaign, 1977, 38:6236-A.

   Develops a world food model which deals with nine commodities: wheat, maize, other grains, soybeans, soybean meal, soybean oil, beef, pork, and chicken; and ten regions: United States, Canada, EC-9, Japan, Australia, USSR, India, China, Argentina, and the rest of the world.

233. Novakovic, Andrew M. "An Economic Analysis of the U.S. Dairy Price Support Program and Alternate Policies." Purdue University, 1979, 40:3431-A.

   A spatial model of the U.S. dairy sector is used to analyze support prices at 75, 80, 90, and 100 percent of parity; supports at 80 percent of parity but with Class I differentials reduced 5, 10, 25, or 50 cents; supports based on the cost of production; a policy of minimal or non-support; and the possibility of increasing dairy imports.

234. Padgitt, Merritt M. "An Analysis of On-Farm Impacts for Soil Conservation and Non-Point Source Pollution Abatement Practices and Policies on Representative Farms in Southeast Minnesota." Michigan State University, 1980, 41:3199-A.

   Estimates on-farm impacts from alternative soil conservation technology and policy options and assesses impact differences among farms because of differences in their size, soil composition and enterprise combinations.

235. Parvin, Gregg L. "An Application of Optimal Control Methods to Agricultural Policy Analysis and Formulation." Oklahoma State University, 1981, 42:4085-A.

Demonstrates that control theory can be used to generate economic intelligence in regard to agricultural policy formulation and analysis.

236. Patton, William P. "The Impact of the 1977 Food and Agriculture Act on Cotton Production in the United States: A Simulation of Policy Alternatives." Texas A&M University, 1980, 41:4455-A.

Estimates the probable impacts of seven alternative cotton policy scenarios on the crop production industry in the Cotton Belt region of the United States.

237. Pederson, Glenn D. "A Conceptualization and Analysis of the Distributional Impacts of Alternative Agricultural Credit Policies." Michigan State University, 1980, 41:3200-A.

The study is made in response to the need for a more thorough understanding of the distribution of benefits from credit. It focuses on a firm-level analysis of the financial impacts which arise under various conditions on loan extension, use, and repayment.

238. Pitt, Mark M. "Economic Policy and Agricultural Development in Indonesia." University of California, Berkeley, 1977, 38:4950-A.

Measures the distorting effects of government intervention in agricultural markets on agricultural supply, and chronicles in some detail the development of the trade regime and rice policy in Indonesia.

239. Plaut, Thomas R. "Urban Growth and Agricultural Decline: Problems and Policies." University of Pennsylvania, 1978, 39:6368-A.

Reviews in detail the nature of the conflict between urbanization and agricultural production, and analyzes the effectiveness of the major techniques aimed at preserving farmland in areas under urban pressures.

240. Poole, Dennis L. "The Impacts of Price Support Policies and Programs on Farm Scale and the Nature of Farm Family Life." Brandeis University, 1979, 39:7525-A.

Identifies the chain of causal impacts extending from price support policies and programs to the changing scale of American farms to the changing nature of farm family life. Focuses primarily on the dairy industry and life on family-operated dairy farms in Maryland.

241. Richardson, James W. "An Application of Optimal Control Theory to Agricultural Policy Analysis." Oklahoma State University, 1978, 39: 5055-A.

Demonstrates the use of an optimal control technique for analyzing farm policy, which enables the researcher to explicitly consider the interests of the various farm policy decision makers.

242. Roberts, Roland K. "Analysis of Selected Policy Impacts on the U.S. Livestock Sector by a Five-Commodity Econometric Simulation Model." Iowa State University, 1979, 40:5946-A.

An econometric simulation model of the U.S. livestock sector including beef, pork, lamb, chicken and turkey is developed.

243. Rose, Frank S. "An Economic Analysis of Alternative Dairy Import Policies for the United States." Michigan State University, 1979, 40: 1613-A.

A comparative static model is developed to permit estimation of the short-run impacts on price and production in the cheese manufacturing and milk production subsectors of the dairy industry as well as the effects on the purchases of the Commodity Credit Corporation under the domestic milk price support program of increasing United States imports of cheese.

244. Skees, Jerry R. "A Multiple Farm Simulation Model of the Impact of Income Tax and Commodity Policies on the Opportunities for Growth of Varied Size Corn/Soybean Farms." Michigan State University, 1981, 42:3686-A.

The study is undertaken in response to re-emerging concerns over structural trends in the agricultural sector. Since these concerns relate to the trend toward larger and fewer farms, this study focuses on the growth phase of the farm firm.

245. Talbott, Irvin D., Jr. "Agricultural Innovation and Policy Changes in Kenya in the 1930s." West Virginia University, 1976, 38:4991-A.

During the depression of the 1930's the government of the Colony and Protectorate of Kenya took various actions to improve the economic viability of the territory. Initially it provided various subsidies for European settler farmers; when these failed, it turned to the promotion of African cash crop cultivation.

246. Thomson, Anne M. "Nutrition, Food Demand and Policy." Stanford University, 1980, 40:740-A.

The work reported in this thesis arose out of a very broad question: how can the nutritional consequences of various types of policy decisions be measured or predicted?

247. Tinberg, Cynthia P. "An Economic Analysis of Agricultural Land Use Policies for Southern Michigan." Michigan State University, 1978, 39: 6253-A.

Provides information prior to the formulation and implementation of new land use policies. Five different and often competing state land use policies are reviewed and evaluated.

248. Walker, David J. "An Economic Analysis of Alternative Environmental and Resource Policies for Controlling Soil Loss and Sedimentation from Agriculture." Iowa State University, 1977, 38:4282-A.

Considers the dual problem associated with water erosion of soil from agricultural lands: diminished productivity of the land and the sediment pollution of surface waters.

249. Walker, Rodney L. "Short-Run Policies for the U.S. Grain and Livestock Sectors: An Application of Control Theory." Purdue University, 1978, 39:3063-A.

Analyzes the tradeoffs among the several goals that policy makers have concerning the U.S. wheat, feed grain, soybean, beef, pork and chicken sectors, and derives these tradeoffs in such a manner so as to reduce the number of alternative policies which can be considered by policy makers to those that optimize the multidimensional objective function of policy makers.

250. Wiese, Allan O. "The Influence of Farm Interest Groups in the Agricultural Policy-Making Process." The University of Oklahoma, 1980, 41:3258-A.

Uses Salisbury's (1969) exchange theory to examine interactions between interest group lobbyists and congressmen. Exchange theory inducements are examined for relationships to interest group goal attainment as are other variables.

251. Williams, Gary W. "The U.S. and World Oilseeds and Derivatives Markets: Economic Structure and Policy Interventions." (Volumes I and II) Purdue University, 1981, 42:2230-A.

The study is a quantitative examination of the complex economic and policy interrelationships in world oilseeds and derivatives markets as they interact with the U.S. oilseeds industry.

252. Zwart, Anthony C. "An Empirical Analysis of Alternative Stabilization Policies for the World Wheat Sector." University of Guelph (Canada), 1977, 38:6237-A.

In this study an empirical model of the world wheat economy is used to analyze the potential impacts of alternative stabilization schemes.

Civil Rights and the
Status of Women

253. Berlowe, James A. "Changes in Admissions Policies at Medical Schools before and after the *Bakke* Decision." Michigan State University, 1982, 42:376-A.

The purpose is to determine whether changes in admissions policies at medical schools were implemented subsequent to the U.S. Supreme Court decision, *Regents of University of California v. Bakke*, 98 S.C. 2733, 1978. The central theme of the underrepresentation of minority students at medical schools is presented, analyzed, and discussed in light of published commentary and research.

254. Bragg, Richard L. "The Maryland Black Caucus as a Racial Group in the Maryland General Assembly: Legislative Communities and Caucus Influence on Public Policy 1975-1978." Howard University, 1979, 40:6401-A.

Examines the role of the Black Caucus members as a racial group in the Maryland General Assembly from 1975-78 to see if this group considered race a key factor affecting the attitudes and behavior of Black Caucus members when making political decisions or whether there were other criteria used by caucus members in determining public policy. Essential to this research is the need to determine whether or not the Black Caucus has influenced public policy at the state level.

255. Brown, Joseph S. "Black Americans: Attitudes toward Population Policies." Purdue University, 1978, 39:3112-A.

The purpose is to explain why black Americans, both leaders and the masses, tend not to support government policies to limit rapid population growth as frequently as white Americans. The study also seeks to determine the extent to which the population attitudes of black leaders are also shared by the black masses.

256. Burt, Larry W. "United States Expansion and Federal Policy toward Native Americans, 1953-60." The University of Toledo, 1979, 40:2220-A.

Describes and analyzes attempts to implement terminationists' ideas after Republican victories in the 1952 elections gave them significant political strength.

257. Canty, Althia. "A Descriptive Analysis of Black College and University Development with Regard to Selected Federal Funding Policies: 1954-1980." The University of Tennessee, 1982, 42:316-A.

Analyzes the patterns of federal funding in fifteen of the black land-grant colleges and universities in the United States.

258. Carter, Herbert L. "The Utilization of Social Indicators in Urban Policy Processes--An Alternate to Recycled Urban Black Violence." University of Southern California, 1979, 39:6958-A.

This exploratory study is directed toward the analysis of theoretical approaches to and programmatic outcomes of urban initiatives which sought to address the quality of life experienced by urban dwellers. Conceptual frameworks underlying policy formulation and execution are examined and several of the relevant theories of black urban violence are explicated.

259. Chertos, Cynthia H. "Social Policy Implementation in Organizations: The Case of Non-Discrimination and Affirmative Action in the University." The University of Michigan, 1982, 42:550-A.

Examines the constraints upon implementation of non-discrimination and affirmative action in one type of work organization: the university.

260. Christian, James E. "A Study of Policies and Practices Which Demonstrate a Commitment to the Achievement of Racial Integration in Selected Oklahoma High Schools." The University of Oklahoma, 1979, 39:6611-A.

Investigates the perceptions of educators regarding the implementation of selected policies and practices which demonstrate a commitment to the achievement of effective racial integration in public secondary educational institutions.

261. Deutsch, Alleen. "Women's Studies as Institutional Policy--An Analysis of the Program Coordinator's Role." Miami University, 1978, 39:4753-A.

Focuses upon the descriptive institutional role components of women's studies program coordinators at twenty-three selected colleges and universities.

262. Doughty, Ronald H. "Public Policy and School Desegregation: An Analysis of Mandatory Busing, Open Enrollment and Community Control." The Ohio State University, 1980, 41:4488-A.

Assesses the degree to which mandatory busing, open enrollment and community control are supported by persuasive evidence and plausible arguments.

263. Fixico, Donald L. "Termination and Relocation: Federal Indian Policy in the 1950's." The University of Oklahoma, 1980, 41:2475-A.

This study of federal Indian policy from World War II through the John F. Kennedy Administration is concerned with the serious repercussions of this critical period of federal-Indian relations.

264. Flannery, Thomas P., Jr. "The Indian Self-Determination Act: An
Analysis of Federal Policy." Northwestern University, 1980, 41:3346-A.

Examines one public policy, federal Indian policy, and traces its development over the years. The development of the current Indian policy, Self-Determination, is examined using a process model of public
policy.

265. Foster, Madison J., II. "Societal Paradigms and Social Policy
Theories: An Analysis of Urban Black Disruption Explanations, 1960-1970."
Bryn Mawr College, 1980, 41:5245-A.

During the middle 1960's, American public officials and social scientists hurriedly developed theories of black urban disruptions. This
study examines the theories and their theoretical origins.

266. Fox, Marion B. "Time Allocation in Planning and Policymaking for
Working Women and Their Households: A Social Indicator Study." University of Pennsylvania, 1978, 39:6366-A.

Links data on the time allocations of a population to three frameworks: population description that might be utilized in urban planning
studies; analysis of time allocation differences, within populations,
that are formulated into a set of normative social indicators; and as
a criterion to be evaluated in policy choice.

267. Haignere, Lois. "Admission of Women to Medical Schools: A Study of
Organizational Response to Social Movement and Public Policy Pressures."
The University of Connecticut, 1981, 42:871-A.

Examines cross-sectionally the responses of medical schools to post-
1970 pressures from the women's movement and its resultant public
policy. In addition, the study investigates historically school response to both antifeminist and feminist movements.

268. Hanna, Allan A. "Settlement and Energy Policy in Perspective: A
Theoretical Framework for the Evaluation of Public Policy." The University of Western Ontario (Canada), 1980, 41:5131-A.

Develops a conceptual framework for understanding the policy field
and a policy planning theory alternative to the three dominant theories: incrementalism, comprehensive rationalism and mixed scanning.

269. Hardy, Richard J. "The Impact of Civil Rights Policies on Achieving Racial and Sexual Income Equality, 1948-76." The University of Iowa,
1978, 39:7511-A.

The Civil Rights Act of 1964 and the policies it engendered represent
a marked shift in the federal government's commitment to end discrimination and improve the status of blacks and women in nearly all
phases of public and private life. The purpose of this thesis is to
assess the impact of these policies on achieving racial and sexual
economic equality.

270. Heflin, John F. "Implementation of School Desegregation Policy:
An Analysis of the California State Department of Education Experience."
Stanford University, 1978, 39:570-A.

Focuses on interactions between the California State Department of
Education and a stratified sample of six local education agencies
during the implementation of state public school desegregation policy.

271.   Hendricks, Judith J.   "Organizational Incentives and Disincentives
for Implementing Innovative Policies: A Study of Affirmative Action in
Delaware." Temple University, 1982, 42:5241-A.

Utilizes organizational theory to examine affirmative action implementation in Delaware and to describe characteristics contributing
to the successful implementation of affirmative action.

272.   Hibbard, Michael.   "Public Epistemologies and Policy Planning: The
Case of American Indian Policy." University of California, Los Angeles,
1980, 40:436-A.

A general model of the relation between public epistemologies and
policy planning paradigms is proposed and tested.

273.   Holm, Thomas M.   "Indians and Progressives: From Vanishing Policy
to the Indian New Deal." The University of Oklahoma, 1978, 39:6915-A.

During the nineteenth century the United States developed an Indian
policy based on the rhetorical ideal of assimilating Native Americans
into mainstream society. To those advocates of the policy, assimila-
tion could only be accomplished through the utter destruction of tribal cultures and values.

274.   Howell, Bing P.   "The Anatomy of Discrimination in the Canal Zone
Vis-a-Vis Stated United States Policy from 1940-1977." University of
California, Los Angeles, 1979, 40:4188-A.

Delves into the discriminatory practices of the United States in the
Panama Canal Zone from 1940 to 1977.

275.   Kerwin, Cornelius M.   "Dimensions of Quality: An Analysis of Policies Affecting the Right to Counsel under the Criminal Justice Act of
1964." The Johns Hopkins University, 1978, 39:1097-A.

The Criminal Justice Act of 1964 provided resources to assure effective representation for indigents in federal criminal proceedings.
The purpose of this research is to analyze the implementation of this
legislation.

276.   Leong, Philip.   "The Conflict in the Requirements of Affirmative
Action and Reduction in Force Policies as They Affect Certified Educational Personnel in Essex County, New Jersey." Rutgers University, 1980,
41:1315-A.

Attempts to determine whether or not affirmative action mandates and
policies were jeopardized by tenure and seniority legislation and
regulations in twenty-one operating school districts in Essex County,
New Jersey.

277.   McCummings, Betty.   "The Incrementalist Nature of Public Policy:
Service Utilization Implications for the Black Elderly under the Older
Americans Act." Syracuse University, 1977, 39:1098-A.

Critically examines and assesses the incrementalist nature of public policy development, and attempts to discern through the analysis of selected performance measures how incrementalism affects the manner in which the black elderly determines to utilize services legislated under the Older Americans Act of 1965.

278. McDermott, Rose M. "The Legal Condition of Women in the Church: Shifting Policies and Norms." The Catholic University of America, 1979, 40:2113-A.

In the Roman Catholic Church lay women and women religious do not share an equal juridical condition with lay men and non-ordained male religious. Although no canon in Church legislation explicitly states this inferior legal status, numerous norms limit women's participation in the teaching, sanctifying and governing mission of the Church.

279. McDonnell, Janet A. "The Disintegration of the Indian Estate: Indian Land Policy, 1913-1929." Marquette University, 1980, 41:4141-A.

Between the passage of the Dawes Act in 1887 and the Indian Reorganization Act in 1934, Indian landholdings shrank from 137 to 48 million acres. Much of this land loss was due to the unsuccessful policies of Commissioner of Indian Affairs Cato Sells (1913-1920) and his successor Charles Burke (1921-1929).

280. Morton, Frederick L. "Sexual Equality and the Family in the United States Supreme Court: A Study of Judicial Policy-Making." University of Toronto (Canada), 1981, 42:4571-A.

This is a critical study of a recent example of judicial policy making--the United States Supreme Court's attempt to promote a greater degree of sexual equality in American society through its interpretation of the Equal Protection Clause of the Fourteenth Amendment.

281. Nielsen, Margaret O. "Enforcing Desegregation Policy: Changing Racial Segregation in Urban School Districts, 1967-1972." The University of Michigan, 1977, 38:6975-A.

Three questions are explored in this research: (1) What is the effect of federal court orders to desegregate school districts among southern and among northern and western cities in the U.S. during the late 1960's and early 1970's? (2) What are the effects of the racial composition, size, spending, and revenue sources of the school district on racial segregation during the same period? (3) What are the effects of structural and compositional characteristics of communities on the segregation of their schools and what is the impact of court orders and district expenditures and revenue sources when the community's socioeconomic status and ecological structure are statistically controlled?

282. O'Brien, David M. "Privacy, Law, and Public Policy." University of California, Santa Barbara, 1977, 39:6929-A.

Attempts an analysis of the parameters, as defined by constitutional law and public policies, of the political ideal of personal privacy.

283. O'Connor, Karen P. "Litigation Strategies and Policy Formulation: An Examination of Organized Women's Groups Use of the Courts, 1869–1977." State University of New York at Buffalo, 1979, 39:7501-A.

Examines three types of litigation strategy: litigation pursued for publicity; litigation to gradually win favorable policy decisions from the courts; and submission of *amicus curiae* briefs. To study these litigation types, several women's groups that have resorted to the courts are examined.

284. Orr, Margaret T. "A Critical Examination of a Policy Process OCR Review of New York City Schools." Columbia University, 1979, 40:6022-A.

Examines an entire policy process, using a case study as the basis of the research. The case study was developed from a field study of the Office for Civil Rights Review of New York City schools.

285. Page, Thornell K. "A Study of the District of Columbia Public Schools Desegregation Policies, 1954–1967." Virginia Polytechnic Institute and State University, 1978, 39:1972-A.

Examines the effect of educational policy decisions approved by the District of Columbia Board of Education to desegregate the public schools between 1954 and 1967.

286. Pilato, Angelica R. "The Judgment Policy Used by Community College Administrators in Judging the Success Potential of Male and Female Administrative Applicants." Oregon State University, 1979, 39:4827-A.

The main focus of this study is to determine how community college administrators used certain personality traits (cues) in judging the success potential of female and male administrative applicants.

287. Pottker, Janice M. "An Analysis of School Resistance to Change Regarding Community Challenges to Sex Biased Policies in Local Schools." Columbia University, 1979, 41:3848-A.

Community task forces formed to eliminate sex bias in local schools emerged throughout the United States in the early 1970's. It is the activities of these school-community task forces, from initiation through policy adoption and implementation, which is the subject of this study.

288. Preer, Jean L. "Law and Social Policy: Desegregation in Public Higher Education." (Volumes I and II) The George Washington University, 1980, 41:2265-A.

Desegregation efforts in public higher education historically have embodied two concerns: the need to overturn legal segregation altogether and the need to improve educational opportunities for black students.

289. Putney, Diane T. "Fighting the Scourge: American Indian Morbidity and Federal Policy, 1897–1928." Marquette University, 1980, 41:4143-A.

Because the Indian health service in the first decades of the twentieth century was unable to correct the economic and political origins of the "Indian health problem," the vigorous and progressive campaigns conducted by that service failed to eradicate significantly disease from among Indian people in the United States.

290. Rand, Wayne D. "An Analysis of Selected Constitutional Rights of Students and the Written Policies and Procedures in Local School Districts Regarding Those Rights." The University of Iowa, 1978, 39:4639-A.

The purpose is to determine the status of the law on selected constitutional rights of students and to delineate legal criteria by which local school board policies and procedures regarding those rights could be analyzed.

291. Rogers, Nancy. "The Development of Federal Policy for the Elimination of Discrimination in the Postsecondary Education of Women." The University of Michigan, 1979, 40:712-A.

Examines the role of women in the formulation and passage of Title IX, the first comprehensive statute directed toward the elimination of sex discrimination in education.

292. Sanders, Mildred E. "Electorate Expansion and Public Policy: A Decade of Political Change in the South." Cornell University, 1978, 39: 2520-A.

Political change in the Deep South presents a unique opportunity to test some propositions central to democratic theory. These propositions concern the significance of the electoral process to policy change: specifically, the nature of responsiveness of elected officials to a new voting group.

293. Scheirbeck, Helen M. "Education: Public Policy and the American Indian." Virginia Polytechnic Institute and State University, 1980, 41: 3455-A.

The subject is the public education of American Indians. Such education is analyzed from the perspective of public policies and actions of federal, state, and local governments toward American Indians.

294. Schrader, Robert F. "The Indian Arts and Crafts Board: An Aspect of New Deal Indian Policy." Marquette University, 1981, 42:4121-A.

Shows that under General Manager d'Harnoncourt the Board assisted in the establishment of standards for the use of official trademarks or certificates of genuineness for Navajo, Pueblo, and Hopi silver, for Navajo woven wool products, and for Alaskan Indian and Eskimo products; encouraged and directed the growth of Indian cooperative production and marketing enterprises; established a wider market for products; and promoted Indian arts and crafts by educating the public about the culture that produced those arts and crafts.

295. Scruggs, Donald L. "Lyndon Baines Johnson and the National Advisory Commission on Civil Disorders (the Kerner Commission): A Study of the Johnson Domestic Policy Making System." The University of Oklahoma, 1980, 40:790-A.

Seeks to accomplish four goals: to describe the political uses of ad hoc advisory groups in the advisory systems created by twentieth century American presidents; to detail the unique contributions of President Johnson to this pattern of political behavior; to advance an original interpretation of the work of one of Johnson's most important advisory groups; to draw conclusions useful in enhancing the theoretical interpretation of the practice of American presidential politics.

296. Soriano, Michael E. "Minority Activism and Media Access: An Analysis of Community Participation in Policy, Programming and Production." Stanford University, 1977, 38:5110-A.

Analyzes the Capital Cities Minority Program Project. Through the project, minority groups in specific cities were provided the opportunity to participate in the formulation of programming and broadcasting policy.

297. Suetopka-Duerre, Ramona N. "A Case Study of Implementing Alaska's Bilingual Education Policy." Harvard University, 1982, 42:1392-A.

Analyzes implementation of Alaska's bilingual-bicultural education policy in the Lower Kuskokwim School District (LKSD) which serves a predominantly Eskimo population. Describes policy implementation, analyzes problems encountered during implementation of LKSD programs under Alaska's bilingual-bicultural education policy, and explains why the programs diverged from the intent of state policy.

298. Sullivan, Harold J. "'De Facto' School Segregation: Private Choice or Public Policy?" City University of New York, 1978, 39:4477-A.

Outlines, compares, and ultimately evaluates a variety of approaches found in court decisions and in the literature to identify the role played by public policy in producing racially isolated schools.

299. Swain, Johnnie, Jr. "Regional Comparison of Black and White Women Economic Activities in Segmented Labor Markets: Implication for Social Policy." Syracuse University, 1977, 39:1143-A.

Attempts to describe and explain black and white labor force participation patterns in American labor markets.

300. Thal, Alexander J. "Fairness in Compensation Procedures: A Case Study of Navajo Tribal Land Acquisition Policies." State University of New York at Buffalo, 1981, 42:1782-A.

Analyzes the effectiveness of the Navajo Tribe's land acquisition policies by evaluating compensation practices in the tribal process of land withdrawal. It is hypothesized that the Navajo Tribe is losing revenues and public services due to a lack of sensitivity to individual landholder interests in the land withdrawal process.

301. Tong, Susan. "College Students' Attitudes toward Affirmative Action Policies for Non-Whites and Women." Western Michigan University, 1981, 42:3316-A.

Assesses college students' attitudes toward affirmative action policies for non-whites and women.

302. Trueheart, William E. "The Consequences of Federal and State Resource Allocation and Development Policies for Traditionally Black Land-
Grant Institutions: 1862-1954." Harvard University, 1979, 40:6170-A.

Analyzes the evolution of land-grant policies from the seminal Mor-
rill-Wade Act of 1862 to the beginning of the era of desegregation
in 1954.

303. Wesman, Elizabeth C. "Public Policies at Loggerheads: The Effect
of Equal Employment Opportunity Legislation on Unions." Cornell University, 1982, 42:5268-A.

Examines organizational and policy implications of Equal Employment
Opportunity legislation, court cases, consent decrees, and affirmative action mandates for unions. The Brotherhood of Railway, Airline
and Steamship Clerks serves as a case study.

304. Zacarias, Ruben. "Attitudes of Selected Superintendency Level Administrators of the Los Angeles Unified School District Regarding Policies
and Practices Affecting the Education of Hispanic American Students."
University of San Francisco, 1981, 42:5039-A.

Assesses the attitudes of selected superintendent-level administrators
of the Los Angeles Unified School District regarding policies and
practices which would facilitate implementation of effective programs
for Hispanic American students.

305. Zelman, Patricia G. "Development of Equal Employment Opportunity
for Women as a National Policy, 1960-1967." The Ohio State University,
1980, 41:3237-A.

Details the events that contributed to the drawing of a legal parallel
between race and sex, and its effect on the development of a feminist
consciousness among officially appointed defenders of women's interests and their allies.

Domestic Taxing and
Economic Policy

306. Afsahi, Shad. "Policy Proposals for Reducing Unemployment in the
United States." University of Southern California, 1979, 39:6867-A.

Simultaneous unemployment and inflation can be resolved within our
present socioeconomic system. The economic tools to combat unemployment are available.

307. Agunbiade, Ajiboye O. "An Analysis of Regional Development Policy
and Economic Growth in Appalachia 1960-1975." The University of Iowa,
1981, 42:2294-A.

The purpose is to determine the extent of structural change and estimate the impacts of region-specific fiscal policies on regional economic growth. The role of regional development policy is evaluated
relative to other potential determinants of regional growth.

308. Akinyemi, Edward O. "A Policy-Oriented Model System for Transportation Regions or Corridors." State University of New York at Buffalo,
1980, 41:3753-A.

A policy-sensitive model system, which can be used for multimodal
transportation analysis in transportation corridors or regions, is
developed.

309. Al-Yamani, Abdullah G. "Alternative Accounting Income Measures and
Dividend Policy." University of Colorado at Boulder, 1980, 42:265-A.

Tests empirically whether dividend policy is better explained by historical cost profit or by replacement cost income measures.

310. Arthur, David L. "An Analysis of the Changing Decision Making
Roles of Business and Government in Regional Development: Related Policy
Issues." University of California, Berkeley, 1977, 38:4920-A.

Focuses on the changing decision-making roles of the private sector
and the public sector as the result of the public recognition of externalities and the desire to eliminate them.

311. Asako, Kazumi. "An Essay on the Announcement Impact and the Role of Stabilization Policy." Yale University, 1979, 40:5955-A.

Shows that the anticipation of future policy actions can indeed influence the real side of the economy, rational expectations and the natural rate hypothesis notwithstanding. Also shows that anticipation or preannouncement of policies can have certain undesirable effects.

312. Austin, Michael L. "Monetary and Fiscal Policy in an Optimal Neoclassical Growth Model." State University of New York at Stony Brook, 1981, 42:2790-A.

Develops an optimal neoclassical growth model which explicitly incorporates fiscal and monetary policy into an economy with consumption, capital goods, government bonds and money.

313. Barsellotti, Dolores A. "Social Responsibility: Organizational Policy Evaluative Criteria with California Savings and Loan Field Test Case Study." Claremont Graduate School, 1979, 39:6849-A.

Derives and develops a qualitative set of criteria or constructs for the evaluation of internal organizational policies, practices and procedures in relation to social responsibility and consumer issue areas.

314. Baum, Christopher F. "Applications of Optimal Control Theory to Macroeconomic Stabilization Policy." The University of Michigan, 1977, 38:6855-A.

Deals with the uses of optimal control theory in the analysis of dynamic macroeconomic models in discrete time. An analytic solution technique is presented and related to other techniques currently in use.

315. Bednarzik, Robert W. "Part-Time Work and Public Policy." University of Missouri-Columbia, 1978, 39:6229-A.

Examines the patterns in the part-time work experience of the United States labor force in recent years. Emphasizes particularly the demographic characteristics of part-time workers and the trends and cyclical variations in voluntary part-time employment.

316. Benjamin, Wahjudi P. "Accounting Policy Interventions and the Behavior of Security Returns." University of Missouri-Columbia, 1980, 42:751-A.

The purpose is twofold: (1) to propose an improved methodology for security market research in general and intervention analysis in particular, and (2) to apply the proposed methodology to two accounting policy interventions.

317. Benson, Bruce L. "A Theoretical Analysis of Regulatory Policy: Bank Mergers and Holding Company Acquisitions." (Volumes I and II) Texas A&M University, 1978, 39:1710-A.

There are two goals pursued in this study: (1) to demonstrate that regulatory policies do not promote the public interest in the case of bank merger and multi-unit bank regulation, and (2) to develop a special interest theory of regulation which explains observed policies toward bank mergers and multi-unit banking.

318. Blumenfrucht, Israel. "An Analysis of the Policies and Practices of the Internal Revenue Service in Implementing the Accumulated Earnings Tax." New York University, 1981, 42:3203-A.

Provides a thorough review and analysis of the accumulated earnings tax in order to determine whether the accumulated earnings tax could be, and indeed should be, applied to publicly held corporations.

319. Borge, Paul D., Jr. "Long Run Consumption and Investment Policies: Adaptive Strategies and Uniform Rules." Harvard University, 1980, 40: 309-A.

Examines the problem faced by an individual who must choose a portfolio risk policy and a consumption policy in each of several successive time periods, taking into account the effects of current strategies on future opportunities.

320. Bowles, David C. "An Information Theoretic Approach to Stabilization Policy." Duke University, 1980, 41:4123-A.

The object of the study is to suggest an alternative (or at least supplementary) approach both to the analysis of causes of economic instability and to the conduct of policy designed to offset this instability.

321. Carmichael, Jeffrey. "The Role of Government Financial Policy in Economic Growth." Princeton University, 1979, 40:4162-A.

Examines the relationship between government financial policy and the dynamic path of a developed capitalist economy. The analysis is concerned for the most part with the efficiency properties of the economy's steady-state growth path, although it does offer some new views and results on issues of concern in the stabilization literature.

322. Cate, Thomas H. "The Intellectual Origins of John Maynard Keynes' Policy Recommendations." The Florida State University, 1979, 40:5138-A.

Investigates the relationship between the policy recommendations which John Keynes (1883-1946) articulates in his phenomenological writings (which are written in response to important historical events or issues) and those of Keynes' two major works.

323. Chaudhury, Ajit K. "Essays on Economic Policy under Non-Market Clearing Conditions." The University of Rochester, 1978, 40:2172-A.

The dissertation should best be viewed as a collection of essays on some selected problems of an economy under non-market clearing conditions.

324. Chessen, James H. "Differential Impact of Monetary Policy: A Sectoral Approach." Virginia Polytechnic Institute and State University, 1981, 42:4519-A.

The proposition tested in the thesis is that actual money growth is not systematically related to output growth of selected manufacturing sectors.

325. Cheung, Chun-Sang. "Optimal Stabilization Policy in a Fixprice-Flexprice Model." University of Illinois at Urbana-Champaign, 1981, 42: 4093-A.

Much of the theoretical work done in the area of wage and price controls suggests that controls are an effective means for reducing inflation. However, in these same studies too little attention has been paid to the shortages created by the controls.

326. Chiu, Cheng Hsiung. "A Two Stage Decision Rule for the Conduct of Monetary Policy." The Ohio State University, 1977, 39:982-A.

Deals with a topic related to one current research stream in monetary economics, that is the finding of optimal monetary strategy with the use of information variables.

327. Chope, Roger A. "Market and Industry Factors, Accounting Policy, and the Time Series Properties of Accounting Earnings." University of Oregon, 1981, 42:4857-A.

Builds a model of individual firm accounting earnings where firm earnings are a function of market-wide earnings, industry-wide earnings, and an individual firm effect. A similar model for common stock returns is also constructed. Firm earnings behavior is then analyzed based on the explanatory power of market and industry-wide earnings, and is compared to results using common stock returns.

328. Considine, Timothy J. "A Regional Economic Analysis of Energy Pricing and Taxation Policies." Cornell University, 1981, 42:3682-A.

Virtually all forecasting models of energy demand at the state level do not explicitly consider the interactions between energy demand and the level of economic activity. The objective of this study is to develop an analytical framework for understanding the nature and extent of these interactions. This framework is then used to evaluate five specific energy pricing and taxation policies for New York State.

329. Culley, John O. "The Need for a Change in Civil Religion in the United States: Implications for School Policy and Curriculum Development." George Peabody College for Teachers, 1980, 41:3979-A.

The civil religion by which we understand ourselves as Americans has greatly contributed to the emergence of the dilemma of whether or not nations should continue to promote economic growth at the expense of nonrenewable resources.

330. Diarraya, Mohamed. "Behavioral Models of Dividend Policy and Their Implications to Financial Management." University of Illinois at Urbana-Champaign, 1980, 41:2679-A.

This thesis examines the intertemporal change of dividend policy.

331. Dickmeyer, Nathan C. "Computer Aided University Budget Policy Making." Stanford University, 1979, 40:3651-A.

The designing and testing of a computer program which displays university budget policy options within a set of financial constraints is the focus of this research.

332. Driskill, Robert A. "Monetary Policy and Exchange Rate Dynamics." The Johns Hopkins University, 1978, 39:982-A.

Examines the adjustment of the exchange rate and the domestic price level of a small, open economy following an unanticipated increase in the money supply. The emphasis is on stock-flow interactions during the adjustment path.

333. Ellis, Charles D. "Investment Policies of Large Corporate Pension Funds." New York University, 1979, 40:3438-A.

After summarizing modern portfolio theory in a brief normative model, a series of hypotheses is specified on the investment policies large corporate pension funds would follow, and these hypotheses are each tested, using data from five years of annual surveys on the actual investment policies of large corporate pension funds and on the beliefs of the corporate executives responsible for supervising these funds.

334. Ellsworth, Richard R. "Corporate Strategy and Capital Structure Policies: A Descriptive Study." Harvard University, 1980, 41:1126-A.

Examines the relationship of capital structure policies to corporate strategy in large, diversified firms.

335. Epstein, Gerald A. "Bank Profits and the Political Economy of Monetary Policy in the United States, 1956-1977." Princeton University, 1981, 42:3230-A.

The argument presented is that the Federal Reserve's need to garner a constituency to protect its independence from the democratic process at the same time compromises its independence by making the Federal Reserve susceptible to influence by the commercial banking community.

336. Erickson, Kenneth W. "Equity and Efficiency of Metallic Mineral Taxation Policies in Wisconsin." The University of Wisconsin-Madison, 1978, 39:1735-A.

The basic problem is to (1) choose a set of metallic mineral tax policy objectives, and (2) select a "tax package" which will assist the state in achieving these objectives.

337. Esaki, Howard Y. "Interest Rates, Short-Run Monetary Policy, and the Federal Reserve Reaction Function." Yale University, 1981, 42:5186-A.

This dissertation is an examination of the monetary policy reaction function of the Federal Reserve.

338. Ezikpe, Jona N. "The Regional Impact of Monetary Policy in the United States." The University of Nebraska-Lincoln, 1981, 42:1707-A.

Investigates the degree of monetary policy pervasiveness in the United States.

339. Fatemi, Seyed. "An Empirical Estimation of Interaction of Financial Policies and Firm Goals." Oklahoma State University, 1979, 40:6346-A.

The purpose of this study is to carry out an empirical analysis of goals and financial policies of owner controlled and management controlled firms.

340. Finch, Brian W. "Econometric Models for Regional Economic Analysis and Policy: Three Applications." University of Georgia, 1978, 39:4398-A.

Three applications utilizing econometric models for regional analysis and policy making are analyzed. The regional focus is Georgia and its substate economies. The econometric model used as the vehicle of analysis is the Georgia Econometric Forecasting Model and its satellites.

341. Fincher, Phillip E. "Some Economic Welfare Implications of a National Minimum Wage Law as a National Economic Policy." The University of Mississippi, 1978, 39:3703-A.

Examines some of the economic welfare implications of a national minimum wage as a national economic policy. Selected theoretical and empirical studies of minimum wage impacts are examined within a welfare framework.

342. George, Wilfred R. "Tight Money Timing: The Impact of Interest Rates and Federal Reserve Monetary Policy on the Stock Market." Golden Gate University, 1979, 40:2188-A.

Explores the impact that changes in interest rates and lending regulations had on the stock market for the period 1914 to 1977. Seeks to determine whether there is a correlation between tight money conditions and a declining stock market and between easy money conditions and a rising stock market.

343. Gertler, Mark L. "Essays on Macroeconomic Methodology and Policy." Stanford University, 1978, 39:3734-A.

Consists of three essays on the equilibrium versus the disequilibrium method in macroeconomics. The theme that links the essays is the belief that the disequilibrium method more accurately characterizes the behavior of the aggregate economy.

344. Gobin, Roy T. "An Analysis of Indirect Taxation in the Caribbean Common Market: Its Impact on Tax Performance and Role in Tax Policy." University of Illinois at Urbana-Champaign, 1978, 39:7455-A.

Analyzes the system of indirect taxes in the four major countries of the Caribbean Common Market (Jamaica, Trinidad, Guyana and Barbados) and in light of the empirical findings, considers the segments of the tax structure which may be reformed in a manner geared to the promotion of national and regional developmental objectives.

345. Groenewold, Nicolaas. "The Effectiveness of Fiscal Policy: A Theoretical Analysis." The University of Western Ontario (Canada), 1979,
40:5535-A.

This thesis is a theoretical examination of the effectiveness of fiscal policy to change output, employment and prices.

346. Guentner, Kenneth J. "The Impact of Monetary Policy on the Government Securities Market: An Econometric Analysis." University of Pittsburgh, 1977, 38:7445-A.

The main objectives are the specification, estimation and simulation
of an econometric model of the U.S. financial sector which emphasizes
the forces of demand and supply in the determination of the model's
basic short- and long-term primary yields.

347. Hakim, Ramzi S. "Policy Capturing of the Aggregate Production
Planning Process by Means of Transform Analysis." University of Houston,
1980, 41:1683-A.

The aggregate production planning decision-making process is studied
at the industry level by means of empirical research and transform
analysis.

348. Halperin, Robert M. "The Effects of an Income Tax Structure Which
Permits Last-In, First-Out Inventory Costing on the Economic Order Quan-
tity Inventory Policy: Analysis and Public Policy Implications." University of Pennsylvania, 1977, 38:6787-A.

The use of the last-in, first-out inventory method is advantageous to
taxpayers in periods of rising inventory prices since it can reduce
the amount of taxes which must be paid on inventory profits.

349. Haritakis, Themis M. "The Impact of Monetary Policy on Residential
Construction Short-Run Cycles: A Comparison of Inventory and Disequilibrium Approaches." Clark University, 1981, 42:1262-A.

The aim is to identify the major underlying factors which cause the
short-run cycle observed in housing construction. Specifically, it
tries to reach some conclusions as to whether the source of this
cyclicality can be found in the profit maximizing behavior of home-
builders or the cycle should be rather attributable to monetary variables.

350. Harris, Robert B. "State and Local Taxation of Commercial Banks:
An Economic Analysis of the Policy Options and Their Implications for the
State of Ohio." The Ohio State University, 1979, 40:2189-A.

Compares the policy alternatives open to Ohio in the tax treatment of
commercial banks after the relaxation of Section 5219 in 1969.

351. Haruki, Kazuhito. "Monetary and Fiscal Policy Effects in a Dynamic
Macroeconomic Model." University of California, Los Angeles, 1979, 40:
4165-A.

A dynamic macroeconomic model is presented to examine several issues;

two in particular are (1) the "crowding out" effect of fiscal policy
and (2) the trade-off between inflation and unemployment.

352. Henderson, Dale W. "Macroeconomic Policy Making in Open Economies:
Four Essays Based on the Portfolio Balance Approach." Yale University,
1979, 40:5937-A.

Represents a contribution to a major effort by economists to provide
a framework for analyzing the implications for national macroeconomic
policy making of the increasingly close financial interrelationships
among nations.

353. Hobeika, Louis G. "Dividend Policy." University of Pennsylvania,
1980, 41:4461-A.

Studies the dividend payout policy of American firms from 1957 to
1976 from the viewpoint of its determinants and the optimality of the
policy followed. Examines the stationarity of dividend policy and
the effect of dividends on stock prices using a new methodology.

354. Howsen, Roy M. "Governmental Policies and Technological Adoption
in the Domestic Steel Industry." University of Arkansas, 1980, 41:2217-A.

The objectives are: (1) to explore what government policies are significant in determining the changes in technology in the domestic
steel industry; (2) to develop a model which includes technological
change and government policies; and (3) to estimate the domestic
steel industry's adoption of the BOF process in the absence of government policies.

355. Igawa, Kazuhiro. "Asset Diversification and Policy Effects under
Flexible Exchange Rates." The Johns Hopkins University, 1981, 42:801-A.

Considering foreign exchange rate movements and uncertainty concerning
future rates, the choice between domestic and foreign assets and the
allocation of real capital investment between domestic and foreign
countries become a serious problem for investors and firms. They will
diversify their financial assets and real capital under flexible rates.

356. Jerison, Michael. "Optimal Public Enterprise Policies in Models of
Monopolistic Competition." The University of Wisconsin-Madison, 1977,
38:7478-A.

Analyzes the optimal output and pricing policies for public enterprises that act "in the public interest" in economies with unregu-
lated oligopolies or monopolies.

357. Johnson, Eldon C. "The Impact of Federal Reserve Membership, Commercial Banking Structures, and Bank Size on the Transmission of Monetary
Policy." University of Colorado at Boulder, 1978, 39:3032-A.

Empirically examines the influence of selected commercial banking
structural factors on Federal Reserve money supply control. Covers a
ten-year period, December 31, 1964 through December 31, 1974, and includes over 80 percent of all insured commercial banks in the United
States.

358.   Johnson, Robert W.   "The Passage of the Investment Incentive Act of 1978: A Case Study of Business Influencing Public Policy."   Harvard University, 1980, 40:313-A.

This thesis is concerned with the process by which business influences the formulation of specific national legislative policies.   The study is based on an in-depth case study of the passage of The Investment Incentive Act of 1978, an initiative to reduce the taxes levied on capital gains.

359.   Joines, Douglas H.   "Government Fiscal Policy and Private Capital Formation."   The University of Chicago, 1979, 40:5529-A.

Examines both theoretically and empirically the relationship between government fiscal policy and private capital formation.

360.   Jones, Robert L.   "Monetary Policy Implications of Bank Liability Management."   University of Notre Dame, 1978, 39:1735-A.

The purpose is to determine the implications of liability management activity for the efficacy of monetary policy, especially a restrictive policy during periods of intense inflationary pressures.

361.   Jung, Woo Sik.   "Expectations and Optimal Stabilization Policies."   University of California, Berkeley, 1979, 40:345-A.

Involves an attempt to resolve some of the apparent conflicts between belief in the rational expectations approach and the application of optimization techniques to economic stabilization.

362.   Kama, Kunio.   "Optimal Monetary Policy and Portfolio Selection in the Overlapping Generations Model."   University of Pennsylvania, 1981, 42:2793-A.

Extends the Lucas equilibrium business cycle model (1972) by incorporating a simple portfolio allocation problem.

363.   Karakitsos, Dimitrios.   "Dynamic Financial Policies of the Firm under Uncertainty."   University of Minnesota, 1979, 40:5951-A.

Addresses the financing problem of a growth firm under conditions of uncertainty in imperfect capital markets.

364.   Kennedy, William F.   "An Empirical Examination of Large Bank Dividend Policy."   Virginia Polytechnic Institute and State University, 1979, 40:2773-A.

Involves an attempt to determine those factors which influence the dividend payout decision at large U.S. commercial banks.

365.   Kerr, Peter M.   "A Guide for Monetary Policy."   University of Kansas, 1979, 40:2804-A.

Provides a guide for the Federal Reserve's monetary policy by selecting a key variable, demonstrating its controllability, making recommendations that would improve its control, and suggesting how it should be controlled.

366. Kessler, Adam. "The Altruism Factor, Social Space and the Structure of Transfer Policies." New York University, 1978, 39:3708-A.

The thesis is concerned with benevolent (and/or malevolent) attitudes and behaviors and their specification for empirical and policy analysis.

367. Kim, Kwangok. "An Econometric Model fo Oklahoma Tax Revenues: An Analysis of Static and Dynamic Implications of Tax Policy Simulation." The University of Oklahoma, 1978, 39:4402-A.

Provides an econometric model which forecasts the various tax revenues and simulates alternative tax policies, and has an implication of the dynamic simulation which traces a change in a tax structure on various tax revenues and state economic conditions. Suggests effective measures for raising the tax revenues for the state government.

368. Kimelman, Nancy J. "Post-War Monetary Policymaking in the U.S." Brown University, 1981, 42:4875-A.

Examines the post-war behavior of the Federal Open Market Committee from a broader perspective than economists have traditionally assumed. Recognizes that policy decision making is a dynamic process in which both economic and noneconomic factors figure. Both historical and empirical evidence is presented to support this point of view.

369. King, Jonathan B. "Ralph Nader and the Problem of Social Cost: An Analysis of Four Public Policy Issues." University of Washington, 1980, 41:2206-A.

Based on the Coasian viewpoint, modified in view of its specific shortcomings, this study examines four public policy issues in which Nader has been actively involved: antitrust law and policy, occupational safety and health, consumer rights, and pension plans.

370. Klein, Bruce W. "The Adequacy of the Earnings Capacity of the Subemployed and Its Policy Implications." The George Washington University, 1981, 42:3674-A.

The plight of the low-income subemployed has been a longstanding issue in labor economics and social welfare policy. This study investigates the impact on the subemployed of their reaching earnings capacity, and discusses policies suggested by the findings.

371. Kuchler, Frederick R. "A Multiperiod Reaction Functions Model with Applications to Antitrust Policy." Virginia Polytechnic Institute and State University, 1981, 42:4538-A.

A market structure in which predatory or exclusionary behavior is feasible is modeled as a multiperiod game.

372. Lam, Chun Hung. "Bank Holding Company: Policy Analysis and Planning Models." Duke University, 1977, 38:7433-A.

Analyzes the behavior of bank holding companies under alternative forms of capital requirements and presents a multiperiod planning model which could help management in strategic decisions.

373. Lee, L. Douglas. "The Congressional Budget Act of 1974: The Impact on Fiscal Policy." The George Washington University, 1978, 39:6261-A.

Provides a qualitative discussion of the legislation, and a quantitative analysis of the impact of the Act on fiscal policy and the growth path of the economy.

374. Lee, William. "Optimal Policy Selection and Evaluation with Rational Expectations." Columbia University, 1981, 42:2794-A.

A theoretical framework is developed for the deprivation and evaluation of optimal policy assuming expectations are rational.

375. Lee, Young-Goo. "Monetary and Debt Management Policy with a Linear Nonhomogeneous Transaction Cost." University of Minnesota, 1981, 42:2794-A.

In "The Inefficiency of Interest-Bearing National Debt" John Bryant and Neil Wallace show the coexistence of fiat money and default-free interest-bearing government bonds by way of a transaction cost. This thesis extends their model.

376. Levy, John M. "'No-Growth' as a Policy Option: Economic and Demographic Consequences." New York University, 1979, 40:1718-A.

To study the consequences of "no-growth" policies, Westchester, New York, a large suburban county, was chosen as the study area. The time period is 1960 to 1970. It is hypothesized that growth controls would most commonly and most forcefully be applied to housing rather than to commercial development.

377. Levy, Mickey D. "Factors Affecting Monetary Policy in an Era of Inflation." University of Maryland, 1980, 42:801-A.

In order to gain a better understanding of Federal Reserve behavior, its objectives are investigated by developing and estimating a money supply-reaction function.

378. Lim, Ungki. "Corporate Liquidity Management in Relation to Dividend and Other Working Capital Policy Decisions: A Time Series Empirical Study." University of Illinois at Urbana-Champaign, 1979, 40:5529-A.

The main thesis of this study is found in its recognition of the interrelated nature between the corporate liquidity decision and other key short-term financial decisions such as dividend payment, inventory, receipt and disbursement policy.

379. Limberg, Stephen T. "An Evaluation of Tax Policy and Investment Structure Uncertainty in Condominium Conversions: A Simulation." Arizona State University, 1982, 42:1207-A.

Examines the tax aspects of condominium conversions. The four research questions focus on two issues: (1) Does current and proposed tax legislation provide an economic incentive for taxpayers to engage in a complex corporate strategy (MMSS) for converting rental units to condominiums? (2) What apportionment of stock ownership is acceptable to all parties in an MMSS?

380. List, Claire. "Private Foundation Cost Patterns, Investment Policies, and Grant Purchase Behavior." Columbia University, 1981, 42:2782-A.

   Explores foundations' "economic behavior" within the framework of the
   traditional theory of the consumer (primarily) and of the firm.

381. Loeys, Jan G. "Policy Invariance in the Financial Sector and the
October 1979 Change in Monetary Policy." University of California, Los
Angeles, 1982, 42:1239-A.

   Investigates the importance of the Lucas-Sargent critique for econometric simulations of financial market behavior on the basis of the
   October 1979 change in monetary policy.

382. McLeod, Phillip. "Regulation and the Capital Expansion Policy of
a Monopoly." Stanford University, 1980, 40:5952-A.

   Using a dynamic investment model of a monopoly, the effects of rate
   of return regulation on a monopoly's investment decisions are examined.

383. McMillin, William D. "A Theoretical and Empirical Analysis of the
Relationship between Fiscal Policy and the Money Supply." The Louisiana
State University and Agricultural and Mechanical College, 1979, 40:2177-A.

   The fiscal policy-money supply relationship is examined within the
   context of a small structural model of the economy.

384. Markovich, Denise E. "Incomes Policy and the Rate of Wage Increase:
A Comparison of Canada and the United States, 1956-76." The University of
Manitoba (Canada), 1979, 40:2176-A.

   Presents a comparative analysis of the rate of wage increase in Canada
   and the United States from 1956-76 and assesses the role that incomes
   policies played in the process of nominal wage determination.

385. Mayers, Kenneth E. "In the Red in Black and White: A Policy Analysis of 'Black Capitalism' in the Light of White Small Business." University of California, Berkeley, 1978, 39:5699-A.

   A strategic question is summarized as follows: Advocates of "Black
   Capitalism" have based their hopes on the potential rewards of business ownership; does the condition of small business in America war-
   rant such hopefulness?

386. Merris, Randall C. "Monetary Policy, Bank Regulation and Banking
Profits." University of Kentucky, 1979, 40:3450-A.

   Investigates the effects of monetary policy actions and bank regulation on the portfolio-selection and rate-setting behavior of commercial banks belonging to the Federal Reserve System.

387. Miller, Randall J. "A Theoretical and Empirical Investigation into
the Regional Impact of Monetary Policy in the United States." University
of Pittsburgh, 1977, 38:5601-A.

   Utilizing a macroeconomic perspective, this thesis assesses the po-

tential and actual impacts of monetary policy actions by the Federal
Reserve on the money supplies and economies of regions in the United
States from an institutional, theoretical and empirical perspective.

388. Mitchell, Douglas W. "Interest-Bearing Checking Accounts and Macro
Policy." Princeton University, 1978, 39:2435-A.

The study is concerned with the macroeconomic implications of allowing interest payments on checking accounts. Emphasis is placed on
the expenditure and interest elasticities of money demand and on the
crucial role of the aggregation process.

389. Moody, Andrew J. "Impacts of State Tax Policy on Manufacturing
Activity in Massachusetts." Boston College, 1979, 40:5952-A.

Analyzes the impact of state tax policy on manufacturing employment
and investment in Massachusetts. Also examines the impact of energy
costs on the variables.

390. Morgan, George E., III. "The Role of Expectations in the Transmission of Monetary Policy." The University of North Carolina at Chapel
Hill, 1977, 39:359-A.

One of the purposes of the study is to demonstrate that the expectations formed by bankers play a role in transmitting actions of the
Federal Reserve to growth in the money stock. The model used is a
two-period model of a rate-setting financial intermediary that operates in imperfect markets under risk neutrality.

391. Musacchio, Robert A. "Optimal Capital Policies of a Regulated
Firm." The University of Wisconsin-Milwaukee, 1980, 41:4795-A.

Investigates the optimal policy of a regulated firm, whose investment
plan is constrained from above by regulated profits and from below by
Arrow's irreversibility assumption.

392. Nichols, Len M. "Market Structure and Stabilization Policy." University of Illinois at Urbana-Champaign, 1981, 42:2769-A.

Uses a macro model with a profit maximizing supply side to derive
policy responses to stagflation. The role of market structure re-
ceives particular concern.

393. Nickerson, David B. "Essays on Neutrality of Monetary Policy."
Northwestern University, 1981, 42:4100-A.

Consists of two essays: the first is concerned with the debate over
policy effectiveness in linear stochastic macroeconomic models with
disequilibrium prices and lagged full information; the second deals
with a cooperative relationship between the monetary authority and
identical price-setting firms which comprise the private sector of
the economy and which face discrete costs of price adjustment.

394. Noble, Nicholas R. "The Formation of Inflationary Expectations:
The Role of Government Policy." University of Cincinnati, 1978, 39:
5629-A.

Examines the role of monetary and fiscal variables in the formation
of inflationary expectations.

395. O'Brien, Joseph P. "Federal Reserve Policies and Variability of
the Money Supply." Oklahoma State University, 1977, 39:397-A.

Attempts to isolate the major contributors to the level of variability
of the money supply achieved during the period 1952 through 1973 and
selected subperiods, and determines the sources of the recent increase
in its variability. The hypothesis is that Federal Reserve policy
measures adopted during the latter half of the 1960's contributed to
an increase in the variability of the rate of change of the money supply.

396. Odogwu, Onwochei. "The Output and Employment Effects of Fiscal Policy in a Classical Model." University of Southern California, 1978, 39:
3068-A.

Establishes formally, within the neoclassical framework, theorems on
the effects of taxes imposed purely for revenue generation purposes,
on factor employment, the returns to these factors, and output.

397. Olson, Clifton V. "Policy Objectives in Airline Regulation: An
Analysis of the Performance of the CAB." Tulane University, 1979, 40:
1606-A.

Develops a procedure to evaluate the policies of the Civil Aeronautics
Board in an attempt to determine who has benefited from regulation of
the airline industry.

398. O'Neill, Timothy J. "The Role of Private Non-Profit Research Organizations in Policy Formation: A Case Study of the Atlantic Provinces Economic Council and the Institute of Public Affairs." Duke University,
1979, 40:6359-A.

The fundamental proposition of this thesis is that, before they have
an influence on policy, the ideas of economists typically are "fil-
tered"--i.e., translated and applied in terms understandable to policy
makers--by individuals such as personal advisors to politicians and by
institutions such as the research units of government departments and
public sector research and advisory agencies like the Council of Economic Advisors.

399. Orr, James A. "A Model of Unemployment in Local Labor Markets with
an Application to Discretionary Fiscal Policies." University of Pennsylvania, 1979, 40:5537-A.

This dissertation is a theoretical and empirical investigation of the
determinants of unemployment in local areas.

400. O'Toole, Thomas P. "Inflation, Flexible Exchange Rates, and Macroeconomic Policy." The Johns Hopkins University, 1980, 41:1164-A.

Studies the macroeconomic behavior of an open economy with a flexible
exchange rate. Of particular interest is the possibility of a "vicious
circle" occurring--a situation in which inflation and exchange rate
depreciation reinforce each other in an unstable spiral.

401. Patankar, Jayprakash G. "Estimation of Reserves and Cash Flows Associated with Different Warranty Policies." Clemson University, 1978, 39:3038-A.

Presents a technique to estimate warranty liability for a fixed lot size of "N" items. The quantities estimated are: expected total warranty reserves, expected present value of total warranty reserves, expected cash flows associated with certain warranty policies, and 95% confidence limits for each of the above quantities.

402. Perryman, Marlin R. "An Indicator of Monetary Policy Derived from a Simultaneous Equation Model." Rice University, 1978, 39:1720-A.

Examines noncyclical indicators of dynamic monetary policy and applies them to policy analysis in several contexts. These policy gauges are designed to measure the stance of Federal Reserve policy relative to the business cycle.

403. Radian, Alexander. "Resource Mobilization in Poor Countries Implementing Tax Policies." University of California, Berkeley, 1977, 38: 5045-A.

Explores two questions: first, why is it that the poor raise (in proportion to GNP) less revenue than the rich; and second, what can be done to strengthen the ability of government to mobilize resources.

404. Rahman, Shah Khondokar. "Some Aspects of Money and Monetary Policy in a Dual Economy: A Theoretical Approach." The University of Manitoba (Canada), 1980, 41:4126-A.

Demonstrates that economic growth and development is not independent of monetary phenomena. Thus, the thesis is a contribution to monetary theory of less developed countries.

405. Rasher, Arthur A. "The Debt and Dividend Policy of a Firm—A Financial Planning Model Using Simulation." Michigan State University, 1982, 42:497-A.

Attempts to fill a void in the literature and develop a financial planning model that is non-optimizing and long term in nature.

406. Ray, John, Jr. "Government Fiscal Policy and the Business Cycle in the United States, 1949-1975." University of California, Riverside, 1980, 41:4791-A.

Using National Bureau of Economic Research methodology, examines in detail the behavior of federal, state and local fiscal variables (expenditures and receipts) over the five post-World War II business cycles.

407. Reese, Craig E. "The Use of Tax Policy to Control Pollution: A Comparative Analysis of the Major Industrialized Countries in North America and Western Europe." The University of Texas at Austin, 1979, 40: 4106-A.

The objectives are: (1) to determine the state-of-the-art in using

three methods of social control to effect environmental quality; and
(2) to develop a comparative analysis of the use of tax policy as a
complement to regulation and direct financial assistance in the control of pollution in the United States and five other industrialized
nations.

408.   Rhoda, Kenneth L.   "A Test of the Relative Effectiveness of Fiscal
and Monetary Policy."   State University of New York at Buffalo, 1978, 39:
374-A.

Fiscal and monetary policies (for example, changes in government purchases or taxes and changes in the money supply, discount rate or the
monetary base) are undertaken for the effects they have on economic
activity.

409.   Ribe, Frederick C.   "Effects of Decentralization on the Efficiency
of Stabilization Policy."   Yale University, 1980, 41:4796-A.

Deals with the effects of differences in the decision problems of
separate monetary and fiscal policy makers on the efficiency of stabilization policy as a whole.   Differences in the policy makers' objectives and estimated economic models are analyzed using Nash equilibrium strategies in nonzero sum games.

410.   Rivard, Richard J.   "A Comparison of Monetary Aggregates as Monetary Policy Targets."   Texas A&M University, 1978, 39:2445-A.

The choice of the best monetary aggregate for use as the target variable in conducting monetary policy has been an unsettled question for
many years in economics.   This study composes seven potential target
aggregates, the monetary base and M1 through M6.

411.   Robertson, John D.   "Post-Industrialism and the Changing Contours
of Public Policy."   University of Illinois at Urbana-Champaign, 1979, 40:
5577-A.

The basic thesis is that as industrial societies evolve toward post-
industrialism, a domestic imbalance between personal consumption and
capital investment develops which increasingly draws public authority
into the economic order of society.

412.   Rogers, Joe O.   "The Impact of Economic Theory on Public Policy:
The Case of Technological Change and Employment Policy."   Duke University,
1978, 39:7459-A.

Since the beginning of the Great Depression, the relationships between
employment, wages, and technological change have been the subjects of
recurring debates among economists and public policy makers.   The purpose of this dissertation is to examine the contribution of economic
theorizing and technological change to the formation of public employment and labor policy.

413.   Rubin, Barry M.   "Regional Econometric Forecasting Models: A Test of
Structural Generality, Disaggregation Effects, and Policy Analysis Poten-
tials with Application to the Milwaukee Metropolitan Area."   The University of Wisconsin-Madison, 1977, 38:6358-A.

Develops two macroeconomic econometric models for the Milwaukee, Wisconsin metropolitan area.

414.   Sav, George T.   "Production and Dynamic Demand Modeling Using Engineering Models and Pseudo Data: The Effects of Tax Policy on the Accelerated Substitution of Solar Energy for Conventional Energy."   The George Washington University, 1981, 42:3693-A.

Analyzes the possible effects of alternative tax policies on the solar for conventional energy substitution process in the production of residential and commercial domestic hot water.

415.   Selvin, Molly.   "'This Tender and Delicate Business': The Public Trust Doctrine in American Law and Economic Policy, 1789-1920."   University of California, San Diego, 1978, 39:2490-A.

Examines the history of the public trust doctrine in American state and federal courts between 1789 and 1920 as a case study in the interplay between law and economic policy.

416.   Shea, Jia-Dong.   "The Policy Implications of the Government Budget Constraint in an Optimal Accumulation Model."   Stanford University, 1978, 39:5653-A.

Investigates the effects of government policies in several different cases with the explicit incorporation of the government budget constraint in an optimal accumulation model, and specifically compares the different impacts of various deficit-financing methods.

417.   Smith, Nancy P.   "A Holistic Approach to Public Policy: Taxation and Environmental Legislation in Maine."   Columbia University, 1979, 40:2864-A.

The subject of this study is a clarification of Lowi's approach by comparing it to others used in policy analysis. Lowi's model of policy types developed for the congressional level is applied to the rural state of Maine. The study is designed specifically to test the explanatory power of this model.

418.   Smith, Stephen D.   "The Differential Impact of Monetary Policy on Common Stock Prices."   The University of Florida, 1980, 42:778-A.

The federal government has a number of tools which it employs for demand management purposes at the macroeconomic level. Income may be redistributed across sectors of the economy when these policies are unexpectedly altered. The impact of unexpected changes in one such tool (the growth rate of the money supply) on the stock market is investigated over the 1960-78 time period.

419.   Southern, Robert N.   "Private Motor Carrier Transportation: Perceived Effects of Changes in Federal Regulatory Policy, 1975-1980."   Arizona State University, 1981, 42:886-A.

Examines the question of how changes in federal regulatory policy from 1975 to 1980 are likely to affect private motor carrier transportation.

420. Speaker, Paul J. "Unemployment and Public Policy with Multiple Labor Market Intermediaries." Purdue University, 1981, 42:3678-A.

The impact of multiple labor market intermediaries in two situations is evaluated. First, an economy is presented where individual sub-markets of labor are characterized by a constant wage environment. Next, using BLS survey data, an empirical interpretation of the results of the model is presented.

421. Stephens, Alan A. "The Identification of Dividend Policies and an Evaluation of Their Impact on Firm Value." The University of Utah, 1980, 41:3183-A.

The purpose is to determine whether the dividend payment pattern a firm adopts affects the value of the firm.

422. Stillman, Robert S. "Examining Antitrust Policy towards Horizontal Mergers." University of California, Los Angeles, 1980, 40:328-A.

Studies a sample of thirty horizontal mergers challenged during the period 1951-74 for evidence that these mergers would have in fact reduced competition by promoting collusion.

423. Storrs, Charles E., Jr. "The Effect of Banking Market Structure upon the Transmission of Monetary Policy." Georgia State University, 1979, 40:5531-A.

Examines the effect of banking market structure upon the speed with which alternative monetary policy measures are transmitted through a commercial banking system.

424. Stout, Gary R. "Tax Policy and Capital Formation: An Empirical Analysis of the Potential Differential Impact of the Investment Tax Credit." University of Southern California, 1977, 38:4903-A.

The research has two objectives: (1) the evaluation of a number of particular aspects of capital formation; and (2) the determination, by empirical methods, of whether the behavioral process of making capital investment decisions within the firm affects the impact of the investment tax credit on the firm's investments in plant and equipment.

425. Swad, Randy G. "ESOPs and Tax Policy: An Empirical Investigation of the Impact of ESOPs on Company Operating Performance." The Louisiana State University and Agricultural and Mechanical College, 1979, 40:6331-A.

The objective is to provide employee stock ownership plan policy makers with empirical evidence which would be useful in the formulation of future ESOP policy.

426. Swaim, Stephen C. "Theory and Policy in the Economic Thought of Leo Rogin: (A Study in the Methodology of Using Economic Theory to Argue for or against Change in Major Economic Institutions)." University of Maryland, 1979, 40:5538-A.

Describes Leo Rogin's ideas about how economists should view the relation of theory to policy, compares those ideas with the approach commonly associated with mainstream economics, and discusses practical implications of Rogin's position.

427. Symansky, Steven A. "Stabilization Policy in an Open Economy: A Simulation Approach with a Rational Learning Rule." The University of Wisconsin-Madison, 1980, 41:4452-A.

With the advent of the monetary approach to the balance of payments, there have been numerous and insightful articles analyzing the efficacy of various stabilization policies in an open economy, most of which has focused primarily on static and long-run equilibrium behavior. The purpose of this dissertation is to fill in a gap by exploring numerous aspects of stabilization policy.

428. Tajika, Eiji. "Optimal Pricing Policies for Economic Development." University of Minnesota, 1981, 42:5204-A.

In the course of economic development the economies of developing countries have been plagued with suboptimal allocations of resources through artificially created distortions as well as through institutional rigidities. The purpose here is to lead developing economies to more efficient use of resources by means of the valuation of goods and services.

429. Tang, Shu Hung. "The Analysis of Interregional Fiscal Policy: A Simulation Approach." McMaster University (Canada), 1980, 41:4121-A.

Provides a theoretical framework for the analysis of interregional fiscal policy.

430. Tareen, Mohammed A. "A Theory of Money Supply and Its Macroeconometric Implementation: Description, Stabilization Policy and Control." University of Pennsylvania, 1978, 39:4387-A.

The debate over whether the Federal Reserve should rely exclusively on the money stock—somehow defined—as an instrument, a target, or an indicator of monetary policy, or all three, continues unabated. A major portion of this study is devoted to reasons, both conceptual and empirical, why the money supply cannot and perhaps should not be used as a target variable in the short run.

431. Thomas, Sharon T. "The Implementation of National Consumer Protection Policies: 1960-1980." University of Houston, 1981, 42:3751-A.

Examines five regulatory agencies, each concerned with implementing consumer protection, to determine the nature of the implementation process.

432. Thompson, Andrew F., Jr. "An Analysis of the Policy Loan Interest Rate as a Decision Variable in Granting Non-Forfeiture Benefits on Ordinary Life Insurance Contracts." The University of Nebraska-Lincoln, 1977, 38:4290-A.

Provides two methods of analyzing loan rate policy as it affects the consumer of insurance and the insurance firm.

433.   Valdivieso Montano, Luis M.   "The Distributive Effect of Alternative Policies to Increase the Use of Existing Industrial Capacity."   Boston University Graduate School, 1979, 39:7443-A.

Constitutes an attempt to develop an analytical framework to understand the effect of alternative multiple shifts micropolicies upon the distribution of income.   Consists of a simulation of the potential distributive and macroeconomic consequences that multiple shiftwork would have in Peru.   The data base for the analysis corresponds to 1969.

434.   Van 'T Dack, Jozef S.   "Short-Run Implications of Exchange-Rate Unification for Monetary and Fiscal Policy."   The University of Michigan, 1981, 42:2785-A.

The effects of monetary policy on the interest-rate levels, the exchange rate with respect to the rest of the world and asset portfolios are analyzed.

435.   Varzandeh, Javad.   "An Econometric Investigation of the Relative Effectiveness of Monetary and Fiscal Policy."   Oklahoma State University, 1981, 42:4081-A.

Attempts to find precise answers to the following econometric equations: (a) Are the dependent variables in single equation models of Friedman and Meiselman, Andersen and Jordan, and their critics exogenous? (b) Is the change in the weighted full employment surplus, used by Andersen and Jordan, a good proxy for measuring fiscal variables? (c) How different would Andersen and Jordan's results be if they used different lag techniques rather than the Almon distributed lag?

436.   Vittoz, Stanley H.   "The American Industrial Economy and the Political Origins of Federal Labor Policy between the World Wars."   York University (Canada), 1979, 40:5147-A.

A recent and still growing body of revisionist scholarship on the sources of American labor movement conservatism places a great deal of emphasis in this respect on the typically duplicitous, opportunistic character of the nation's trade union leadership, reckoning it as perhaps a decisive ingredient in the remarkable assimilative capacity of the "corporate liberal," or "state capitalist," regime.

437.   Vorst, Karen S.   "Analysis of Uncertainty in Monetary Policy Determination."   Indiana University, 1980, 41:5193-A.

The purpose is to derive empirically a method by which Federal Reserve policy actions could reflect its perceptions of uncertainty.

438.   Waldo, Douglas G.   "Long-Term Contracts and Monetary Policy."   The University of North Carolina at Chapel Hill, 1980, 41:1709-A.

The broad issue addressed here is the existence and identification of nonneutralities which can be exploited by the monetary authority in order to dampen business cycles.

439. Winant, Howard A. "Taxation with Representation? Economic Policy-Formation and State Structure in the Early 1960s USA." University of California, Santa Cruz, 1980, 41:2320-A.

Examines economic policy-formation processes in the early 1960's USA, with particular reference to tax reduction and reform issues addressed by the federal state in 1963-64.

440. Wojcikewych, Raymond. "The Interdependence of Monetary and Fiscal Policy." The Pennsylvania State University, 1981, 42:1727-A.

Analyzes the interdependence between monetary and fiscal policy for the period 1960-1974. Specifically investigated is the direction of causality that exists (if any) between these two policy weapons.

441. Wolkoff, Michael J. "An Analysis of the Use of Tax Abatement Policy to Stimulate Urban Economic Development" The University of Michigan, 1981, 42:4144-A.

Analyzes the use of property tax abatement to induce urban economic development.

442. Woolley, John T. "The Federal Reserve and the Political Economy of Monetary Policy." The University of Wisconsin-Madison, 1980, 42:371-A.

This is an examination of the relationship of the Federal Reserve System to its political environment and of the ways that relationship affects the process of policy making within the Federal Open Market Committee. The focus is on domestic monetary policy from the mid-1960's to the late 1970's.

443. Yoshikawa, Hiroshi. "An Essay on Macroeconomics and Monetary Policy." Yale University, 1978, 40:394-A.

Analyzes the short-run stability of the macro economy, and its bearing on alternative monetary policies.

444. Yoshino, Naoyuki. "Optimal Choice of Monetary and Fiscal Policy under Uncertainty." The Johns Hopkins University, 1979, 40:394-A.

The purpose is to show that previous work on the choice of monetary policy instrument under uncertainty obtained some incorrect conclusions, and correct conclusions are shown here. The thesis demonstrates that under certain conditions the expected value of the loss function is determined by the authorities' choice of endogenous variables and not by their choice of policy instrument.

Educational Policy

445. Abuhl, Ralph E. "A Study of the Tenure Policies and Practices of Colleges Which Are Members of the Council for the Advancement of Small Colleges." Michigan State University, 1978, 39:4748-A.

Determines the tenure policies and practices of the colleges associated with the Council for the Advancement of Small Colleges, and deals with faculty ratio, procedural due process, reasons for the dismissal of both tenured and non-tenured faculty members, alternatives to tenure, and faculty involvement in the acquisition of tenure.

446. Adams, Janet. "Planning as Policy: The Attempt to Institutionalize Educational Quality Assessment in Pennsylvania." University of Pittsburgh, 1978, 39:2569-A.

Planning is conceptualized here as a form of policy process in which the utilization of technical information is a major attribute. The case study which forms the core of this research focuses on identification of conditions which promote or impede the utilization of this information.

447. Afe, John O. "Institutional Policies and Procedures for the Admissions of Foreign Graduate Students: A Descriptive and Exploratory Study of Selected Institutions." Temple University, 1981, 42:5033-A.

An attempt is made to determine the commonalities and variations in admissions policies and procedures for foreign graduate students in selected institutions of higher education in the United States, and to establish a conceptual framework that will form a multidimensional basis for understanding admissions processes for foreign graduate students.

448. Allen, Eugene D. "A Study of the Opinions of Selected South Carolina School Board Members and Educators toward Teacher Participation in Policy Making Decisions." University of South Carolina, 1980, 41:858-A.

Investigates the attitudes of South Carolina educators, including teachers and principals, and those of school board members toward the concept of collective negotiations and meet and confer.

449. Alley, Reene A. "Evaluating Role Performance of High School Principals: School District Policies and Procedures and Their Impact on Those Evaluated." Indiana University, 1981, 42:3353-A.

   Examines the nature of performance evaluation of high school principals as it occurs in Indiana school districts.

450. Altes, Jane W. "Policy-Making Behaviors and Circumstances in a Typological Context: The Enactment and Implementation of Section 1202 (State Postsecondary Education Commissions) of the Higher Education Amendments of 1972." Saint Louis University, 1982, 42:1686-A.

   Establishes an outline of the processes which occur in policy development. The circumstances and behaviors expected in the typologies of Lowi, Edelman, Salisbury and Heinz are then associated with the process items.

451. Antonelli, Patrick T. "Impact of Professional Educators' and Community Members' Percpetual Input on the Formulation of Pupil Personnel Policy." Fordham University, 1981, 41:4896-A.

   The purpose is to determine, compare and rank board of education members' perceptions of the degree of adequacy of the nine major service dimensions of pupil personnel policy before and after exposure to the transmittal data regarding the importance of delivery of pupil personnel services as rendered by professional educators and community members.

452. Aseltine, James M. "Reduction in Force Policies of Connecticut Public School Systems as Compared to the Policy Model of Educational Policies Service/National School Boards Association." The University of Connecticut, 1980, 41:1851-A.

   Compares reduction in force policies and practices employed by selected Connecticut public school systems, with the Educational Policies Service/National School Boards Association Model.

453. Bartlett, Clyde R. "A Study to Determine Desirable Standards, Policies and Practices for School Personnel Administration." Ohio University, 1978, 39:2637-A.

   The purpose of the study is to determine desirable standards, policies and practices in school personnel administration for the American Association of School Personnel Administrators.

454. Bass, Gail V. "Alternatives in American Education: District Policies and the Implementation of Change." University of California, Los Angeles, 1978, 39:33-A.

   Analyzes the establishment of public alternative schools and programs from the perspective of school district management. The study analyzes the experiences of four districts that have introduced alternative programs in their schools.

455. Bender, Frances K. "A Study of Financial Retrenchment Policies and Procedures for Personnel and Program Reduction in Selected Four-Year Institutions." The University of Tennessee, 1979, 40:3138-A.

Suggests appropriate guidelines for personnel reduction in higher education based on documented data about present program and personnel reduction policies of selected four-year public and private institutions, and provides information about the planning for future reduction being done by those institutions which had not experienced such reduction.

456. Bergman, Janet L. "Student Rights and Responsibilities: An Analysis of Student, Teacher, and Administrator Knowledge in a School System Where a Well Established Policy Exists." University of Maryland, 1979, 40:4815-A.

The study concerns itself with the amount of knowledge of student rights and responsibilities possessed by administrators, teachers, and students in a school system where a well-defined, widely disseminated student rights and responsibilities policy exists.

457. Berke, Iris P. "Evaluation into Policy: Bilingual Education, 1978." Stanford University, 1980, 41:2050-A.

Traces the influence of the AIR *Evaluation of the Impact of the ESEA Title VII Spanish/English Bilingual Education Program* on the 1978 reauthorization of The Bilingual Education Act.

458. Billy, Theodore. "The Political Involvement of Minnesota Superintendents in the State Level Educational Policy System." University of Minnesota, 1978, 39:5218-A.

Examines the political involvement of Minnesota school superintendents in the state education policy system. Analysis is confined to the superintendent's political involvement as manifested through campaigning and lobbying, and the relationship of the involvement to selected personal characteristics of superintendents and to selected characteristics of their districts.

459. Bisesi, Michael R. "General Education: Case Studies and Policy Implications for Texas Colleges and Universities." University of Houston, 1980, 41:1966-A.

Examines the current status and possible future trends of general education requirements for bachelor's degrees in the four-year public senior colleges of Texas.

460. Bolden, Samuel H. "Current Status, Policy and Criteria for the Evaluation of Tenured Faculty in Alabama's Four-Year Public Institutions of Higher Education." Auburn University, 1979, 40:5330-A.

Determines the status, policy, and criteria for the evaluation of tenured faculty in Alabama's four-year public institutions of higher education.

461. Bourexis, Patricia S. "Implementation Factors Related to Schools' Compliance with Special Education Policy." Syracuse University, 1979, 40:6081-A.

Describes and analyzes implementation factors related to schools'

compliance with special education policy. Boston Public Schools
served as the field study site.

462. Bradley, Carl C. "Perceptions of Public School Teachers toward In-
Service Programs in Region VII of the State of Texas as They Relate to
Policies and Procedures in Special Education." East Texas State Univer-
sity, 1981, 42:5083-A.

Evaluates the perceptions of special and regular educators toward
policies and procedures resulting rrom Public Law 94-142.

463. Bragg, Stephen M. "The Relationship between Student Interstate
Migration and Financial Aid Practices and Policies." The Pennsylvania
State University, 1980, 41:3897-A.

Establishes the nature of the relationship between college student
interstate migration and financial aid practices and policies.

464. Bridges, Edgar F. "Consequences of Florida's University Admission
Policies on Black and White Entering Freshmen (1975-1976)." The Florida
State University, 1978, 39:1207-A.

Examines differential enrollment, survival, progress, and academic
success of both black (N=259) and white (N=3,270) first-time-in-col-
lege students as a function of three admission categories (unrestric-
tive, restrictive, and special), which was defined by scores on the
mandatory Florida Twelfth Grade Test.

465. Brown, Hugh A., III. "A Study of the Probation Intervention Policy
and Procedures at the University of Utah." The University of Utah, 1982,
42:4983-A.

The study was designed to determine if (1) the intervention treatment
at The University of Utah has an effect on the probation population's
academic performance and/or retention, and (2) if the semantic differential could be used as a predictor of probation.

466. Bryant, Barbara J. "The Effect of Faculty and Administrative Attitudes towards Students over Twenty-Five Years of Age on the Policies and
Programs of Selected Universities in Texas." Texas A&M University, 1977,
38:6424-A.

Attempts to determine the effect of administrative and faculty attitudes toward students at the undergraduate level who are twenty-five
years of age or older on the programs and policies offered at three
selected institutions of higher education in Texas.

467. Carignan, Richard H. "An Evaluation of the Competency Based Aspects
of the Educational Administrator Certification Program at the Center for
Educational Policy and Management, University of Oregon." University of
Oregon, 1979, 40:4817-A.

Attempts to: (1) determine the current relevance and importance of
CEPM's twenty-six competency statements as perceived by Oregon school
principals and superintendents; (2) identify the commonly accepted
components of competency based education as revealed in the pertinent

literature; (3) determine the extent instructors of certification courses apply the components of competency based education; and (4) determine the extent to which CEPM implemented a competency based certification program.

%68. Chuntz, Howard. "The Effect That Collective Bargaining Has Had on Workload Policies and Practices for Full-Time Faculty: A Case Study of the Coast Community College District." University of California, Los Angeles, 1981, 42:1924-A.

Attempts to determine the educational orientations and the interpersonal behaviors of postsecondary occupational-technical instructors, and to examine the proposed relationship between interpersonal behaviors, demographic variables, and educational orientations of occupational-technical educators.

469. Cline, Daniel H. "Service Delivery Models in Special Education Inservice Training for Regular Educators: Status of the Federal Initiative with Policy Recommendations for Local, State, and Federal Planners." Indiana University, 1981, 42:4788-A.

Investigates a federal initiative in in-service teacher education related to the statewide Comprehensive System of Personnel Development mandated by Public Law 94-142, the Education for All Handicapped Children Act of 1975.

470. Cody, Caroline B. "A Case Study on Policy Implementation: Minimal Competency Testing Policy, Birmingham City Schools." The University of Alabama, 1979, 40:35-A.

Investigates the impact of a minimal competency testing policy on the administration of local schools and on instruction in the Birmingham City Schools.

471. Cohen, Elissa D. "Policy Guidelines on Student Rights and Responsibilities in Florida Public Schools." University of Miami, 1979, 40:36-A.

Attempts to determine the status of each Florida public school district's compliance with Florida Statute 230.23(6)(d). This project also serves as a resource document for Florida school district policy makers and administrators in establishing or updating their student rights handbooks consistent with state law.

472. Cornelsen, LeRoy A. "A Theoretical Construct for Adult Education Public Policy." The University of Alabama, 1977, 39:5870-A.

Identifies and discusses elements and components necessary for developing public policy to guide educational agencies, institutions and legislative bodies in determining priorities among and between the various education needs of adults and the programs designed to serve them.

473. Couture, Jerry L. "Teacher Perception of Influence Patterns Affecting the Development of Student Behavior Policies and Practices." University of Oregon, 1981, 42:3360-A.

Attempts to determine how teachers perceive the patterns of influence that affect the development of student behavior policies and practices.

474. Cross, Malcolm L. "Determinants of Superintendent Tenure and Fiscal Policy in Modern Urban School Districts." University of Missouri-Columbia, 1980, 42:3747-A.

Measures the impact of the formal legal structure of the modern school district's government on the tenure of its superintendent and the nature of its fiscal policy.

475. Crowley, John D. "The Federal College Work-Study Program, University Policy Making and the Graduate Student." Syracuse University, 1977, 38:5039-A.

Explores several propositions, in light of the College Work-Study Program's legislative history, related to the ways in which the forty-eight members of the Association of American Universities have implemented this federal aid program, especially for their graduate and professional students.

476. Cullar, Wendy M. "State Policy for the Education of Exceptional Students in Florida, 1869-1979." The University of Florida, 1981, 42:2608-A.

The purpose of this historical analysis of provisions for educating exceptional students in Florida is to (1) determine state policy as defined by the legislature, state board of education, state department of education administrative and leadership activities, and other state executive offices; and (2) identify forces that influenced these provisions.

477. Davis, Carl L., Jr. "An Examination of Tenure and Promotion Policies in State Universities and Land-Grant Colleges and Their Relationship to Selected Current Issues." The University of Alabama, 1980, 41:3341-A.

Examines tenure and promotion policies in state universities and land-grant colleges, the criteria used for determining tenure and promotion, and the relationships of selected current issues to tenure and promotion policies.

478. Deselms, Harold D. "A Descriptive Study of Practices and Policies for Selected Schools and Communities with Programs of Shared Facilities." The University of Nebraska-Lincoln, 1978, 39:4675-A.

Identifies the types and extent to which public facilities were utilized jointly by selected school districts and communities; and determines the practices, procedures and policies employed by these school districts and municipalities in the provision, maintenance and operation of joint school and community facilities.

479. Detzel, Denis H. "The Schooling Method: Policies, Practices, Romantic Alternatives." Northwestern University, 1981, 42:1871-A.

Presents a critical examination of the roles of contemporary schooling from the Romantic or Libertarian perspective. The schools' roles as the dominant provider of food, day care, socialization, culture and information, and as an agent for the enforcement of government policy are examined and the social, economic and political implications of delivering these services through government schooling is discussed.

480. Doscher, Mary-Lynn. "Guessing Distortions and Implications for Educational Policy: Extensions of the Classical Test Theory Model." University of California, Los Angeles, 1979, 40:5410-A.

Examines the potential distortions in standardized achievement tests scores due to guessing.

481. Dubose, Peggy H. "Explanations of Public Policy: Environment and Power in Public Education Policy in Georgia, 1930-1970." Vanderbilt University, 1977, 38:5021-A.

Constitutes an effort to improve and expand explanations of variation in public policy using education policy in Georgia counties as the basis for a quantitative longitudinal analysis covering five decades from 1930 to 1970.

482. Dunn, Sally A. "Educational Policy Making in an Urban School System with Regard to an Operating Levy." The University of Toledo, 1980, 41:2850-A.

Examines the involvement of individuals and groups in a large city public school campaign to determine their influence on educational policy making with regard to the outcome of an operating levy.

483. Ellsworth, Jill H. "Policy, Policy Formulation and Civic Literacy/ Futures-Invention." Syracuse University, 1979, 40:6108-A.

The purpose of this conceptual, formative inquiry is to explore the meaning and nature of adult education policy through an examination of policy, education policy and adult education policy. It postulates certain claims about policy and the formation of policy.

484. Emslie, Marion F. "A Study of the Status, Policies and Practices of the Endowed Academic Chair in Selected American Colleges and Universities." University of Virginia, 1977, 38:3973-A.

Seeks information from selected institutions about policies and practices governing the endowed chair; determines whether there were commonalities and disparities among institutions in those policies and practices; inquires into the scope of the endowed chairholder's activities; and seeks information about the endowed chairholder's activities in relation to the administration of the academic department.

485. Eveslage, Sonja A. "Implementing an Innovative Policy: A Comparative Analysis of Four State Universities." University of Minnesota, 1977, 38:5942-A.

External studies is the illustrative innovation investigated in four of Minnesota's six four-year state universities. This board office proposal, requiring competency evaluation of learning through life

experiences, undergoes case study analysis tracing the course of institutional scrutiny from initiation to outcome stages. Easton's
(1965) political systems framework is used.

486. Flamer, Herbert J. "A Policy Study of the Educational Opportunity
Fund Graduate Grant Program." Rutgers University, 1978, 40:118-A.

Examines public policy in New Jersey as it relates to expanding access
for minorities in graduate and professional education. The primary
focus is the Educational Opportunity Fund's Graduate Grant Program.

487. Forbes, Norma E. "Federal Policy and the Small School District: A
Field Study of the Effects of the Indian Education Act." University of
Alaska, 1977, 39:5385-A.

Reports a field study of educational change in a small Alaskan school
district, initiated by the acceptance of Indian Education Act funds.
The emphasis is on the interaction between the Indian parent committee
and the school personnel.

488. Francis, Richard H. "The Effect of Public Policy on Interstate
Student Migration." University of Maryland, 1977, 39:1096-A.

The study is concerned with the influence that state public policies
have on interstate migration of undergraduate students to public and
private institutions of higher education.

489. Garner, Linda W. "Continuing Education Policies of the Professions:
An Analysis and Description of Content." Texas A&M University, 1981, 42:
2968-A.

Analyzes and describes the policies established by professional associations and licensing boards to direct and regulate continuing professional education. Fifty-three professional groups, representing
eighteen professions, were surveyed.

490. Garrett, Larry N. "The Foreign Student in American Higher Education: A Study of the Policies and Practices of Selected Host Institutions
as They Relate to English Language Proficiency and Academic Advisement."
George Peabody College for Teachers, 1979, 40:124-A.

Investigates and reports the stated policies and actual practices of
selected American host institutions as they regard certain prescribed
academic foreign student affairs.

491. Garrison, John H. "Interest Group Responses to Student-Initiated
Pressures for Change: An Application of the Baldridge Political Model to
University Policy Formulation Processes." The University of Texas at
Austin, 1978, 39:1950-A.

Attempts to determine the utility of the J.Victor Baldridge political
change model for diagnosing and categorizing the interest articulation
behavior of pressure groups in policy issues which are initiated by
students in institutions of higher education.

492. Gaswirth, Marc S. "Teacher Militancy in New Jersey: An Analysis of

Organizational Change, Public Policy Development, and School Board-Teacher
Relationships through January, 1975." Rutgers University, 1977, 38:3835-A.

    Examines teacher militancy in New Jersey within the context of teacher
organizational change, public policy development, and increased school
board-teacher bargaining through January, 1975.

493. Gibson, Samuel N. "Public Policy in the Expansion of Higher Education in the State of Alabama, 1963-1978: A Case Study in the Politics of
Higher Education." University of Pittsburgh, 1980, 41:2465-A.

    This case study in the politics of higher education has as its purpose
to identify and to analyze the ingredients of public policy which were
significant in the remarkable expansion of higher education in the
State of Alabama between 1962 and 1978.

494. Gorman, William T. "An Analysis of School Committee Decision-Making
and Policy Manuals." Boston College, 1978, 39:1220-A.

    Compares the operations of school committees with respect to (1) gen-
erality or specificity of decisions, (2) distinction between their
policy-making function and the superintendents' policy-executing function, (3) repetition of decisions in recurrent situations, and (4)
types of topics voted upon.

495. Gorrell, William T. "Educational Policy-Making and the Illinois
State Senate." Southern Illinois University at Carbondale, 1979, 40:
3142-A.

    Examines the role of the Illinois State Senator in the educational
policy-making process.

496. Gould, Renee V. "The Early Childhood Education Act of 1972, (SB
1302): A Study in Policy Transformation." University of California, Los
Angeles, 1979, 40:1992-A.

    The Early Childhood Act of California or Senate Bill 1302 is used as
a case study to illustrate the process of policy-formulation.

497. Greer, Darryl G. "Politics and Higher Education: A Case Analysis
of Coordination and Policy Implementation by the Ohio Board of Regents."
Stanford University, 1979, 40:1069-A.

    Analyzes through case analysis the process by which the Ohio Board of
Regents, Ohio's state-level coordinating board for higher education,
approaches coordination of institutions of higher education and implementation of public policy goals in a political setting.

498. Halpert, Leon. "Legislative Oversight of Elementary and Secondary
Education Policy: Theory and Analysis." The University of Michigan, 1977,
38:6909-A.

    This is a study of legislative oversight based on four educational
programs: the Elementary and Secondary Education Act, the Teacher
Corps, the Emergency School Aid Act, and legislation creating the
National Institute of Education. Includes both the Johnson and Nixon
Administrations (1965-1973).

499.   Halverson, John W.   "The Private and Social Net Present Value of Medical and Dental Education at the University of Michigan and Analysis for Policy."   The University of Michigan, 1979, 40:987-A.

Develops a model for determining the private and public net present value of dental and medical education at The University of Michigan, and analyzes the results in order to assess the private and public financing of these activities.

500.   Hamilton, Bette E.   "Federal Policy Networks for Postsecondary Education."   The University of Michigan, 1977, 38:6561-A.

Examines the role played by participants in the postsecondary education policy system in working to effect four legislative policy "innovations" contained in the 1976 Education Amendments, P.L. 94-482.

501.   Hammond, Michael P.   "An Analysis of the Effectiveness of a Calculative Involvement Policy in Reducing Absenteeism among Secondary Students in Metropolitan Nashville Public Schools."   George Peabody College for Teachers, 1977, 38:4478-A.

Gathers and analyzes information which would assist in assessing the effectiveness of a calculative involvement policy for attendance in reducing absenteeism among secondary students in the Metropolitan Nashville Public Schools.

502.   Hartmark, Leif S.   "The Effects of Rationalistic Budgeting and Legislative Staff upon University Policy-Making Independence: The Wisconsin Experience."   State University of New York at Albany, 1978, 39:1829-A.

The dissertation is an exploratory study of the accountability relationships between The University of Wisconsin System and the Wisconsin State Legislature during the 1973 to 1975 period, dealing with the legislative budgetary process.

503.   Hatridge, Douglas G.   "Public School Principal Performance Appraisal Policies in Missouri."   University of Missouri-Columbia, 1978, 40:48-A.

Gathers information from public school principals in Missouri concerning their school districts' principal performance appraisal policies and procedures.

504.   Heath, Fred M.   "The Policy Role of the Virginia State Council of Higher Education (SCHEV)."   Virginia Polytechnic Institute and State University, 1980, 41:3351-A.

Describes and analyzes the contribution to policy development of the State Council of Higher Education for Virginia.

505.   Heck, Susan.   "Perceived Outcomes and Concurrent Conditions of Parent Participation in School Policy-Making."   Stanford University, 1977, 38:5384-A.

Describes school advisory committee activities and influence as perceived by committee members and isolates some of the factors associated with both activity and influence.

506. Hendricks, Leon. "An Analysis of State Statutes, Policies, and Practices Related to Public Financing of Urban Non-Public Parochial Schools: Elementary and Secondary." Loyola University of Chicago, 1979, 39:6432-A.

   Attempts to present a nationwide appraisal of existing state statutes, policies, and practices related to financing of urban non-public parochial school programs and services on the elementary and secondary levels.

507. Henson, Charles J. "An Examination of the Perceptions of Selected Educational Leaders and Policymakers in Alabama Relative to the Desired Governance Structure for the State's 43 Public Two-Year Institutions." The Florida State University, 1981, 42:971-A.

   Examines the perceptions of selected educational leaders and policy makers relative to the desired governance structure for the State's forty-three public, two-year institutions.

508. Hindes, Sally K. "Perceived Effectiveness of In-Service Programs for Educational Mainstreaming and Its Relationship to Local Mainstreaming Policies." Rutgers University, 1981, 42:177-A.

   Two survey instruments are developed to obtain administrative data on mainstreaming policies and teachers' perceptions of the in-service programs of forty-seven districts in New Jersey participating in a three-year Mainstream In-Service Project.

509. Hocutt, Anne M. "Parent Involvement Policy and Practice: A Study of Parental Participation in Early Education Projects for Handicapped Children." The University of North Carolina at Chapel Hill, 1980, 41: 2552-A.

   Clarifies the policy of parent involvement for the Handicapped Children's Early Education Program to determine the closeness of fit between the clarified policy and the practice of parent participation in these projects, and to determine those project characteristics which are related to implementation congruent with that in the clarified policy.

510. Holbrook, Margaret W. "An Analysis of Policies and Programs for Increasing Student Retention in Institutions of Higher Education in Georgia." University of Georgia, 1981, 42:4322-A.

   Attempts to determine the types of policies and programs Georgia's colleges have implemented in an effort to improve student retention.

511. Hubbell, Brook A. "Grade Retention Policies at the Elementary School Level." Brigham Young University, 1980, 41:2932-A.

   A survey of grade retention policy and practice is conducted among 124 elementary schools in Ventura County, California, during the 1979-1980 school year.

512. Irish, Joan. "Board-School-Community Relations and Educational Policy Making." Columbia University, 1980, 41:1312-A.

Makes recommendations for educational policy making and the management of school-community relationships in the West Valley, New Jersey
school system, and draws inferences for the consideration of the profession of educational administration.

513.   Jackson, Ruth E.   "An Elementary School Model Student Placement
Policy: A Study to Identify the Rationale, Processes, and Criteria Used
to Develop a Policy." Brigham Young University, 1977, 38:4482-A.

Identifies rationale, processes, and criteria to be used by school
personnel in developing an elementary school model placement policy.

514.   Johnson, Mary S.   "Political Cleavages and Public Policy: Adult
Education in France and the United States." University of Virginia,
1978, 40:1052-A.

The particular programs adopted by each of the countries have differed
significantly in scope, intent and administrative detail. This dissertation looks to political cleavages to explain at least some of
the variance in national adult education policies.

515.   Johnston, Thomas E.   "An Assessment of Attitudes of State and Institutional and Association Policy Makers on the Coordination and Planning of Higher Education in Michigan." Michigan State University, 1977,
39:151-A.

The study is directed at the identification of an operational definition of institutional autonomy and statewide coordination and planning of public higher education in Michigan through assessing the
attitudes of policy makers from the institutions, state government,
and educational associations regarding specific programmatic, fiscal,
facilities, personnel and governance questions.

516.   Jones, Walter M., Jr.   "Applications of the Law Governing the Student Newspaper in the Policies and Practices of Selected Institutions of
Higher Education." University of Georgia, 1977, 38:3977-A.

Presents an examination of the academic change process in undergraduate higher education during the experimental movement of the 1960's,
as exemplified by the creation and early operation of Livingston College, a federated college of Rutgers University.

517.   Kahane, Ernest S.   "The Justification of Special Admissions Policies." University of Illinois at Urbana-Champaign, 1981, 42:3902-A.

Addresses the problem of presenting a satisfactory justification for
special admissions policies using race or sex as often decisive criteria for entrance to higher educational and professional school opportunities.

518.   Kane, William M.   "The Effects of an Attendance Policy Enforced by
Suspension and Expulsion among High School Students." University of Oregon, 1977, 38:5824-A.

Investigates the effect an attendance policy, which specified suspension and expulsion as the consequences of truancy, had among students

in a large Oregon high school. Also identifies perceptions of persons affected by the policy, characteristics of students truant with the policy in effect, and the cost of operating the policy.

519. Kelly, Raymond F. "Educational Policy Change for International Professional Training and Development: A Study of the Maryknoll Fathers, 1912-1978." New York University, 1980, 41:2536-A.

This is a study of the Maryknoll Fathers, 1912-1978, with emphasis upon the educational policy change for professional development and training.

520. King, Roger B. "The Role of Educational Concerns in Rational Acts of Adopting and Implementing Educational Policies." Syracuse University, 1977, 38:4763-A.

In an attempt to throw some light on the extent to which public schools, when rationally operated, are conducive to education, the author inquires into the role of educational concerns in rational acts of adopting and implementing educational policies.

521. Knibbs, Linda G. "A Comparative Study of the Higher Education Policies in the Fifty American States." University of Illinois at Urbana-Champaign, 1981, 42:4132-A.

The need for a more systematic examination of state higher education policies is the inspiration for the study. Three dimensions of state higher education policy were selected: the state's fiscal commitment, faculty prestige, and types of degrees awarded.

522. Kornegay, Judge N., Jr. "A Survey of the Perceptions of Chief Student Personnel Administrators in Selected Colleges and Universities for Determining Trends, Policies, Practices and Models Utilized in Staff Development Programs in Divisions of Student Affairs." Iowa State University, 1980, 41:959-A.

Attempts to determine the perceptions that chief student personnel administrators have regarding the structure, practices, procedures, and budget considerations of professional staff development programs in divisions of student affairs in selected public and private institutions.

523. Largue, Eula M. "Retrenchment: Practices, Policies, and Effects in the Colleges of Education in the Florida State University System." The Florida State University, 1980, 41:873-A.

This is a descriptive study designed to determine the aspects of retrenchment within the Colleges of Education in the nine public universities of Florida.

524. Law, William D., Jr. "The Effects of Systemwide Instructional Cost Policies on Selected Undergraduate Curricula." The Florida State University, 1977, 39:1372-A.

Four academic curricula--business, education, mathematics, and psychology--common to the University of Florida, The Florida State Uni-

versity, and Florida Technological University are studied to see if
any changes in their curricular structure could be attributed to two
cost-of-instruction policies adopted by the Florida Board of Regents.

525. Leventhal, Richard C. "The Extent to Which State Policies in the
Financing of Public Colleges and Universities in the State of Colorado
May Affect the Higher Educational Opportunities of High School Students."
University of Denver, 1978, 39:2089-A.

Attempts to determine what factors exist in Colorado which may be
producing barriers to those students with annual family incomes of
less than $6,000 in their efforts to attend a public institution of
higher education and to determine whether such barriers are directly
related to the manner in which a state (Colorado) operates its student financial aid program(s).

526. Levinson, Nanette S. "College Teacher Preparation in Ph.D. Programs
at the University of Hawaii: Policies, Practices, and Faculty Attitudes."
Harvard University, 1979, 40:3149-A.

Studies by Hollis in 1945 and Berelson in 1960 have examined the attitudes of faculty toward college and university teacher preparation in
Ph.D. programs. A literature review reveals a need for a multivariate
study of faculty attitudes toward college and university teacher preparation in Ph.D. programs at one institution as well as for a study
of college and university teacher preparation components in these programs.

527. Lilker, Martin. "Educational Policy and Decision-Making in the
Jewish Secondary Schools." Yeshiva University, 1977, 38:6442-A.

Investigates policy and decision making in selected representative
Jewish secondary schools and in selected representative private non-
sectarian schools.

528. Lofrese, James J. "An Analysis of Existing Attendance Policies and
Their Relationship to Secondary School Student Attendance Rates in the
Newport News (Virginia) Public Schools (1977-1978)." Virginia Polytech-
nic Institute and State University, 1978, 40:2394-A.

The purpose of this investigation is to determine the extant relationship between formal statements of attendance policy, as implemented by each school administrator, and the associated student ab-
sentee rates.

529. Lotto, Linda S. "Educational Knowledge Dissemination and Utilization and Schools of Education: Assessment of Current Involvement, Projected Responses to External Interventions, and Federal Policy Recommendations." Indiana University, 1979, 40:699-A.

The objectives are to: (1) provide a normative depiction of current
SCDE schools of education involvement in dissemination and utilization (D and U); (2) project the likely responses of SCDE's to federal
interventions in D and U; and (3) recommend effective and feasible
federal policies and programs utilizing SCDE's in education D and U.

530. Love, Jane H. "Inferential School Board Policy." West Virginia University, 1977, 38:4486-A.

Analyzes the policy-making process of the members of a school district board of education as they execute their roles in policy formulation and implementation during one school year.

531. Lummis, Adair T. "Especially Union? Educational Policy and Socialization in an Elite Boundary Professional School, Union Theological Seminary, New York." Columbia University, 1979, 40:472-A.

Focuses on events in the early seventies at this seminary in exploring the degree to which external social conditions and changes in value priorities of the seminary's university and occupational constituencies affected the internal responses to various pressures and its socialization practices.

532. Lysakowski, Richard S. "Cues, Participation and Corrective Feedback in Relation to Learning: A Quantitative Synthesis for Educational Policy." University of Illinois at Chicago Circle, 1981, 42:1554-A.

This investigation has synthesized a large body of research on quality of instruction, cues, participation, and corrective feedback. Quantitative synthesis of outcomes was performed on the reported outcomes of fifty-four studies (1964-1980) in the educational and psychological literature.

533. McGuigan, Hugh E. "A Descriptive Case Study of a School Closing Decision-Making Process and Its Implications for Educational Policymaking and Operations." New York University, 1981, 42:325-A.

Develops a case study of the phases and forces involved in the process of decision making concerning school utilization in a community experiencing enrollment decline, and analyzes the study in terms of implications for educational policy making and operations of an educational organization.

534. Machi, Lawrence A. "A Research Study Measuring the Relationship of Program Policy and Program Cost to Student Achievement with Ninth Grade Disadvantaged Students in Reading Programs in the East Side Union High School District, San Jose, California." University of San Francisco, 1979, 40:2572-A.

Two specific inquiries are made: (1) Is there a significant difference in adjusted post-test reading scores between compensatory and non-compensatory programs? (2) Is there a significant difference in the adjusted reading scores between high-cost and low-cost reading or equivalent programs?

535. McSpadden, Lucia. "Teacher Judgments of Educational Policies Appropriate for Mexican-American Elementary Students." University of Utah, 1978, 38:7199-A.

All the elementary teachers in the Salt Lake City and Tooele County public school systems are surveyed in order to ascertain their judgments as to appropriate educational policy for Mexican-American elementary students.

536. Maiberger, George L. "Comparative Analysis of Three Groups of
Policy-Makers Concerning Selective Components of Rural Community Education." The Florida State University, 1980, 41:961-A.

    Analyzes three groups of policy makers from the western counties of
    the state of Florida concerning four components of rural community
    education.

537. Maikowski, Thomas R. "Assumed and Preferred Functions of Significant Individuals and Groups Formulating Educational Policies and Regulations for the Catholic Elementary Schools of New Mexico." Saint Louis
University, 1980, 41:3356-A.

    Attempts to determine and compare role expectations and perceptions
    of selected groups involved with the governance of the Roman Catholic
    elementary schools in the State of New Mexico, concerning their own
    roles and the roles of the other selected groups in this governance.

538. Malbon, Lee C. "A Multivariate Model to Predict Changes in Student
Behavior and Achievement Attributable to a Set of Attendance Policy Practices for Secondary School Students." Boston College, 1979, 40:5675-A.

    Evaluates and predicts, using a multivariate model, the changes in
    student achievement and behavior attributable to a set of attendance
    policy practices for secondary school students.

539. May, Leslie S. "The Development of the Massachusetts Basic Skills
Improvement Policy." Harvard University, 1979, 40:3090-A.

    Describes and analyzes the development of the Massachusetts Basic
    Skills Improvement Policy, and analyzes how state level educational
    policy making, as evidenced by the Massachusetts experience in adopt-
    ing a minimum competency program, is conducted.

540. Miller, Dennis A. "Perceptions of Relative and Ideal Levels of Influence in the Formation of Public School Educational Policy." The University of Michigan, 1979,40:5274-A.

    Examines perceptions of professional educators, board of education
    members, and lay citizens of their relative power to influence the
    formation of educational policy; explores perceptions of ideal levels
    of influence for each group; and examines the differences in the per-
    ceptions of the legitimate levels of influence of citizen advisory
    groups in selected aspects of educational decision making.

541. Miller, Pamela F. "Educational Policies and State Characteristics
Influencing State Response to Gifted and Talented Education between 1977
and 1980." Southern Illinois University at Carbondale, 1981, 42:4234-A.

    Several educational policies and state characteristics have been cited
    in the literature as having a beneficial influence upon state response
    to gifted and talented education. This study seeks to acertain the
    influence of these educational policies and state characteristics on
    the level of state services provided gifted and talented students and
    state expenditures provided to support such services observed across
    states between 1977 and 1980.

542. Mitchell, Edward H. "Governor's Study Commission on Structure and Governance of Education for Maryland: An Analysis of a Public Policymaking Process." University of Maryland, 1977, 38:3856-A.

The research effort is designed to analyze a public policy process that has frequently been employed in Maryland to effectuate changes in public education, the gubernatorial study commission. The Governor's Study Commission on Structure and Governance of Education for Maryland was chosen for analysis. Eight issues which confronted the Commission were selected for in-depth study.

543. Murphy, Sheila E. "A Study of Policies for Part-Time Instruction in the Community College." Arizona State University, 1980, 41:3362-A.

Examines the status of policies relating to the use of part-time instructors in a sample of public community colleges in Arizona and California.

544. Novembre, Anthony. "An Analysis of Tenured Teacher Evaluation Policies of New Jersey School Districts in Relation to the State Board of Education's Established Rules and Regulations." Rutgers University, 1981, 42:1416-A.

Descriptively and analytically investigates tenured teacher evaluation policies in the 566 public school districts in New Jersey, with the intent to determine if the policies incorporated all the elements of the New Jersey Administrative Code 6:3-1.21.

545. O'Connell, Colman. "The Influence of Organizational Policies and Arrangements of Faculty Development Programs upon Faculty Participation and Changed Teaching Behavior." The University of Michigan, 1979, 40:5276-A.

Examines the organizational factors and institutional policies which influence faculty participation in faculty development programs and changes in teaching behavior.

546. Olivas, Michael A. "Public Policy Dimensions of Statewide Coordination in Higher Education: Agenda Building and the Establishment of the Ohio Board of Regents." The Ohio State University, 1977, 38:4611-A.

Examines seven major issues in the establishment of the Ohio Board of Regents. Each of these issues, as well as the pattern of events surrounding each issue, is examined by means of the Cobb and Elder model.

547. O'Malley, Charles J. "A Study of the Influence of the Independent Colleges and Universities of Florida, Inc., (ICUF) and the Florida Association of Private Schools, Inc. (FAPS) upon Selected Policy Concerning Private Postsecondary Education." The Florida State University, 1979, 40:5337-A.

Analyzes the influence of the two private postsecondary advocacy groups, the Independent Colleges and Universities of Florida, Inc. and the Florida Association of Private Schools upon state educational policy.

548. Ortenzio, Paul J. "The Problem of Purpose in American Education: The Rise and Fall of the Educational Policies Commission." Rutgers University, 1977, 38:6572-A.

Traces the history of the Educational Policies Commission (EPC) and investigates its influence during its thirty-three years of service to American education. Examines and assesses the origins, membership, support, and criticism of the EPC. The actions which led to the demise of the EPC in 1968 are given careful coverage.

549. Osborn, Franklin E. "The Structure and Justification of Educational Policy." Indiana University, 1978, 39:4115-A.

What is the structure and institutional function of educational policy? What is an adequate theory of educational policy justification? To provide answers is the task of this study.

550. Page, Lenore R. "An Analysis of the Collaborative Structures of the Policy Boards of the Sixty Federally Funded Teacher Centers--FY 1979." George Peabody College for Teachers, 1980, 42:945-A.

Analyzes the perceptions and attitudes of policy-board members of the first teacher centers federally funded under P.L. 94-482.

551. Palaich, Robert M. "The Emergence and Development of Federal Education Policy: A Dimensional Analysis of Congressional Roll Call Voting, 1909-1968." Columbia University, 1981, 42:2837-A.

This study of roll call voting in the United States House of Representatives explores the relationship between the legislative agenda and legislative outcomes in the policy area of education during the 1909-1968 period.

552. Parker, Darrell T. "Policies and Procedures for the Evaluation of the Elementary School Principal as a Function of Authority System Stability." University of Southern California, 1980, 41:2866-A.

Attempts to determine the extent to which policy statements and administrative procedures for appraisal systems for elementary school principals are supported by practicing principals and their primary evaluators.

553. Parker, Dorothy B. "A Study of Policies and Procedures for Utilization of School Facilities with Declining Enrollments on the State and Local Levels." Vanderbilt University, 1981, 42:1419-A.

Determines the extent to which policies and procedures for utilizing school facilities with declining enrollments exists on state and local levels.

554. Patterson, Mary. "A Study of Congruence between Delphi Validated Policies and Procedures Which Promote Learning among High-Risk Students and Current Practices in Selected Community Colleges." The University of Texas at Austin, 1980, 41:2867-A.

Individuals knowledgeable about educational policy and learning specialists in the areas of the community college, high-risk students, and adult education were conjoined as a Delphi panel to develop a set of policies and procedures which can consistently result in high levels of learning and retention among high-risk students. This set of Delphi-validated policies and procedures was then tested in a selected sample of community colleges.

555. Perry, Philip J. "A Study of Change in Student-Teacher Attitudes towards Child-Centered Policies and Practices." University of Washington, 1981, 42:2579-A.

Attempts to effect change in student-teacher attitudes toward child-centeredness by revealing their attitude discrepancies to experimental subjects.

556. Petak, Dorothy M. "An Analysis of Student Suspension Factors in Relationship to School Board Policies and Other Selected Variables." Loyola University of Chicago, 1981, 41:4567-A.

This investigation, which was conducted during the school year 1977-78, seeks to discover whether or not there were significant relationships between suspension rates in Chicago Public High Schools during the five-year span between 1972-73 and 1976-77.

557. Pickett, William L. "An Assessment of the Effectiveness of Fund Raising Policies of Private Undergraduate Colleges." University of Denver, 1977, 38:3983-A.

Addresses the problem of identifying the fund-raising policies which are likely to increase the gift income of private undergraduate colleges.

558. Planek, Joanne M. "An Analysis of Factors Which Interfere with the Full Implementation of Archdiocesan Policies by Local Schoolboards in the Archdiocese of Chicago." Loyola University of Chicago, 1981, 42:1421-A.

Analyzes factors affecting the full implementation of archdiocesan policies by local school boards.

559. Rash, Chester L. "The Coleman Report: A Case Study of the Linkage between Social Science Research and Public Policy." State University of New York at Stony Brook, 1980, 41:1245-A.

The general theoretical concern of this thesis is the relationship between the men of ideas and the men of action.

560. Rasmussen, Kenneth S. "Reduction in Force Principles, Practices, and Policies for Public K-12 Education in Nebraska." The University of Nebraska-Lincoln, 1979, 40:5277-A.

Investigates the personnel implications of reduction in force for public K-12 education in Nebraska.

561. Roberts, Godfrey. "Population Policy and Population Education." Rutgers University, 1977, 38:4076-A.

The relationship between national population goals as identified by
population policy and population education programs are examined in
three countries: the United States, India and Sri Lanka.

562.   Roberts, Ronald E.   "A Study of the Policy-Making Relationships of
Ten Texas Public Community College Governing Boards, the College Administration, Faculty, and the Impact of the Community Environment."   University of Houston, 1978, 39:4008-A.

Attempts to ascertain differential perceptions regarding philosophy
of policy making as manifested by the various sample groups: governing board members, administrators, and faculty members.

563.   Robledo, Amado.   "The Impact of Alien Immigration on Public Policy
and Educational Services on Selected Districts in the Texas Educational
System."   University of Houston, 1977, 38:7034-A.

Addresses several important issues which have directly affected American society.   Shows the degree of impact alien immigration is having
on the Texas educational system, and makes recommendations on public
policy that have implications in the educational field.

564.   Rollin, Jean M.   "Bilingual Adult Education: A Preliminary Analysis
and Assessment of Policy and Implementation."   The Florida State University, 1979, 40:5285-A.

This descriptive study is an attempt to link the research areas of
litigation and legislation with the area of program implementation
to provide a data base for the expanding field of bilingual adult
education.

565.   Rosser, John R.   "Extent of Congruence of Adult Educators with Basic
Educational Policy Changes Advocated by USOE Proponents of Career Education."   The George Washington University, 1978, 39:1997-A.

Assesses the extent of agreement with USOE's Career Education Policy
Paper among adult educators, as a prelude to infusion of career education into existing programs.   The primary concern is with attitudes
of staff according to variables that differentiate among subpopula-
tions of adult educators; and to provide implications for management
and in-service training strategies.

566.   Rothrock, Paul D.   "Legal Foundations for West Virginia School Board
Business Management Policies."   Virginia Polytechnic Institute and State
University, 1977, 38:5837-A.

Synthesizes the pertinent legal requirements for the business management operations of West Virginia county boards of education, and helps
fill a void in the policy formulation process for West Virginia boards
of education.

567.   Ryan, Mark E.   "Puerto Rico's Educational Policy and Its Relation
to Political Power: 1898-1976."   Arizona State University, 1981, 42:
3894-A.

Focuses on the following question: How has the political relationship between the United States and Puerto Rico affected language policy within the Puerto Rican schools?

568. Sakal, Edward L. "A Study of School Board Member Involvement in Policy Determination." Syracuse University, 1977, 39:594-A.

Examines the role perceptions of school board members in policy-making situations, and measures the extent to which board members believed that they shared their responsibilities in various policy-making areas with superintendents, and examines the variability of board member role perceptions in relation to some of the characteristics of board members and school districts.

569. Sanera, Michael R. "Political Skill in the Formulation and Legiti-mation of Public Policy: The Case of Education Vouchers at Alum Rock." University of Colorado at Boulder, 1979, 40:4741-A.

To investigate Bardach's theory to political skill, this research ex-plores policy-making activities emanating from the Office of Economic Opportunity attempt to establish an experiment with education vouchers at Alum Rock School District, San Jose, California.

570. Schuerman, William C. "A Model Institutional Policy on the Privacy of Student Records in Compliance with the Family Educational Rights and Privacy Act of 1974 as Amended." The American University, 1980, 41: 2964-A.

Develops a model for a written institutional policy on the privacy of student records in American four-year colleges and universities that complies with the Family Educational Rights and Privacy Act of 1974 as Amended.

571. Schwamm, Jeffrey. "The Politics of Implementation: A Comparative Study of the Influence of School Committees and Superintendents on Special Education Policy." Brandeis University, 1977, 39:226-A.

Investigates and analyzes the educational ideology and political-economic orientation of local educational decision makers, and looks at the extent of special education policy implementation in Massa-chusetts.

572. Seifelnasr, Ahmed. "Uncertainty and Policy Analysis in Educational Flow Models." The Johns Hopkins University, 1979, 40:5216-A.

Presents several algorithms for analyzing the effect of uncertainty about the values taken by parameters and/or exogenous variables on the results generated using educational flow models.

573. Shawver, S. Herbert, III. "Laws, Policies, Practices and Problems of Securing Compulsory Attendance in Kansas." University of Kansas, 1977, 38:3867-A.

Identifies Kansas attendance laws, and the policies, practices, pro-cedures used and problems of securing attendance experienced by ad-ministrators and jurists in Kansas.

574.   Shelton, David E.   "The Legal Aspects of Male Students' Hair Groom-
ing Policies in the Public Schools of the United States."   The University
of North Carolina at Greensboro, 1980, 41:1335-A.

Examines court decisions from the judicial circuits of the United
States Courts of Appeals concerning length of male students' hair in
the public schools of the United States.

575.   Sieradski, Philip.   "Beyond In Loco Parentis: An Analysis of Determinants of College and University Policy toward Student Felonious Behavior."   New York University, 1980, 40:490-A.

Seeks to examine whether institutions of higher education still evidence some characteristics of a sanctuary.   Specifically, how do colleges and universities deal with felonious behavior committed by their
students?

576.   Singer, Jerry D.   "Evaluation and Analysis of High School Attendance
Policies in the State of Kansas."   University of Trinity College (Canada),
1981, 42:1891-A.

Attempts to determine the perceptions of student council presidents,
building representatives of the teacher organization, school board
presidents, and principals toward characteristics found in attendance
policies used in the State of Kansas.

577.   Skinkle, John D.   "Certification Standards for Vocational Educators:
The Implications for Professional Development Policy."   University of Minnesota, 1978, 39:7310-A.

The purpose is to ascertain the present standards for the certification of vocational educators and to determine the subsequent implications for the continuance, expansion, and qualitative improvement of
professional development programs and policy.

578.   Slack, James D.   "Policy Implementation and Intergovernmental Relations: The Case of the Emergency School Aid Act."   Miami University,
1981, 42:4144-A.

Examines from an intergovernmental perspective the implementation of
the Emergency School Aid Act enacted by the U.S. Congress in 1972.

579.   Smith, Jack.   "Manpower Planning and Higher Education: National
Policy in the United States and England."   The University of Arizona,
1982, 42:694-A.

National policy for higher education in the United States and England
is examined with respect to provision of highly qualified manpower.
Four agencies concerned with manpower policies were selected in two
centers of national government, Washington, D.C. and London.   Each
is analyzed in terms of the contribution made to decision making and
policy formulation.

580.   Solfronk, Donald F.   "An Analysis of Certain Beliefs Regarding Public Junior Colleges Held by Selected Groups Responsible for Educational
Policy Formulation and Implementation within the State of Alabama."   Auburn University, 1978, 39:5861-A.

Assesses and compares certain educational beliefs of selected groups
of educational policy makers and implementors regarding the role and
function of public, tax-supported junior colleges; and provides additional field testing of the study instrument, Auburn Scale of Community College Beliefs, and compares the results with earlier uses of
the instrument.

581. Spigler, Frederick H., Jr. "The Education Coordinating Committee
as an Influence on Educational Policy Making in Maryland." University
of Maryland, 1981, 42:3468-A.

Examines an educational coordinating mechanism in Maryland, the Education Coordinating Committee, which links the public school and postsecondary sectors for the cooperative development of educational policy at the state level.

582. Stein, David T. "The Evolution of Policy Development for Programs
of Higher Education in the Lutheran Church Missouri Synod and Its Relationship to Internal and External Governance 1944-1975." Saint Louis
University, 1979, 40:2509-A.

Investigates a reasonable period of time, believed to be significant,
in the organizational and institutional life of the Lutheran Church-
Missouri Synod. The years from 1944-1975 are studied for the evi-
dences of policy development and evolution in programs of higher education.

583. Stevens, Leonard B. "Bankrolled Educational Opportunity: A Policy
Study." University of Massachusetts, 1978, 39:2860-A.

This policy study on school dropouts recommends that the federal government provide education entitlements to citizens with less than a
high school education.

584. Stoll, Ned C. "Policy Guidelines Developed from an Analysis of
Emerging Legal Challenges to the Academic Autonomy of Public Institutions
of Higher Education." The University of Utah, 1980, 41:1438-A.

The legal research method is pursued to study judicial opinions contained in case reports, treatises, and legal periodicials with a view
toward answering three questions.

585. Sundberg, Ronald E. "A Study of Community College Administrator
Values toward Selected Policies and Practices in Higher Education Governing Admissions." Boston University School of Education, 1979, 40:2435-A.

Analyzes the values of community college administrative personnel
toward selected policies and practices in higher education governing
the admissions process, and attempts to discover if any relationship
exists between those value preferences held and implementation of
policies and practices of the same type in the field.

586. Taylor, Bonita M. "A Policy Analysis of Institutional Career Education Goals and the Implications for Academic Planning: Articulated Perceptions of Faculty and Administrators at a State University." University of
Massachusetts, 1979, 39:7105-A.

As an exploratory study, this research examines whether the construction of the *Goals Assessment Inventory* is appropriate for measurement of attitudinal differences regarding career education at the higher education level.

587.   Timmermann, Sandra.   "Older Learners in an Aging Nation: Projections and Guidelines for Planners and Policymakers."   Columbia University Teachers College, 1979, 40:2418-A.

Attempts to identify the significant trends affecting programming and policy in education for older persons and to develop speculations and guidelines that will be of value to policy makers and programmers now and in the future.

588.   Walton, Barbara F.   "Policy Delphi: Issues in School to Work Transition."   Arizona State University, 1978, 39:5475-A.

Examines the acceptability of policy issues concerning school to work programs and services as viewed by forty selected leaders from education and the community.

589.   Weaver, Mary L.   "Policy and Its Consequences: Higher Education in the United States and Great Britain, 1957-1977."   Cornell University, 1980, 41:1204-A.

The argument here is that it is the type of policy--its form rather than its substance or genesis--that not only creates the condition for policy success or failure but also leads to constraints upon government which are unintended.

590.   Weichenthal, Phyllis B.   "Impact of a Shift in National Public Policy on Continuing Education Administration in Institutions of Higher Education."   University of Illinois at Urbana-Champaign, 1980, 41:2401-A.

This nationwide research project analyzes the impact of the 1976 shift in Title I Part A of the Higher Education Act and what was implemented under it.

591.   Wells, James N.   "Status and Substance of Missouri School Districts' Policies Dealing with Corporal Punishment."   University of Missouri-Columbia, 1979, 40:4346-A.

Determines the percentage of Missouri school districts in this study that allow the use of corporal punishment and whether or not the school districts have written board policies concerning corporal punishment; and identifies the elements in the policies that limit, govern, or control the use of corporal punishment and the frequency by which they occur.

592.   Wertz, Janis M.   "The Accused Student and Student Offender: Criteria of a Policy Framework for the University of Massachusetts to Collaborate with the Courts and Correctional Facilities on Educational Interests of Students."   University of Massachusetts, 1978, 39:2783-A.

A history, rationale, and basis for policy action regarding student offenders at the University of Massachusetts is developed.

593. Wharton, Liberty C. "The Policy-Making Process in Higher Education in the State of Maryland, 1973-1976: A Case Study of SB 347." The George Washington University, 1982, 42:4743-A.

Focuses on the policy-making processes of two mechanisms: the Rosenberg Commission and the Wilner Task Force. Attempts to: (1) provide insights into the political processes in Maryland that shaped higher education policy formulation from 1973 to 1976; (2) provide educators with a better understanding of political processes; and (3) contribute to the scholarly study of higher education.

594. Whiteis, David H. "Analysis of Categorical Expenditures in Georgia Institutions of Higher Education and Its Implications for Statewide Planning and Public Policy." University of Georgia, 1979, 40:5756-A.

Develops one aspect of a cost data base for higher education in Georgia (per student categorical expenditures) and analyzes the importance of the information in providing for more effective planning and more informed public policy for higher education in Georgia.

595. Woelfer, Carlyle P. "A Study of Concepts, Policies and Procedures to Accomplish Vocational and Technical Education Program Articulation between Secondary Schools and Institutions of the Community College System of North Carolina." North Carolina State University at Raleigh, 1977, 38:4563-A.

Develops five operational concepts for the articulation of occupational programs based upon a variety of sources. Support for the concepts is derived primarily from reviews of literature and from data obtained by the conduct of an attitudinal survey among selected occupational educators in North Carolina.

596. Wright, Aaron E. "Educational Policymakers' and Practitioners' Perceptions of the Future Role of the High School in the State of Nebraska." The University of Nebraska-Lincoln, 1982, 42:752-A.

Attempts to determine if there existed consensus between educational policy makers and practitioners in their perceptions of the desirability, impact, and implementation of selected reform recommendations designed to affect high schools as reported in *Giving Youth a Better Chance: Options for Education, Work, and Service.*

597. Wright, Annette E. "The Nature of Legislated Policy: A Comparative Analysis of Selected Educational Legislation." The University of British Columbia (Canada), 1979, 40:1813-A.

This interprovincial comparative study examines selected Canadian provincial educational legislation as meta-policy, that is, as policy which guides the educational policy-making process.

598. Wyly, James R., Jr. "Positions of Policymakers on Factors Affecting the System of Statewide Coordination of Higher Education in Arkansas." University of Arkansas, 1978, 39:3416-A.

Surveys policy makers in higher education to determine their positions on certain factors which affect the statewide system of coordination of higher education in Arkansas and determine if a climate for change exists.

599.   Yost, Marlen D.   "An Analysis of Changes in Staffing Patterns and Personnel Policies in Ohio School Districts with Substantial Enrollment Decreases from 1970 to 1976."   The Ohio State University, 1978, 39:2683-A.

Describes changes in staffing patterns in local school districts and assesses the nature and extent of personnel policies adopted pertaining to declining enrollment.

600.   Young, Assunta.   "An Analysis of Social Consequences of Policy Implementation: A Study of the Community Clinical Nursery School (CCNS) Transfer of Children to the Local Educational Agencies (LEAs)."   Brandeis University, 1979, 39:7539-A.

Evaluates one of the implementation processes of Chapter 766, The Comprehensive Special Education Law, passed in Massachusetts on July 17, 1972, through analyzing the "social consequences" or "impacts" of a specific policy decision on the consumers involved.

601.   Youngs, Elizabeth H.   "Nonpromotion Policy: Criteria and Rationale for Grade Retention in Colorado Elementary Schools."   University of Colorado at Boulder, 1980, 42:53-A.

The problem is to determine the bases for retaining students in grades in Colorado elementary schools.

U.S. Foreign Policy

602. Abramson, Arthur C. "The Formulation of American Foreign Policy towards the Middle East during the Truman Administration, 1945-1948." University of California, Los Angeles, 1981, 42:371-A.

Models derived from two schools of thought, along with the traditional, Presidentially-centered, national-security paradigm, are used herein as a means of ordering and identifying the major factors involved in the Truman Administration's foreign policy formulation process toward the Middle East during the time frame covered in this study.

603. Ahmad, Rashid S. "Politics and Foreign Policy Making: A Critical-Theoretical Perspective." University of Hawaii, 1978, 39:3813-A.

Develops an alternative to the epistemological perspective implicit in the existing approaches to foreign policy-making analyses.

604. Anderson, Helen. "Through Chinese Eyes: American China Policy, 1945-1947." University of Virginia, 1980, 41:2247-A.

This study of the Chinese press during the civil war period reveals the fallacy of certain assumptions and suggests a strikingly different interpretation: the Nationalist dependence on American aid was itself one of the factors in the ultimate Kuomintang failure.

605. Anderson, Paul A. "Bureaucracy, Goal Seeking, and Foreign Policy." The Ohio State University, 1979, 40:2248-A.

Constitutes a theoretical inquiry into the foreign policy behavior of bureaucratic governments. It is based upon the view that the capabilities of the mechanism which underlies foreign policy behavior of governments are important in explaining foreign policy performance.

606. Andrews, John D. "Eisenhower and Middle Eastern Foreign Policy: A Rhetoric of Consensus." Northwestern University, 1978, 39:4588-A.

The study is an analysis of presidential rhetoric and its effect on the maintenance of a foreign policy consensus.

607. Baron, Michael L. "Tug of War: The Battle over American Policy toward China 1946-1949." Columbia University, 1980, 40:793-A.

The process of policy making is reevaluated in this study of American policy toward China from 1946 to 1949.

608. Beck, Kent M. "American Liberalism and the Cold War Consensus: Policies and Policymakers of the Moderate Democratic Left 1945-1953." University of California, Irvine, 1976, 38:4321-A.

Most historians and informed political commentators agree that American liberalism became more moderate and more realistic between 1945 and 1953 but they sharply disagree on the wisdom of this move toward the middle. Studying the views of five important liberals between 1945 and 1953 illuminates the extent to which unity and diversity coexisted within the moderate Democratic left.

609. Benjamin, Charles M. "Developing a Game/Decision Theoretic Approach to Comparative Foreign Policy Analysis; Some Cases in Recent American Foreign Policy." University of Southern California, 1981, 42:5234-A.

Develops a game/decision theoretic approach to comparative foreign policy analysis. Five cases in recent American foreign policy are described and analyzed: (1) Angola, 1975-76; (2) Cyprus, 1974; (3) Chile, 1962-73; (4) the Kurds, 1972-75; and (5) Cuba, 1961-62.

610. Berger, Jason. "A New Deal for the World: Eleanor Roosevelt and American Foreign Policy, 1920-1962." City University of New York, 1979, 40:2834-A.

Through extensive research as well as through the use of oral history projects and the author's own interviews with Mrs. Roosevelt's contemporaries, this dissertation examines an often neglected area of Mrs. Roosevelt's career.

611. Blum, Robert M. "Drawing the Line: The Origin of the American Containment Policy in Southeast Asia." The University of Texas at Austin, 1980, 42:3270-A.

After September 1949 and before the outbreak of the Korean War, the Truman Administration, responding to the crisis in Asia and using the contingency fund Congress gave it for use in the "general area of China," began to bend the Pacific containment line to the left, constructing it across the subcontinent of Southeast Asia.

612. Brown, Donald E. "Fulbright and the Premises of American Foreign Policy." State University of New York at Binghamton, 1982, 42:4923-A.

This study of the public career of J. William Fulbright examines the evolution of his foreign policy outlook during his three decades in Congress and attempts to relate changes in his views to broader changes that occurred in the nation at both mass and elite levels.

613. Burke, Mary P. "United States Aid to Turkey: Foreign Aid and Foreign Policy." The University of Connecticut, 1977, 38:5030-A.

Examines and analyzes United States economic aid to Turkey in an effort to gain insights into the aid relationships--goals of both donor and recipient, aid's process and limitations, where aid succeeded, where it did not, and why.

614. Cahn, Linda A. "National Power and International Regimes: United States Commodity Policies 1930-1980." Stanford University, 1981, 41: 4828-A.

Through three case studies of U.S. commodity policy over a fifty-year period, the research focuses on identifying and explaining various forms and patterns of leadership and analyzes the dynamics of change that occur over time as a result of international and national factors.

615. Canh, C. Nguyen. "United States Policy toward Vietnam, 1950-1954." Bowling Green State University, 1982, 42:1263-A.

The U.S. policy toward Vietnam from 1950-1954 was influenced by American domestic politics and American policy makers' Cold War beliefs. Due to strong anticommunism at home and to the apparent threat of Soviet expansionism in China and Korea, the Truman and Eisenhower Administrations were compelled to help the French prevent a victory by the Communist-led national liberation forces of Ho Chi Minh.

616. Carpenter, Ted G. "The Dissenters: American Isolationists and Foreign Policy, 1945-1954." The University of Texas at Austin, 1980, 41: 4810-A.

Isolationism represents one of the most misunderstood components of America's foreign policy tradition. Few historians have examined the dubious assumption that isolationism vanished in the post-World War II period. This dissertation endeavors to remedy that deficiency in the historical literature.

617. Champney, Leonard W. "Foreign Policy and International Organizations: An Analysis Based on State Behavior." Rutgers University, 1981, 42:372-A.

Attempts to determine if foreign policy behavior conducted in the context of international organizations is patterned differently than foreign policy behavior conducted in other contexts and to determine if the use of these institutions by states contributes to a reduction in the levels of conflict behavior on the part of these states.

618. Chen, Helen. "Chinese Immigration into the United States: An Analysis of Changes in Immigration Policies." Brandeis University, 1980, 41: 2292-A.

Focuses on the social control dimension of Chinese immigration. It is, essentially, a study of policy analysis which explores the forces governing Chinese immigration.

619. Clemens, Carol. "Issue Areas and United States Foreign Policy Processing: Interoceanic Canal Facilities 1920-1940." University of Notre Dame, 1981, 41:4822-A.

If one accepts the theory that the issue and its effect on the domestic situation determine the policy process, then it would follow that
the policy process would differ significantly if the same issue were
presented in different ways. The issue of improving interoceanic
canal facilities is a clear example of such an issue.

620. Colombo, Claudius M. "Chinese Communist Perceptions of the Foreign
Policy of John F. Kennedy, 1961-1963." New York University, 1982, 42:
519-A.

Examines Sino-American relations during the Kennedy Administration.
Particular emphasis is placed on Peking's perception of Kennedy's
foreign policy.

621. Cozean, Jon D. "The U.S. Elite Press and Foreign Policy: The Case
of Cuba." The American University, 1979, 40:4216-A.

Special attention is focused on the historically political role of
the news media with emphasis on the tremendous influence of the *New
York Times* and the *Washington Post*. A related topic concerns attempts
to limit the sweeping legal immunities granted the news media by the
First Amendment.

622. Crutchfield, Stephen R. "Management of Foreign Fishing Rights:
Theory and Policy." Yale University, 1980, 41:4773-A.

The traditional economic analysis of exploited fisheries is expanded
to include the possibility of joint harvesting of fish by two nations
with different demand and cost structures.

623. Culbreth, B. Spencer. "American Foreign Policy in the 1920s: Isolation or Involvement? A Problem in Instruction and Learning." Middle Tennessee State University, 1978, 39:1757-A.

Examines the primary and secondary sources, relevant to both the generalizations and the criticism of them, in an attempt to develop the
most suitable generalization for describing American foreign policy
in the 1920's.

624. Dixon, William J. "Multiple Stratification Systems and Intergovernmental Foreign Policy Behavior: A Test of Two Models." The Ohio State
University, 1980, 40:391-A.

Represents an empirically based assessment of two approaches to the
study of international systems.

625. Dobbs, Charles M. "American Foreign Policy, the Cold War, and
Korea: 1945-1950." Indiana University, 1978, 39:1057-A.

As the sun dawned on the morning of June 25, 1950 the world awoke to
learn that North Korean troops had invaded the Republic of Korea.
What had happened in the previous five years to bring about this situation? How had American foreign policy contributed to the deepening
crisis that gripped the peninsula?

626. Donnelly, Dorothy. "American Policy in Vietnam, 1949-1965: A Per-

ceptual Analysis of the Domino Theory and Enemy Based on the Pentagon Papers." University of Pittsburgh, 1980, 41:2756-A.

Utilizing the three editions of the Pentagon Papers and other relevant publications available to the author by the late 1970's, this dissertation analyzes the progressive American involvement in Vietnam from the end of World War II through the decision by President Johnson in 1965 significantly to increase military participation.

627. Dreier, John A. "The Politics of Isolationism: A Quantitative Study of Congressional Foreign Policy Voting, 1937-1941." University of Kentucky, 1977, 39:3770-A.

This analysis of Congressional foreign policy voting in the years preceding America's entry into World War II reveals voting patterns that were not unique, but were an outgrowth of alignments constructed in the struggle over the domestic New Deal.

628. Dura, Juan. "United States Policy toward Dictatorship and Democracy in Spain, 1936-1953: A Case Study in the Realities of Policy Formation." University of California, Berkeley, 1979, 41:1732-A.

(Abstract not available.)

629. Edelman, Eric S. "Incremental Involvement: Italy and United States Foreign Policy, 1943-1948." Yale University, 1981, 42:2261-A.

In the absence of any coherent policy of their own, American confusion and ignorance, the pace of events, and British preconceptions shaped American behavior in Italy during most of 1943. Increasingly, however, the State Department pushed for an active role in determining the political future of Italy.

630. Edwards, Catherine R. "U.S. Policy towards Japan, 1945-1951: Rejection of Revolution." University of California, Los Angeles, 1977, 38:6920-A.

U.S. occupation of Japan undertook the disarmament of Japan, instituted a reparations program, inaugurated a civil liberties policy, implemented the purge of militarists, created a labor union movement, ordered the dissolution of *zaibatsu* (large financial combines), and encouraged land reform.

631. Eggleston, Noel C. "The Roots of Commitment: United States Policy toward Vietnam, 1945-1950." University of Georgia, 1977, 38:4323-A.

The historic roots of America's intervention in Vietnam during the 1960's extend deep into the early postwar years of the Truman Administration. While the policy developed during these first five years did not inalterably dictate the future decisions of later administration, it did significantly influence the direction of United States involvement over the next twenty years.

632. Ellis, Kail C. "United States Policy toward Lebanon in the Lebanese Civil Wars of 1958 and 1975-76: A Comparative Analysis." The Catholic University of America, 1979, 40:4736-A.

Seeks to compare United States policy in Lebanon's two civil wars to
determine whether in the interval a change had occurred in the United
States' perception of its vital interests and if the ability of the
United States to act in the international system had been significantly constrained in the same period of time.

633. Elterman, Howard A. "The State, the Mass Media and Ideological
Hegemony: United States Policy Decisions in Indochina, 1954-1975--Histori-
cal Record, Government Pronouncements, and Press Coverage." New York University, 1978, 39:2556-A.

Concerns itself with government policies adopted during ten episodes
of the Indo-China War, comparing in each instance, a historical account of the policies adopted with the corresponding pronouncements
of government spokespersons, and with the accounts given in the national, foreign and alternate press.

634. Erickson, Stephen. "United States-Panamian Relations vis-a-vis the
Panama Canal: A Historical and Policy Analysis." Tufts University, 1978,
39:6318-A.

A comprehensive historical analysis comprises a substantial portion
of the study. It is intended that the historical analysis be as objective as possible such that the treaty and policy analysis may be
presented with a minimum of distortion.

635. Feaver, John H. "The Truman Administration and China, 1945-1950:
The Policy of Restrained Intervention." The University of Oklahoma, 1980,
41:1186-A.

The basic contention of this study is that, for military and strate-
gic reasons arising out of the concern about Soviet expansionism, the
Truman Administration never seriously considered withdrawing from
China prior to the Korean War.

636. Fejes, Fred A. "Imperialism, Media, and the Good Neighbor: New Deal
Foreign Policy and United States Shortwave Broadcasting to Latin America."
University of Illinois at Urbana-Champaign, 1982, 42:4634-A.

Presents an historical account of the expansion of United States interests in Latin American communications in the first half of this
century. Particular emphasis is laid on how United States shortwave
broadcasting was used as a vehicle for the penetration and dominance
of Latin American mass communication systems. Such penetration is
analyzed in relation to the overall context of the goals and activities of the Good Neighbor Policy of Franklin D. Roosevelt.

637. Foltos, Lester J. "The Bulwark of Freedom; American Security Policy
for East Asia, 1945-1950." University of Illinois at Urbana-Champaign,
1980, 41:2734-A.

Examines the roots of America's security policy for the postwar years
and the development of that policy in the early Cold War period from
1945-1950.

638. Fritz, David L. "The Philippine Question: American Civil/Military

Policy in the Philippines, 1898–1905." The University of Texas at Austin, 1977, 38:4324–A.

The objective is to learn whether American policy for the Philippines was benevolent or selfish in intent and execution, and why its stated philanthropic purposes did not culminate in a closer union between the Philippines and the United States.

639. Gale, Roger W. "Micronesia: A Case Study of American Foreign Policy." University of California, Berkeley, 1977, 38:5032–A.

It is the main theme of this study that a combination of systemic transformation in the international arena and bureaucratic inarticulateness within the United States has led to a situation in which it is impossible, with the traditional tools of political science, to categorize Micronesia simply, as either an integral part of the U.S. or as an entity with a defined international personality.

640. Ganguly, Shivaji. "The United States and South Asia: A Study of Policy and Process." University of Illinois at Urbana-Champaign, 1977, 38:6300–A.

Analyzes the sources and pattern of U.S. policy process regarding South Asia in conflictual and nonconflictual situations. This is a comparative analysis of foreign policy orientations of a major global power with reference to four select issue areas as faced by three different administrations.

641. Garfinkle, Adam M. "United States Foreign Policy and the Jordan Crisis of 1970: A Cognitive Approach." University of Pennsylvania, 1979, 40:1672–A.

Many proponents of the so-called cognitive approach have claimed that the application of concepts from cognitive and social psychology can solve most or all of the theory of decision making in foreign policy problems. Investigates the extent to which the claims made on behalf of the cognitive approach are justified.

642. German, Lawrence P. "Power and Interdependence: United States Policy toward Nigeria, 1960–1978." The University of Wisconsin-Madison, 1980, 42:842–A.

Focuses on United States foreign policy toward Nigeria during the period from 1960 through 1978. Attempts to offer a descriptive account of what has happened in an important area of U.S. policy and to test competing hypotheses about relationships between environmental factors and foreign policy behavior.

643. Godfried, Nathan. "An American Development Policy for the Third World: A Case Study of the United States and the Arab East, 1942–1949." The University of Wisconsin-Madison, 1980, 41:4477–A.

Describes and analyzes American economic development policy toward the underdeveloped world in general and the Arab East in particular during the 1940's.

644. Hadian, Ronald F. "United States Foreign Policy towards Spain, 1953-1970." University of California, Santa Barbara, 1976, 40:1064-A.

Analyzes the origins and implications of U.S. foreign policy toward Spain during a period crucial to both countries.

645. Hagan, Joe D. "Regimes, Oppositions, and Foreign Policy: A Cross-National Analysis of the Impact of Domestic Politics on Foreign Policy Behavior." University of Kentucky, 1980, 42:372-A.

Examines the cross-national relationship of domestic politics to foreign policy. The analysis considers the foreign policy behavior of the regimes of thirty-eight nations for the years 1959-1967.

646. Hamre, John J. "Congressional Dissent and American Foreign Policy: Constitutional War-Making in the Vietnam Years." The Johns Hopkins University, 1978, 39:2509-A.

The dissertation is broadly concerned with the response of Congress to the Vietnam war.

647. Hannigan, Robert E., Jr. "Dollars and Diplomacy: United States Foreign Policy, 1909-1913." Princeton University, 1978, 39:3773-A.

The purpose of the study is to present an integrated analysis of American foreign policy in the Taft era.

648. Harrington, Daniel F. "American Policy in the Berlin Crisis of 1948-49." Indiana University, 1979, 40:5558-A.

Drift characterized American policy toward the Berlin question from 1944 to 1949. When the blockade began in the summer of 1948 it seemed that judgments could no longer be postponed.

649. Harris, Scott A. "Domestic Politics and the Formulation of United States China Policy, 1949-1972." The University of Wisconsin-Madison, 1980, 42:373-A.

Consists of an investigation of the impact of domestic politics on the making of American China policy from 1949 to 1972.

650. Head, William P. "America's China Sojourn: United States Foreign Policy and Its Effects on Sino-American Relations, 1942-1948." The Florida State University, 1980, 41:1186-A.

The work is an analysis of the events and circumstances in China from the beginning of World War II to the election of 1948. It reveals how the U.S. foreign policy during this era affected the relationship between China and America.

651. Henderson, John T. "Leadership Personality and War: A Biographical Approach to Assessing the Impact of the Head of Government on Crisis Foreign Policy Decision-Making in the United Kingdom and United States." Duke University, 1977, 38:5032-A.

Eight case studies are examined, made up of four "pairs" of British

Prime Ministers and American Presidents possessing a similar degree of foreign affairs experience (expert or amateur), and displaying a similar degree of dogmatism (open or closed behavior) while seeking to cope with broadly similar war or war-threatening situations.

652. Herr, Donald F. "Presidential Influence and Bureaucratic Politics: Nixon's Policy toward Cuba." Yale University, 1978, 39:2527-A.

Focuses on an administration review of American policy toward Cuba that began in early 1969 and was completed in early 1970, and the crisis of September 1970 when the U.S.S.R. sent equipment to Cienfuegos, Cuba, for the servicing of nuclear submarines. The bureaucratic political situation in each instance is examined at working levels and at the top.

653. Hinojosa, Jose R. "Discretionary Authority over Immigration: An Analysis of Immigration Policy and Administration towards Mexico." University of Notre Dame, 1980, 41:1758-A.

Analyzes American immigration policy and its administration toward Mexico by examining the development and implementation of immigration policies and their relationship to the political environment.

654. Hollihan, Thomas A. "The Public Controversy over the Panama Canal Treaties: A Fantasy Theme Analysis of Foreign Policy Dramas." The University of Nebraska-Lincoln, 1978, 39:5801-A.

Criticizes public rhetoric surrounding the ratification of the Panama Canal treaties.

655. Humeston, Helen M. "Origins of America's Japan Policy, 1790-1854." University of Minnesota, 1981, 42:4554-A.

Analyzes the factors that animated America's Japan policy.

656. Jarvis, Thomas M. "The Founding Fathers and the Future of American Foreign Policy: Unity and Disunity, 1783-88." The American University, 1980, 40:771-A.

The study is a comparative analysis of the foreign policy views of seven key founding fathers (Washington, Jefferson, Hamilton, Adams, Jay, Madison, and Monroe) from 1783 to 1788. Examines areas of unity on broad aspects of foreign policy and areas of disunity on specific problems confronting the United States.

657. Johnson, Nelson E. "New England Congressional Attitudes Concerning American Policy toward the Philippines, 1899-1908." Middle Tennessee State University, 1979, 40:5540-A.

From 1899 through 1908, issues surrounding the questions of how the Philippine Islands should be governed, what tariff preferences, if any, should be extended to Philippine products, and when the Filipinos should be granted their independence were often before Congress. The leading spokesmen for and against the Republican administrations' policies were from New England.

658.   Johnson, Sterling.   "Nation-State and Non-State Nations: The International Relations and Foreign Policies of Black America."   The Ohio State University, 1979, 40:5581-A.

Describes the international and transnational activities of major black organizations.

659.   Joseph, Robert G.   "Commitments and Capabilities: United States Foreign and Defense Policy Coordination, 1945 to the Korean War."   Columbia University, 1978, 39:5132-A.

Because the Korean War produced a reassessment and integration of foreign and defense strategies and propelled the enlargement of conventional forces to a level congruent with commitments, it was chosen as the end-point of this investigation.

660.   Karl, John F.   "Compromise or Confrontation: James F. Byrnes and United States' Policy toward the Soviet Union, 1945-1946."   University of Toronto (Canada), 1976, 39:2528-A.

The argument is that James F. Byrnes as Secretary of State pursued a policy based on compromise with the Soviet Union.   Byrnes was determined to use his political skill for engineering compromise to bring about an agreement with the Soviet Union which would lead to an era of peace.

661.   Kassis, Jihad G.   "U.S. Foreign Policy-Making in Middle East Crises: The 1973-74 Oil Embargo."   University of Notre Dame, 1981, 42:1304-A.

Deals with decision making under conditions of crisis.   Specifically, the study deals with the foreign policy behavior of the U.S. during the 1973-74 Arab oil embargo.

662.   Kendrick, Joseph T.   "The Consultation Process--The Legislative-Executive Relationship in the Formulation of Foreign Policy."   The George Washington University, 1979, 40:3510-A.

Drawing largely upon the unpublished stenographic notes of the recent Murphy Commission on the Organization of the Government, explores the nature of foreign policy consultation, its role in the political process, and how it might be improved.   The question is examined from the Constitutional, historical, and political perspectives.

663.   Kenney, Stephen F.   "Vietnam Decision-Making: A Psychological Perspective on American Foreign Policy."   Boston University Graduate School, 1978, 38:7542-A.

Analyzes American decision making in Vietnam from a psychological perspective and attempts to isolate certain factors which contributed to distorted perceptions within the U.S. government regarding the situation in Indochina.

664.   Kepley, David R.   "Challenges to Bipartisanship: Senate Republicans and American Foreign Policy, 1948-1952."   University of Maryland, 1979, 40:6393-A.

During 1947 and 1948, Senate Republicans worked with Democrats to
pass a spate of historic foreign policy programs.

665. Kern, Montague. "The Presidency and the Press: John F. Kennedy's
Foreign Policy Crises and the Politics of Newspaper Coverage." The Johns
Hopkins University, 1979, 40:5168-A.

Examines the press-presidential relationship in a policy context and
in relation to other categories of influence on newspapers: public
opinion, interest groups, politicians, foreign governments and the
prestige press.

666. Khare, Harish C. "Perceptions and Policy Choices: United States
Relations with India, 1962-1971." Yale University, 1979, 42:1780-A.

Seeks to determine patterns in American perceptions and policies toward India in the context of a basic assumption that in the postwar
period the American foreign and defense policy postures at any particular time have been determined by two variables: a conception of a
preferred world order, in which the United States would enjoy military
dominance, and a perceived need to endure a "balanced" interaction
among the superpowers.

667. Klingaman, William K. "Congress and American Foreign Policy for
the Middle East, 1956-58." University of Virginia, 1978, 39:5105-A.

Studies congressional-executive relations in the field of American
foreign policy for the Middle East in the years 1956-58, and attempts
to describe and analyze the role of Congress in the formulation of
American Mideast policy, and also to examine the basis of legislative
support and criticism of that policy, to determine the intellectual
foundations of congressional opinions.

668. Laffey, Robert M. "United States Policy toward and Relations with
Syria, 1941 to 1949." University of Notre Dame, 1981, 42:1271-A.

America had few interests in the Arab world until World War I; these
were primarily cultural, philanthropic, and commercial. The First
World War, however, marked a turning point in U.S. relations with
that region because of President Woodrow Wilson's participation in
the postwar settlement of the political problems of the Middle East.

669. Lairson, Thomas D. "Decision-Making in Groups: Social Paradigms
and Postwar American Foreign Policy." University of Kentucky, 1980, 40:
795-A.

Foreign policy decisions are most often made by groups, not by individuals calculating in isolation. This work is devoted to an examination of the formation of this context for American foreign policy
in the period following World War II, attempting to delineate its substantive configuration and trace its impact on the process of policy
deliberation.

670. Leeds, Roger S. "The Origins of the Alliance for Progress: Contin-
uity and Change in U.S. Policy toward Latin America." The Johns Hopkins
University, 1976, 40:796-A.

Analyzes the origins of the Alliance for Progress. The principal
hypothesis is that, contrary to many accounts of the Alliance, the
Kennedy-initiated program was not particularly new or unique in the
annals of U.S.-Latin American relations.

671. LeGette, Caroline M. "Income Redistribution and Foreign Policy:
Presidential Influence and Congressional Response." State University of
New York at Buffalo, 1977, 38:5685-A.

Seeks to clarify both the relationship between the President and Congress and the relationship between citizens and their representatives.
The President's standing with the mass public (Presidential popular-
ity) is posited to cause Presidential success in the House of Representatives.

672. Lenczowski, John. "Soviet Perceptions of U.S. Foreign Policy in the
Context of the Struggle between the Two Social Systems." The Johns Hopkins University, 1980, 40:392-A.

Examines in systematic fashion how the Soviets view American foreign
policy as one component of the "correlation of forces" between the
superpowers.

673. Lockwood, Jonathan S. "The Evolution of the Soviet View of US
Strategic Doctrine (1954-1976): Its Implications for Future US Strategic
Policy Decisionmaking." University of Miami, 1980, 41:1759-A.

Soviet pronouncements and evaluations on various U.S. strategic doc-
trinal concepts over the period from 1954-1976 are analyzed.

674. Loevinsohn, Ernest. "Some Normative Issues Relevant to Foreign
Policy." Princeton University, 1980, 41:1639-A.

Three issues are discussed in the study: (1) If moral relativism is
correct, what limits should be placed on foreign policy in the human
rights area? (2) Should a government, in shaping policy, give more
weight to the national interest of its own country than to the national interest of any foreign country? (3) Is it just as bad, moral-
ly speaking, for a government to allow undeserved harm to befall
citizens of foreign countries as it is to actively inflict undeserved
harm upon such persons?

675. Loftus, Robert A. "The American Response to the Berlin Blockade:
Bureaucratic Politics, Partisan Politics, and Foreign Policy Improvisa-
tion." (Volumes I and II) Columbia University, 1979, 40:5582-A.

During the 1948 Berlin crisis, Washington officials formulated American policy only on a partial basis. The American commander in Germany, General Lucius D. Clay, often exercised predominant influence
over American policy, and the actions of foreign governments often
limited the options open to Washington decision makers.

676. McGinnis, Joseph S., Jr. "The Belief Systems of Foreign Policy
Decision-Makers: Values and Consistency." The American University, 1978,
39:3818-A.

Explores the proposition that stability, or consistency, in foreign
policy beliefs has resulted in a fairly constant American response
to events in the international system.

677. McGinnis, Kathleen. "The Foreign Policy Committees and the Congressional Research Service." University of Virginia, 1977, 39:4481-A.

Focuses on the question: Is the congressional role in foreign policy
curtailed by its inability to obtain the necessary information to make
decisions and influence policy or has its unwillingness to play an
active role in foreign policy decision making been responsible for
its being inadequately informed?

678. Maghroori, Gholam R. "United States Policy toward the Arab-Israeli
Conflict, 1969-1976: Changes and Continuities." University of California,
Riverside, 1978, 39:6954-A.

It is the American policy during the period of 1969 to 1976 which is
the main focus of the study. By means of description and analysis,
endeavors to penetrate and understand the forces behind the formation
of U.S. foreign policy.

679. Mahoney, Richard D. "The Kennedy Policy in the Congo 1961-1963."
The Johns Hopkins University, 1980, 40:393-A.

The Kennedy Administration's role in Africa was a notable exception
to our generally unhappy and occasionally disastrous experience on
the continent. The Congo was the centerpiece of U.S. African policy
in the early 1960's.

680. Manning, Donald J. "Soviet-American Relations, 1929-1941: The Impact of Domestic Considerations on Foreign Policy Decision-Making."
Michigan State University, 1978, 40:1031-A.

The diplomatic relationship between the U.S. and the U.S.S.R. in the
interwar period was unstable, this being a function of domestic considerations which both nations projected onto a changing international
environment. These domestic considerations consisted of economic,
political, bureaucratic, ideological, institutional, and organizational pressures which coalesced into definite, if frequently self-
contradicting, foreign policies.

681. Mark, Eduard M. "The Interpretation of Soviet Foreign Policy in
the United States, 1928-1947." The University of Connecticut, 1978, 39:
6918-A.

The study is an attempt, based upon official records, periodicals,
scholarly writings, and personal papers, to treat the interpretation
of Soviet foreign policy as intellectual history.

682. Matray, James I. "The Reluctant Crusade: American Foreign Policy
in Korea 1941-1950." University of Virginia, 1977, 39:4448-A.

Investigates American foreign policy in Korea from the beginning of
World War II until the outbreak of the Korean War. Focuses particularly on evaluating the wisdom of American leaders in recognizing

the limitations on the power of the U.S. in formulating policy objectives in Korea.

683. Mauck, Kenneth R. "The Formation of American Foreign Policy in Korea, 1945-1953." The University of Oklahoma, 1978, 39:6919-A.

Explores at the highest levels of the U.S. government the formation of U.S. policy toward Korea in the 1945-53 period, which resulted in a bilateral security pact that is still in effect today.

684. Mayer, Laurel A. "Third World Arms Transfers and U.S. Foreign Policy." Miami University, 1977, 38:7543-A.

Sequentially examines the Third World arms transfer system, evaluates U.S. foreign policy objectives associated with its arms transfers, and analyzes the arms transfer program formulation and implementation processes.

685. Mayville, William V. "A Study of the Influence of Federal Policy on Curricula in United States Institutions of Higher Education, and Its Implications for Developing Nations, with Focus on the People's Republic of China." The George Washington University, 1980, 41:2469-A.

Examines federal action that has influenced, either directly or indirectly, the curriculum of higher education as a way to (1) comprehend the process by which education policy decisions are reached by the government and (2) determine what institutions of higher education have to do with this process.

686. Miner, Deborah N. "United States Policy toward Japan 1941: The Assumption That Southeast Asia Was Vital to the British War Effort." Columbia University, 1976, 39:5710-A.

Examines a crucial assumption underlying U.S. policy toward Japan in 1941, the assumption that Southeast Asia was vital to the British war effort.

687. Minix, Dean A. "The Role of the Small Group in Foreign Policy Decision-Making: A Potential Pathology in Crisis Decisions?" University of Cincinnati, 1979, 40:2252-A.

Measures, compares, and evaluates differences between individual and small group decisional units within the foreign policy process. The research stems from the work in psychology, sociology, and social-psychology in group dynamics known as extremization or polarization.

688. Modisett, Lawrence E. "The Four-Cornered Triangle: British and American Policy toward Yugoslavia 1939-1945." (Volumes I and II) Georgetown University, 1981, 42:893-A.

Anglo-American discord over Yugoslavia reflected differing views on global priorities, dealing with Moscow, and the aims of wartime diplomacy. These differences prevented a coordinated approach to Yugoslav issues and allowed the roots of postwar tensions to grow unchecked.

689. Morley, Morris H. "Toward a Theory of Imperial Politics: United States Policy and the Processes of State Formation, Disintegration and Consolidation in Cuba, 1898-1978." State University of New York at Binghamton, 1980, 40:6433-A.

Aims at providing a sustained and coherent reinterpretation of the logic of events and trends constituting the history of U.S.-Cuban relations since the end of the nineteenth century.

690. Mumme, Stephen P. "The United States-Mexico Groundwater Dispute: Domestic Influence on Foreign Policy." The University of Arizona, 1982, 42:916-A.

Examines the groundwater controversy in U.S.-Mexico relations and the role domestic political structures are likely to play in shaping a bilateral agreement apportioning transboundary groundwater.

691. Ngoh, Victor J. "The United States and the Nigerian Civil War, 1967-1970: An Analysis of the American Policy toward the War." University of Washington, 1982, 42:901-A.

The research problem consists of two parts: determining the policy which was adopted by the American government toward the Nigerian civil war and analyzing the policy.

692. Ninkovich, Frank A. "U.S. Foreign Policy and Cultural Relations, 1938-1950." The University of Chicago, 1978.

Cultural relations as a foreign policy approach were not institutionalized until the founding in 1910 of the Carnegie Endowment for International Peace. With the encouragement of corporate philanthropy, over the next thirty years there evolved an interlocking system, national and international, of private organizations dedicated to promoting international understanding through intellectual contacts.

693. O'Donnell, Thomas A. "Cognitive Structure and Organizational Factors as Sources of Foreign Policy Attitudes among Foreign Service Officers: Perception and Misperception of the Arab-Israeli Dispute, 1973." Rutgers University, 1979, 40:446-A.

This is a study of foreign policy attitudes of Foreign Service officers and how they are shaped by factors arising from their organizational environment and their cognitive structure.

694. Picraux, Danice K. "The Relative Roles of Humanitariansim and National Interest in the Formation of Foreign Policy: American Policy towards the Jewish State, 1914-1951." Claremont Graduate School, 1979.

Evaluates the degree to which humanitarian and national interest actions at the state level affects the course of American foreign policy. Also examines whether the security of the U.S. is compromised when a factor other than national interest motivates foreign policy.

695. Price, Morris. "The Nixon Years (1969-1974): Duplicity in United States Policies toward Southern Africa." St. John's University, 1977, 38:6877-A.

A number of examples is offered of how during the Nixon term of office, the Administration, despite numerous public statements of ab-
horrence of apartheid and of support for black-majority rule in southern Africa, quietly worked against this position and strove to maintain white-majority rule in the Portuguese colonies of Angola and
Mozambique, in Rhodesia, and in South Africa.

696. Purkitt, Helen E. "Issues in Foreign Policy Behavior: Southern
Africa, 1973-1975." University of Southern California, 1978, 39:3126-A.

Investigates the role of issue variables for understanding variations
in foreign policy behavior.

697. Raphael, Theodore D. "The Cognitive Complexity of Foreign Policy
Elites and Conflict Behavior: Forecasting International Crises--The Berlin
Conflict, 1946-1962." The American University, 1980, 41:5237-A.

Focuses on the evaluation of a cognitive complexity-international
conflict behavior model which seeks to forecast the onset of international crises.

698. Reuter, Paul H., Jr. "William Phillips and the Development of
American Foreign Policy, 1933-1947." University of Southern Mississippi,
1979, 40:1653-A.

William Phillips, a career diplomat in the American State Department
during the twentieth century, merits a study in order to determine
with particularity the extent to which he influenced the development
of American foreign policy between 1933 and 1947, the years of great
turbulence in American foreign policy.

699. Roehm, John F., Jr. "Congressional Participation in Foreign Policy:
A Study of Congress' Role in U.S. Middle East Policy vis-a-vis the Confrontation States in the Arab-Israeli Conflict from the Yom Kippur War to
the End of the Ford Administration." University of Pittsburgh, 1980,
41:2758-A.

The dissertation is a case study of an effort by the Executive Branch
and Congress to establish their "proper" roles in one vital U.S. foreign policy issue area.

700. Rollings, Andrew E. "The State, Capital, and the Structure of the
World System: American Foreign Policy Formation towards Japan in the
Interwar Period." New York University, 1981, 42:3744-A.

Uses an historical case study (American foreign policy toward Japan)
to test the relative adequacy of the instrumental and structural
theories of the state as explanations of foreign policy formation
within advanced capitalist society.

701. Rosenberg, Jerry P. "Berlin and Israel 1948; Foreign Policy Decision-Making during the Truman Administration." University of Illinois at
Urbana-Champaign, 1977, 38:6301-A.

The study is an application of a new framework to two case studies:
the decision to recognize the State of Israel and the decision to

remain in Berlin in the face of the 1948 Russian blockade of that
city.

702.   Rosenberger, Leif R.   "The Evolution of the Nixon-Kissinger Policy
toward the Soviet Union: An Analysis of the Cold War Legacy and the Ambi-
valent Pursuit of Detente."   Claremont Graduate School, 1980, 40:5177-A.

   During the Cold War years, U.S. presidents operated under the premise
   that American military superiority over the Soviet Union was essential for the national security.   Nixon abandoned the Cold War concept
   of American military superiority, at least in the domain of strategic
   nuclear weapons, and began to accept the Soviet Union as a military
   equal.

703.   Sabrier, Jules G., Jr.   "United States Atlantic Alliance Policy and
the Problem of France, 1963-1969."   Tulane University, 1978, 39:6899-A.

   Demonstrates that despite the demands of the Vietnam war and numerous
   frustrations, both domestic and international, President Johnson remained a faithful proponent of Atlantic partnership.

704.   Sanford, Jonathan E.   "American Foreign Policy and the Multilateral
Banks: The Actors and Issues Affecting U.S. Participation in the International Development Lending Institutions."   The American University,
1977, 38:6924-A.

   Assesses the issues and policy process affecting U.S. particpants in
   the multilateral development banks.   Based on public documents and
   ninety confidential interviews with executive and legislative branch
   officials, it describes the political and organizational geography
   for this significant area of U.S. foreign economic policy.

705.   Schmickle, William E.   "For the Proper Use of Victory: Diplomacy
and the Imperatives of Vision in the Foreign Policy of Woodrow Wilson,
1916-1919."   Duke University, 1979, 40:2253-A.

   The central presupposition of this work is that politics, properly
   conceived, is preeminently a form of moral endeavor and an art rather
   than a science.

706.   Schneider, James C.   "The Anxieties of Neutrality: Chicago Public
Opinion and American Foreign Policy, 1939-1941."   The University of Wisconsin-Madison, 1979, 41:2262-A.

   Many historians have examined the intense foreign policy debate which
   took place across the U.S. in the 1939-1941 period.   No one concentrated upon the debate itself.   This study attempts to begin filling
   that gap by focusing on the city of Chicago, one of the debate's
   stormcenters.

707.   Schneider, Michael D.   "World View and Role Awareness in Foreign
Policy Decision Making: The Berlin Crisis of 1961."   The American University, 1978, 39:4483-A.

   Through a study of the Berlin Crisis of 1961, this dissertation seeks
   to analyze the influence of decision makers' world view and role awareness on foreign policy choices.

708. Scranton, Margaret E. "Changing United States Foreign Policy: Negotiating New Panama Canal Treaties, 1958-1978." University of Pittsburgh, 1980, 41:2758-A.

Uses policy process analysis to explore two questions: how and why attempts to change American foreign policy are made, and how and why some attempts succeed while others fail.

709. Seigal, Albert. "United States Policy toward Okinawa, 1945-1972. A Study in Organizational Interaction in Policy-Making." West Virginia University, 1978, 39:1814-A.

Shows that U.S. policy toward Okinawa from 1945 to 1972 was influenced by a changing balance of strategic and political requirements which led to competitive interaction between the State Department and the military, and that this interaction further led to changes in U.S. policy toward Okinawa and to a shift toward predominant influence from the military to the State Department.

710. Seiler, John J. "The Formulation of U.S. Policy toward Southern Africa, 1957-1976: The Failure of Good Intentions." The University of Connecticut, 1976, 38:5034-A.

U.S. foreign policy making for Southern Africa is examined within a political systems framework, using analysis of media content to ascertain both frequency of coverage and the predominant perspectives conveyed as an indirect guide to probable public opinion.

711. Shiels, Frederick L. "The American Experience in Okinawa: A Case Study for Foreign Policy and Decision-Making Theory." Cornell University, 1977, 39:456-A.

Seeks to offer a framework for analyzing acts of choice making in foreign affairs through an in-depth examination of a series of decisions related to the American rule of the Ryukyu Islands during the period 1945-1969.

712. Siegel, Howard B. "Strengths and Limitations of Informal Resources for Presidential Influence on Foreign Policy Legislation: The Truman Years." Brown University, 1978, 39:6320-A.

Seeks to analyze and precisely explain the nature of some of the informal resources and factors which are an important part of presidential influence in foreign policy legislation.

713. Simon, Jeffrey D. "Public Opinion and American Foreign Policy: 1952-1972." University of Southern California, 1978, 39:1093-A.

The research consists of three parts: (1) replication of Johan Galtung's research on social position and foreign policy opinion; (2) formulation and testing of an alternative theory of public opinion and foreign policy; (3) development of a classification scheme for foreign policy attitudes.

714. Smith, Emory T. "The United States, Italy and NATO: American Policy toward Italy, 1948-1952." Kent State University, 1981, 42:3726-A.

The policy of the U.S. toward Italy from 1948 to 1952 is the major area of focus for the dissertation, which examines the U.S. decisions and their impact on Italy.

715. Strikwerda, Charles E. "The House Foreign Affairs Committee and Changing Executive-Legislative Relations in Foreign Policy." University of Kentucky, 1977, 39:1816-A.

Since the end of World War II the Congress had left the direction of foreign policy primarily in the hands of the Executive Branch. Domestic dissent, however, coupled with a lengthy and complex Vietnam conflict brought about a congressional movement to reassert the institution's constitutional role in foreign policy. This study examines the particular role of the House Foreign Affairs Committee in this process.

716. Stuart, Douglas T. "The Relative Potency of Leader Beliefs as a Determinant of Foreign Policy: John F. Kennedy's Operational Code." University of Southern California, 1979, 40:448-A.

Seeks to improve the research potential of the operational code approach by considering the interrelationship between idea elements. It is proposed that under certain circumstances one particular operational code belief (a subject's image of a significant opponent) will perform the role of "master" belief, structuring other contingent aspects of the overall world view.

717. Thies, Wallace J. "Coercion and Diplomacy: Force and Foreign Policy in the Vietnam Conflict, 1964-1968." Yale University, 1977, 39:2533-A.

Focuses on the Johnson Administration's efforts to compel the government of North Vietnam to abandon its efforts to reunify Vietnam under Communist control.

718. Thompson, Joseph E. "American Foreign Policy toward Nigeria, 1967-1970." The Catholic University of America, 1977, 38:4360-A.

Offers a case study of U.S. involvement in the Nigerian-Biafran Civil War. The purpose is to further understand American foreign policy toward the Third World as well as U.S.-Nigeria relations. The explanation for policy formulation and for policy change in this paper is conducted within the decision-making framework of Graham Allison's models.

719. Townsend, Joyce C. "Retrieving Lost Ideals: United States Foreign Policy toward Brazil, 1960-1968." The University of Oklahoma, 1980, 41:3253-A.

The analysis combines the bureaucratic politics model with an extensive analysis of Brazilian society, economy, and the political system in 1960.

720. Treadway, Sandra G. "Terra Incognita: The Philippine Islands and the Establishment of American Colonial Policy: 1898-1904." University of Virginia, 1978, 40:1034-A.

Explores America's encounter with the Philippines at the turn of the twentieth century and seeks to determine how and why the United States became a colonial power.

721. Vannucci, Albert P. "United States-Argentine Relations, 1943 to 1948: A Case Study in Confused Foreign Policy-Making." New School for Social Research, 1978, 39:3128-A.

Examines the foreign policy-making process in the U.S. Attempts to identify and analyze the many and often conflicting sources of a foreign policy.

722. Vivian, John P. "United States Foreign Policy in the Inter-American System: An Evaluation of Competing Analytical Frameworks." Miami University, 1980, 41:4830-A.

Evaluates the accuracy of four different analytical frameworks of foreign policy making (realist, radical, liberal and world politics) that purport to describe and explain U.S. relations with Latin America.

723. Vocke, William C., Jr. "Detente: A Quasi-Experimental Evaluation of the Policy's Impact." University of South Carolina, 1981, 42:3293-A.

Evaluates the impact of detente on Soviet and American behavior.

724. Weber, William T. "Agricultural Exports and Decision-Making in American Foreign Policy." University of Virginia, 1977, 38:4361-A.

The bureaucratic perspective can be disaggregated into five useful models: the Electoral Politics, Bureaucratic Politics, Organizational Process, Shared Values and Personal Values Models. Together with Irving Janis' Groupthink Model, their empirical validity and utility can be tested against the record of American foreign policy.

725. Winship, James A. "Millenial Misperception: The Theological Component in American Foreign Policy Thinking." The Johns Hopkins University, 1981, 42:1783-A.

Seeking to trace the intellectual geneses of the exceptionalist ideal and destinarian ideology the present work attempts to bridge the rather wide gulf between American diplomatic and intellectual history as well as that between American political theory and the consideration of religious/theological factors as they shaped the political culture of the new world.

726. Winter, Francis J. "German Reunification: A Problem for American Foreign Policy." The University of Iowa, 1979, 40:6415-A.

While American policy makers have continued to insist steadfastly that the exercise of self-determination leading to German reunification in peace and freedom remains the fundamental objective of American policy, they have at crucial junctures opted for approaches which, while presumably designed to accomplish this, were in fact oriented toward the achievement of other seemingly more important goals.

Governmental Regulation of Morality: Sex, Drugs, and Abortion

727. Bermas, Neal F. "Practitioners' Attitudes toward Current Conceptions of Alcoholism: Policy Implications for Treatment and Control."
Brandeis University, 1980, 42:416-A.

Could any rational theory, differential diagnosis, specific treatment, or successful outcome be derived from the current experiences
of practitioners in the field? To that end, practitioners were surveyed at eighteen alcoholism treatment centers in six states under
private, state, and federal auspice.

728. Bovelle, Elliott I. "A Critical Assessment of the National Institute on Alcohol Abuse and Alcoholism (NIAAA) Funding Policies and Practices of Alcoholism Research." Brandeis University, 1980, 41:2316-A.

The general aim is to capture and describe the objectives of alcohol
research proposals that have been funded by the NIAAA and then to
determine whether or not they reasonably reflect, constitute, or are
representative of the broad range of available research options that
could have been brought to bear upon the problem within the context
of statutory laws that govern the NIAAA.

729. Browning, Ronald S. "Consumer Borrowing in the Gaming Industry:
The Development of Casino Credit, Credit Practices and Promotional Pol-
icies in Nevada with Particular Emphasis upon the Period 1971-1975."
University of Arkansas, 1978, 39:3687-A.

The four main purposes are: (1) to trace the historical development
of casino credit in Nevada; (2) to identify its role in the Nevada
gaming industry and estimate its impact on the regional economy;
(3) to estimate the volume of casino credit used; and (4) to analyze
customer credit characteristics from a sample of Las Vegas Strip
casinos.

730. Colon, Israel. "Alcohol Control Policies and Their Relation to
Alcohol Consumption and Alcoholism." Brandeis University, 1980, 40:
6443-A.

Incompatible policy and program strategies for minimizing alcoholism
are proposed by two competing prevention models, the sociocultural
and the single distribution models.

731. Compton, Donald W. "School Policies about Smoking: Suggestions
from an Empirical Study of Adolescent Cigarette Smoking." University of
Minnesota, 1980, 41:4614-A.

The dissertation is intended to make modest contributions to smoking
behavior theory, youth development theory and to provide implications
for a tentative school smoking policy which is sensitive to youth development issues.

732. Formicola, Jo R. "The American Catholic Church and Its Role in the
Formulation of United States Human Rights Foreign Policy 1945-1978." Drew
University, 1981, 42:1296-A.

Asks the question: What role did the American Catholic Church play in
the formulation of U.S. human rights foreign policy from 1945-1978?

733. Giaquinta, Gerald J. "The U.S. Prescription Drug Delivery System:
A Comparative Analysis of Policy Options." University of Southern California, 1980, 41:2760-A.

Attempts to respond to the question of how actors engaged with the
prescription drug delivery system establish their positions regarding acceptable risk to benefit ratio for drug therapy.

734. Green, William C. "Courts, Parliament, and Obscenity Policy: A
Case Study of the Obscene Publications Act of 1959." State University
of New York at Buffalo, 1977, 38:5684-A.

The policy role of the English courts in the controversy over liter-
ary obscenity and the parliamentary response to that behavior is the
subject of the study. The central concern is to explain who makes
obscenity policy in England.

735. Halem, Lynne C. "Divorce and the Law: Pathology, Policy, and Practice." Harvard University, 1977, 38:7595-A.

Examines the ideological shifts in thought on divorce and its impact
on the law's regulation of family policies. Depicts the outcomes of
these transitions and the conflict from which they emanated.

736. Keiser, Gayle L. "Dynamics of Policy Politics: The Cases of Abortion Funding and Family Planning in the State of Oregon." University of
Oregon, 1981, 42:4919-A.

Constructs a model of three critical stages of policy formation--
adoption, implementation and administration--and explores the nature
of politics at each of these stages. The dynamics of the model are
developed as policy authority, the ability to make a necessary policy
decision or take appropriate action, shifts from one policy partici-
pant to another.

737. Kirk, Lewis M., Jr. "Laetrile Legalization Policies in the American States: A Multi-Explanatory Analysis of Health Policy Adoptions and
Nondecisions." University of Kentucky, 1980, 40:786-A.

Seeks to empirically test six explanations related to the health policy process and public policy making using the current controversy over the adoption of Laetrile legalization policies in the American states.

738. Klein, Dorothy A. "Methadone Maintenance: Issues in Drug Policy." University of California, Berkeley, 1979, 40:4247-A.

Examines the rise of methadone maintenance as the federal strategy to cope with the perceived plague of illegal heroin use and street crime in the U.S. in the early 1970's and interprets it from an historical perspective on drug use and control.

739. Monti, Joseph E. "Ethics and Public Policy: The Conditions of Public Moral Discourse." Vanderbilt University, 1981, 42:3191-A.

Addresses the crisis in the policy process--a crisis of fragmentation, reductionism, and isolation among the policy sciences. Argues that a new self-understanding is necessary for the policy process, one based on a restructuring of the conditions for an adequate participatory dialogue about policy questions.

740. Morgan, Patricia A. "The Political Uses of Moral Reform: California and Federal Drug Policy, 1910-1960." University of California, Santa Barbara, 1978, 39:3859-A.

Examines the transition of drug control policy from medical regulation to the criminalization of narcotics users in comparison with major past sociological examinations, expecially the notions of moral crusades, bureaucratic environment, and class interest.

741. Neef, Marian H. "Policy Formation and Implementation in the Abortion Field." University of Illinois at Urbana-Champaign, 1979, 40:5586-A.

Examines the Supreme Court's decision of 1973, *Roe v. Wade*, which attempted to establish a national abortion policy.

742. Rittweger, Louis R. "An Analysis of Virginia's Public School Policies on Religion: From Historical, Public Policy, and Evangelical Christian Perspectives." Virginia Polytechnic Institute and State University, 1978, 40:2364-A.

Specifies the relationship between religion and public education and develops a framework for analysis from a historical, evangelical and public policy perspective.

743. Scott, Joel E. "The Public Schools and Problem Drinking of Professionals: Development of Policy Guidelines." Arizona State University, 1978, 39:6453-A.

Attempts to determine whether a problem with alcoholism/problem drinking exists among educators and, if so, to determine what is being done about the problem.

744. Shirley, Edward W. "Teacher Dismissal for Immorality: A Model Policy Statement for Local School Boards." West Virginia University, 1979, 40:1199-A.

It is the expressed purpose of the dissertation to develop a model
policy statement which could be effectively utilized by a local board
of education when confronted with a problem related to teacher dismissal for immorality.

Housing Policy

745. Bell, Robert K. "Constructing the Public Interest: A Sociological Analysis of Administrative Deliberation and the Interpretation of Federal Subsidized Housing Policy." University of California, Berkeley, 1980, 42:391-A.

Examines the processes by which government organizations interpret their responsibilities and some social factors that affect how well they do so.

746. Clark, Alex R. "Low-Income Housing for the Elderly in Baltimore: A Spatial Analysis of a Social Policy." The Pennsylvania State University, 1979, 40:460-A.

Adopts a holistic framework for analyzing the locations of housing projects in Baltimore. An ecological approach is employed to examine the locations of existing projects in Baltimore. The city is analyzed with respect to three important subsystems, social structure, housing morphology, and population.

747. Davidson, Flora S. "City Policy and Housing Abandonment: A Case Study of New York City, 1965-1973." Columbia University, 1979, 40:2879-A.

Examines the evolution of public policy on housing abandonment throughout the Lindsay Administration when it first became a policy problem and political issue.

748. Finkler, Merton D. "The Influence of Municipal Fiscal Policy on Single Family Residential Property Value." University of Minnesota, 1979, 40:5949-A.

The initial objective of this research was to determine how the levels of municipal and school district bonded indebtedness matter to residents of the relevant cities. Here the aim is the specific influence of local governmental debt on residential property values. Since finding this impact proved to be somewhat difficult, the scope of the research was expanded to address how the set of fiscal policies available to local governments (i.e., public services and financing decisions) affected the distribution of single family residential property values across cities in a region.

749.   Goodrich, James A.   "The Political Economy of Housing Policy: A
Comparative Study in Central America."   University of California, Los
Angeles, 1979, 40:2880-A.

   This study of housing policy in three Central American republics--
   Costa Rica, El Salvador, and Honduras--compares policy choices and
   performance in these countries through an analysis of different national initiatives to deal with housing problems.

750.   Hiltz, Daniel J.   "An Evaluation of Subsidized Homeownership as an
Anti-Poverty Policy."   University of Notre Dame, 1979, 39:6358-A.

   In this study comparing a group of Section 235 Subsidized Homeownership Program participants (N=313) with a group of non-participants
   (n=186) who have met the same selection criteria, the effectiveness
   of Section 235 as an anti-poverty program is examined.

751.   Jackson, Philip L.   "An Investigation of the Spatial Aspects of
Tornado Hazard and Mobile Housing Policy in Kansas."   University of Kansas, 1977, 39:1160-A.

   The objectives are to identify patterns of relative tornado hazard
   on a substate basis, to identify patterns of mobile home residency,
   to investigate public policy on the mobile home-tornado hazard issue,
   and finally to ascertain the response of local governments to the
   relative tornado hazard.

752.   Keating, Edward L.   "Subsidized Housing, Filtering and Housing
Policy."   The University of Wisconsin-Madison, 1978, 39:3881-A.

   Filtering, or the notion that new construction for the wealthiest
   households will eventually lead to an improvement in housing conditions for the poor, has been the pillar of America's amalgam of housing policies and programs for decades.   This research presents an
   expanded set of definitions of filtering.

753.   Kurtz, Larry R.   "Public Policy and the Housing Problem: Goals,
Programs and Policy Constraints."   University of Toronto (Canada), 1977,
39:2536-A.

   Argues that the housing "problem" in Canada is rooted in conflicting
   socioeconomic value premises which simultaneously impel governments
   to posit adequate housing at affordable prices as a social right, and
   constitute the crucial policy constraints to government action capable of giving substance to this "right."

754.   Morrow-Jones, Hazel A.   "The Impact of Federal Housing Policy on
Population Distribution in the United States."   The Ohio State University,
1980, 41:3262-A.

   In the process of assessing the FHA's spatial impact, an updated history of federal housing programs is developed, and the FHA's place
   in a theoretical framework of urban land use is discussed.

755.   Nugent, Anne E.   "Toward a Housing Policy Proposal for the Elderly
Homeowner."   University of Idaho, 1980, 41:1211-A.

Focuses on the spatial distribution of the elderly in the ninety-five census tracts in Omaha in order to establish trends and patterns of the target population and to create a statistical data base for the purpose of housing policy analysis.

756. Oguri, Yukio. "A Metropolitan Residential Relocation Model for the Evaluation of Housing Policies of the Tokyo Region." University of Pennsylvania, 1978, 39:6368-A.

Develops a residential model which causally and quantitatively relates phenomena and projects how the households would be accommodated in the region under different sets of housing policies.

757. Peterson, Nils G. "Income, Fiscal Policies and Residential Location." Syracuse University, 1977, 38:5053-A.

It is postulated that the tax and expenditure levels of communities influence the residential location of families which, in turn, influence the income levels of communities across a metropolitan area. To explore this topic two models are tested using data from areas in two fiscally different states: New Jersey and New York.

758. Vento, Carol S. "Homesteading: A Value Analysis of Policy Formation in the Urban Neighborhood." Temple University, 1979, 39:6966-A.

Studies the reality of urban homesteading as opposed to its symbolism by: (1) assessing the policy impact of urban homesteading in the six cities in which it has operated the longest, and (2) determining the salient characteristics of urban homesteading cities as opposed to non-homesteading cities in order to see if there are basic differences between the cities which choose different rehabilitation approaches.

759. Zisook, Stuart W. "Housing for the Physically Disabled: A Public Policy Analysis." University of Washington, 1981, 42:2903-A.

Examines federal housing policies and programs designed to meet the housing needs of physically disabled persons. Underlying this analysis is the belief that policy makers have favorably responded to the emotional appeal of a politically sympathetic interest group.

Energy and the
Environment

760. Akridge, Paul B. "The Politics of Energy Policy: Regulation of
Electric Utility Rate Structure Design by the Public Service Commission
of Wisconsin." The University of Wisconsin-Madison, 1979, 40:4739-A.

Examines the regulation of electric utility rate structure design by
the Public Service Commission of Wisconsin and investigates the seminal national test case of 1972-74 (Re. *Madison Gas and Electric Company*) which resulted in the revision of the traditional declining
block rate structure and the adoption of the time-of-use/peak-load
pricing rate design.

761. Alger, Dean E. "Environmental Policy-Making and Metropolitan Governance: Lessons from the San Francisco Bay and Los Angeles Regions."
University of California, Riverside, 1978, 39:3795-A.

The two research questions are: (1) Does the traditional array of
municipal and county institutions result in appreciably different
policy outputs on the environment than a metropolitan governing arrangement? (2) Does a more general purpose form on a regional level
result in appreciably different policy outputs than a set of single
purpose ones?

762. Anderson, Paul D. "The Environmental Policy Arena and Public Interest Politics." Purdue University, 1979, 40:5163-A.

The policy arenas approach, identified with Theodore J. Lowi, has
been applied to public policy research. The sulfur dioxide emission
limitation program in Ohio provides a case study of public interest
politics and nonincremental policy making, a model of policy making
devised by Paul R. Schulman.

763. Boggess, Trent E. "Fiscal Policy in a Growing Economy." University of Kansas, 1980, 41:5197-A.

In order to arrive at statistical estimates of the effect of fiscal
policy on the level of output growth, an econometric model is developed to estimate the relationship between fiscal policy and the ratio
of labor and capital inputs, a variable closely tied to the level at
output growth.

764. Bond, Jon R. "Oil and the Policy Process: The Causes and Effects of the Oil Depletion Allowance." University of Illinois at Urbana-Champaign, 1978, 39:439-A.

Tests hypotheses that attempt to explain why the oil depletion allowance varied over time and what effect it had on oil producers over the period 1900 to 1974.

765. Bouchard, Thomas P. "Environmental Decision-Making: The Wisconsin Environmental Policy Act and the Department of Natural Resources." University of Washington, 1978, 39:3835-A.

Investigates the effects of a state environmental policy act on the policies, procedures, projects, and decision making of a state agency with major environmental responsibilities.

766. Braden, John B. "Natural Gas from the Great Lakes: Economics, Environment, and Policies." The University of Wisconsin-Madison, 1979, 40:4148-A.

In this study: (1) economic and environmental prospects for Lake Erie gas development are appraised; (2) the institutional setting within which development might occur is summarized; (3) a management approach emphasizing incremental evaluation of all feasible policy alternatives is proposed; (4) a simulation framework conforming to the proposed management approach is suggested for evaluation of offshore development policies; and (5) policy issues arising when independent jurisdictions become embroiled in a common environmental problem are discussed.

767. Brooks, Edward B. "The Impact of Rural Water Districts on State Water Policy: A Case Study of Institutionalization in Southeastern Oklahoma." The University of Oklahoma, 1982, 42:541-A.

This is a case study of institution building, concerned with the formation of rural water districts and how they affect state and national water policy.

768. Brown, Richard R. "A Multi-Factor Business Policy Model for Successful Diversification of Aerospace Firms into Energy Related Areas." University of Washington, 1978, 39:3028-A.

The purpose is the development of a policy model for the diversification of aerospace companies into energy areas. This model should assist executives by emphasizing important factors while still allowing for individual perceptions, aspirations, and values.

769. Bucknell, Howard, III. "The Energy Question: A Case Study in Major Public Policy Development in a Quasi-Free Enterprise Society." University of Georgia, 1977, 38:5037-A.

Addresses the question of analyzing public policy as well as the factors involved in developing public policy. The energy situation is used as an example.

770. Cibas, Gediminas A. "Economic Impact on New Mexico of the Natural

Gas Policy Act of 1978 and the New Mexico Natural Gas Pricing Act." The
University of New Mexico, 1980, 42:2231-A.

Investigates the longer-term impact--up to the year 2000--of the pricing provisions of the Natural Gas Policy Act of 1978 on New Mexico in
terms of a set of policy-relevant economic measures, namely, future
natural gas production, state and producer revenues, and direct consumer costs.

771. Cna'an, Ram A. "Forecasting Environmental Reaction to Policy Initiation by an Organization." University of Pittsburgh, 1980, 41:5244-A.

Develops a model which enables any organization which seeks change to
forecast the reaction of other organizations within its environment
to this planned change.

772. Cohen, Steven A. "Citizen Participation in Bureaucratic Decision
Making: With Special Emphasis on Environmental Policy Making." State
University of New York at Buffalo, 1979, 40:5178-A.

Analyzes the citizen participation "movement" in the context of the
historical evolution of the American system of representation. Assesses the degree to which direct citizen involvement in water quality decision making enhances (or detracts from) the potential repre-
sentativeness of water quality policy.

773. Cowhey, Peter F. "The Problems of Plenty: Energy Policy and International Politics." University of California, Berkeley, 1977, 39:1091-A.

Analyzes the options for international cooperation on energy problems
in three parts: (1) Part One argues that economic and technological
"fixes" for energy problems are unlikely to work; (2) Part Two is a
case history of the evolution of national and international energy
policies; (3) Part Three builds on the literature in economics, public policy, organization theory and international relations to construct a typology of nine strategies for international cooperation
on managing energy problems.

774. Culhane, Paul J. "Politics and the Public Lands: Local Policy Processes of the U.S. Forest Service and the Bureau of Land Management."
Northwestern University, 1977, 38:5039-A.

The main theoretical focus of the dissertation is on interest group
theory, particularly its proposition about group influence on policy,
as well as its normative implications. The politics of public land
management provides the setting for the investigation.

775. Dejax, Pierre J. "An Economic Analysis of Pollution Control Policies." Cornell University, 1977, 38:4936-A.

Characterizes pollution control policies for their efficiency, applicability and fairness to both the polluters and the victims of the
pollution.

776. Dickens, Robert E. "A Policy Analysis of the Sawtooth National
Recreation Area--Idaho." The University of Arizona, 1978, 39:3799-A.

For over 200 years, the natural resources contained on this nation's public lands have been put to a variety of uses. This study analyzes the establishment of the Sawtooth National Recreation Area in Idaho.

777. Dryzek, John S. "Public Policy When Values and Rights Conflict: Natural Resource Management in Alaska." University of Maryland, 1980, 42:2278-A.

The study is an attempt to come to grips with the problems that conflicting values present to both the design of public policies and policy research directed at the public decision process.

778. Duguid, Stephen R. "Technocrats, Politics and Planning: The Formulation of Arab Oil Policy, 1957-1967." Simon Fraser University (Canada), 1977, 38:5637-A.

The central concern is the relationship of politics, national and international, to the ideology and behavior of a particular elite group in the Arab Middle East, the oil technocrats. The study focuses on the impact of foreign ideas and interests in shaping the options and policies pursued by policy makers in the field of Arab oil.

779. Durant, Robert F. "EPA, TVA, and Pollution Control: A Comparative Analysis of Intragovernmental Policy Implementation." The University of Tennessee, 1981, 42:4928-A.

Of late the substance, organization, and context of federal policies have been altered. The study examines one manifestation of these developments: the burgeoning necessity of one federal agency having to hold another accountable to national policy goals. Its analytical focus is the Environmental Protection Agency's experience with the Tennessee Valley Authority during the former's implementation of the Clean Air Act and the Federal Water Pollution Control Act.

780. Eboh, Cyprian K. "The Management of Natural Resources: A Comparative Analysis of Energy Conservation Policy in a Developed and a Developing Country." University of Houston, 1980, 41:5239-A.

Focuses on the inability or unwillingness of policy makers in the U.S. and Nigeria to enact effective energy conservation policies in the face of increasing shortages of nonrenewable energy resources.

781. Ethridge, Marcus E., III. "The Effect of Administrative Procedure on Environmental Policy Implementation: A Comparative State Study." Vanderbilt University, 1979, 40:3525-A.

Assesses the empirically verifiable components of several arguments concerning the policy consequences of administrative procedure.

782. George, Stephen S. "Short-Run Residential Electricity Demand: A Policy Oriented Look." University of California, Davis, 1979, 40:5510-A.

Concerned with the short-run demand for electricity in the residential sector, the study investigates several different questions which are of concern to the policy-oriented user of residential electricity demand models.

783. Giaquinto, Eli J. "The Urbanization of National Forest Policy in the South." University of Georgia, 1981, 42:2289-A.

Examines the impacts of urbanization upon southern national forest renewable resources policy relationships with the purpose of better understanding conservation politics pertaining to the national forests of the South.

784. Goulder, Lawrence H. "A General Equilibrium Analysis of U.S. Energy Policies." Stanford University, 1982, 42:1226-A.

Involves the construction and application of a large-scale simulation model designed to assess the effects of changing energy conditions and policies on the U.S. economy.

785. Granger, Mitchell P., II. "An Inquiry into the Social Accounting Practices and Disclosure Policies of Selected Firms in the Pulp and Paper Industry of the Southern Pine Forest Region." University of Arkansas, 1979, 41:2175-A.

Uses an interview technique within two firms selected from the pulp and paper industry of the southeastern U.S. in an effort to describe disclosure policies and accounting practices and procedures relating to corporate social responsibility.

786. Green, Janet J. "Government and Wildlife Preservation, 1885-1922: The Emergency of a Protective Policy." York University (Canada), 1975, 40:4174-A.

Between the years 1885 and 1922, a concern for wildlife preservation gradually evolved within the Canadian Federal Government. These two dates mark the reservation of what was to become Canada's first national park--Rocky Mountain--and the holding of the first Dominion-Provincial Conference on Wild Life Protection which established wildlife conservation as a part of regular government policy.

787. Griffin, Ronald C. "Irrigated Agriculture and Nitrate Pollution of Rural Water Supplies: Economics for Policy in Central Wisconsin." The University of Wisconsin-Madison, 1980, 41:4453-A.

Examines the economic structure which characterizes the nitrate pollution of groundwater by irrigated agriculture in the Wisconsin Central Sands Region.

788. Gross, Meir. "The Impact of Transportation and Land Use Policies on Urban Air Quality." University of Pennsylvania, 1979, 40:1717-A.

Describes the development and testing of a comprehensive transportation, land use and air quality simulation system, which is intended for use by planning agencies.

789. Hall, Timothy A. "Energy Conservation: An Analysis of Public Policy Formulation, Implementation, and Alternatives." The University of Oklahoma, 1978, 39:6324-A.

The study is designed with the dual research goals of defining the

substantive political issues and the policy-making system which led
to the formulation and implementation of public policy with regard
to energy conservation and identifying, evaluating, and comparing
policy alternatives to improve and/or change conservation policy making and policy results in the consuming sectors.

790. Hamblin, Daniel M. "Automobile Demand Models for Evaluating the
Impacts of Fuel-Efficiency Energy Policies." State University of New
York at Buffalo, 1978, 40:2174-A.

On April 29, 1977 a national energy plan was proposed. Embodied in
the National Energy Act, the plan included "The Fuel Efficiency Incentive Tax" and a "Standby Gasoline Tax." Evaluates two dimensions
of the automobile sales impact of this "originally proposed" legislation.

791. Hamilton, Larry L. "The Diffusion of Technological Innovations:
Nuclear Energy Development and New Considerations for the Making of Public Policy." University of South Carolina, 1980, 42:364-A.

Examines the current controversies and problems in the field of nuclear energy from the perspective of public policy analysis. A major
assumption of the study is that the success of new technologies with
potential long-term hazards is threatened because an unprecedented
crisis of credibility has developed.

792. Hammerstrom, Gary A. "Nuclear Power and Nuclear Weapons Prolifera-
tion: A Policy Analysis and Forecasting Model." Syracuse University,
1978, 39:3817-A.

Develops a forecasting model for the identification of states which
are likely to adopt a policy position for the development of nuclear
weapons.

793. Hammoudeh, Shawkat M. "Optimal Oil Pricing Policy for Saudi Arabia." University of Kansas, 1980, 41:5175-A.

Presents an institutional description of Saudi Arabia's and the
world's oil industries and analyzes the factors which are apt to shape
the Kingdom's long-run oil pricing policy; analyzes the Kingdom's
optimal oil pricing policy; and two of the theoretical models are
applied and the long-run optimal oil prices computed.

794. Hooper, Peter F. "The Administrative Policy Process for Science:
A Case Study of Organizational-Environmental Dynamics." The University
of Connecticut, 1979, 41:3705-A.

The research is a case study of the policy process for a federal
agency that supports large-scale basic scientific investigations.
The agency studied is the Office for the National Science Foundation.
The study adopts an institutional approach, focusing on the organizational and clientele factors that shaped the program's development
and implementation.

795. Jurewitz, John L. "The Internalization of Environmental Costs in
the Private Electric Utility Industry: A Theoretical Analysis of Alterna-

tive Environmental Policies under Rate-of-Return Regulation." The Univeristy of Wisconsin-Madison, 1978, 39:5075-A.

Private electric utilities are subject to rate-of-return and price regulation by state public service commissions as well as environmental regulation by local, state and federal governments. This creates three sets of second-best policy issues which require investigation.

796. Kim, Choon Keun. "Technocrats and Coastal Policies: Long Beach and Santa Barbara." University of Southern California, 1979, 40:4222-A.

Examines the role and influence of technocrats in the community decision-making process of Long Beach and Santa Barbara in regard to the outer continental shelf oil and gas development as well as related industrial and coastal environmental activities.

797. Kim, Song Ki. "Control Policies for Reporting and Investigating Cost Variances." The University of Texas at Austin, 1979, 40:1562-A.

Critically examines a variety of issues relating to the determination of control policies for reporting and investigating cost variances. A cost control model which is aimed at determining the optimal combination of reporting interval and timing of investigation is developed.

798. Kramer, Kenneth W. "Implementing Environmental Policy: Air and Water in Texas." Rice University, 1979, 40:1676-A.

The concept of policy type is, in some senses, part of the concept of policy environment. Two different kinds of environment surround the implementation of policy: (1) the external environment, and (2) the immediate policy environment.

799. Kuczynski, Irving H. "British Offshore Oil and Gas Policy." Harvard University, 1978, 39:2401-A.

The study is the historical analysis of the evolution of British government policy in its indigenous oil and gas industry, and describes the pattern of policy making which unfolded as oil and gas developments proceeded and analyzes the factors behind policy formulation and the choice of instruments for controlling the oil and gas industry.

800. Kwast, Myron L. "Household Energy Demand: An Investigation into the Welfare Economics of Energy Prices and Policy." The University of Wisconsin-Madison, 1977, 38:6848-A.

Develops an analytical and empirical framework for examining the impact of an individual household of alternative pricing policies designed to achieve a given degree of energy conservation in the household sector. Household energy demand is defined as a residential consuming unit's demand for electricity, natural gas, and fuel oil. The impact of policy is measured by the net change in consumer's surplus caused by the pricing policy.

801.   LaForte, Joseph D.   "Water Pollution Control Costs and Public Policy for the Paper Industry with Application to Western Massachusetts."
The University of Connecticut, 1977, 38:4957-A.

   Examines the economic impacts of pollution abatement costs for a group
   of non-integrated small mills located along the Connecticut River in
   western Massachusetts.

802.   Lareau, Thomas J.   "A Welfare Analysis of Alternative Air Pollution
Control Policies." Indiana University, 1978, 39:4380-A.

   Addresses the question of the extent to which society bears an unnec-
   essary cost to achieve its clean air goals.

803.   Laurich, Gary E.   "Political Theory, Administrative Structure, and
Public Policy: A Theoretical Analysis of Bureau Politics and Pollution
Control." Wayne State University, 1977, 38:6929-A.

   The logical and epistemological structure of the value orientation of
   pollution control officials is explored. The connection between subjective frameworks and the outcome of pollution control policy is the
   main intended contribution to the study of politics.

804.   Laursen, Finn. "The Making of U.S. Ocean Policy, 1970-78." University of Pennsylvania, 1980, 41:1207-A.

   Analyzes two major aspects of U.S. ocean policy making--the politics
   of new coastal zones of resource-related coastal state jurisdiction
   and the politics of deep seabed mining.

805.   Lee, Martin.   "Patterns of Gasoline Consumption in Michigan and
Their Implications for Rationing and Alternative Conservation Policies:
A Disaggregate Analysis." The University of Michigan, 1980, 40:829-A.

   Planning of policies to reduce gasoline consumption in the U.S. requires data on the dependence of different populations on gasoline
   and an ability to predict the distributional impact of restrictions
   on gasoline or travel. This study develops, and meets, requirements
   for new data sources.

806.   Leung, Thomas K.   "Institutional and Community Factors Affecting
Intergovernmental Cooperation: Implementing the Regionalization Policy in
Water Pollution Control." University of Illinois at Urbana-Champaign,
1979, 40:5500-A.

   Examines the various social and political factors which enhance or
   impede the implementation of a federal policy in water pollution control.

807.   Mangun, William R.   "The Public Administration of Environmental
Policy: A Comparative Analysis of the United States and West Germany."
Indiana University, 1977, 38:5702-A.

   Provides information about the similarities and differences in the
   systems of environmental administration in the U.S. and West Germany.

808. Matthes, Dieter. "Regulating the Coal Industry: Federal Coal Mine Health and Safety and Surface Mining Policy Development." University of Pittsburgh, 1977, 39:447-A.

   Seeks to clarify the conditions and process by which an industry comes to be regulated by the federal government. Two legislative thrusts in particular are examined--the Federal Coal Mine Health and Safety Act of 1969 and the Surface Mining Control and Reclamation Act of 1977.

809. Megatali, Abderrahmane. "Petroleum Policies and National Oil Companies: A Comparative Study of Investment Policies with Emphasis on Exploration of SONATRACH (Algeria), NIOC (Iran) and PEMEX (Mexico), 1970-1975." The University of Texas at Austin, 1978, 39:4372-A.

   By means of an extensive interview program with top executives and managers of these three state corporations and with government officials of Algeria, Iran, and Mexico, the objectives and principles of national petroleum policies which are the basis of the investment decision of SONATRACH, NIOC, and PEMEX are identified for each country and compared with each other.

810. Milon, Joseph W. "Evaluating Economic and Thermodynamic Policy Models: A Study of the Effect of Residential Solar Water Heating on Electric Utilities in Florida." The Florida State University, 1978, 40:970-A.

   Advocates of a public policy model using energy units as a measure of value have argued that economic analysis is inappropriate for allocating energy resources because of pricing inefficiencies in energy markets and the exclusion of zero-priced environmental resources which contribute to energy production. In order to evaluate the merits of this new approach, a model is constructed to determine the benefits and costs of integrating residential solar water heating into the demand pattern of two electric utilities in Florida.

811. Mueller, Michael J. "Oil Shale, Economic Rent, and Public Policy." The University of Michigan, 1978, 39:6237-A.

   Reviews the institutional, historical, and technical aspects of the oil shale industry. Institutional aspects of oil shale use are reviewed with particular emphasis on land and water laws and water supply.

812. O'Connell, James C. "Technology and Pollution: Chicago's Water Policy, 1833-1930." The University of Chicago, 1980, 41:1188-A.

   Examines how Chicago managed its water pollution problems from its founding in 1833 until 1930, when the U.S. Supreme Court ordered it to provide complete sewage treatment.

813. Ogden, Gerald R. "Forestry for a Nation: The Making of a National Forest Policy under the Weeks and Clarke-McNary Acts, 1900-1924." The University of New Mexico, 1980, 41:2261-A.

   Details, analyzes, and demonstrates the results of the campaigns for and the legislative histories of the Weeks and Clarke-McNary Acts.

814.   Outen, Ronald B.   "The National Commission on Water Quality: A Case Study in Congressional Policy Analysis." The University of Texas at Dallas, 1980, 42:377-A.

The National Commission on Water Quality, a congressional commission numerically dominated by members of Congress, is analyzed and evaluated as a mechanism for research and policy analysis in an issue area of great scientific and technical complexity.

815.   Padungchai, Sumol. "An Economic Analysis of Water Quality Improvement Policies: The Optimal Combination of Salinity Control Techniques." Utah State University, 1980, 41:1152-A.

The theory of water pollution control with the dilution possibility is developed, and it is proved that simultaneous management of waste load and of stream dilution capacity is the least-cost policy to achieve a given level of water quality.

816.   Page, Ann L.   "Energy Policy and Ruling Class Hegemony: The Dissemination of Corporate Policy Preferences via Teachers and Textbooks." The University of Tennessee, 1979, 40:1099-A.

The objectives are: (1) to develop a model of corporate policy preferences concerning energy and to use this model to describe the attitudes of a sample (N=253) of science teachers and the content of a sample (N=15) of science textbooks; and (2) to compare teachers who were characterized by the corporate energy model to teachers who were not.

817.   Page, G. William, III.   "Toxic Substances in Water: Patterns of Contamination and Policy Implications." Rutgers University, 1980, 41: 1808-A.

The central research question addressed is how the contamination of ground water with toxic substances compares to the contamination of surface water with toxic substances in New Jersey.

818.   Paterson, Alan M.   "Rivers and Tides: The Story of Water Policy and Management in California's Sacramento-San Joaquin Delta, 1920-1977." University of California, Davis, 1978, 39:3781-A.

Examines water development policies and practices affecting and affected by the Sacramento-San Joaquin Delta, a northern California estuary that joins San Francisco Bay to the great rivers of the state's interior valley.

819.   Pohl, Gerhard W.   "Costs and Benefits of Residential Energy Use and Conservation in the United States: A Public Policy Perspective." New York University, 1981, 42:786-A.

The U.S. government has espoused a particular blend of energy conservation policies, combining subsidies toward energy consumption with quantitative restraints through energy conservation regulations. The study deals with one major subsector of energy use, residential space heating.

820. Rhodes, Steven L. "Organizing for Energy: The Federal Nuclear Model and Contemporary Solar Energy Policy." University of Colorado at Boulder, 1980, 41:1753-A.

Examines how internal factors influence the ability of the federal government to bring nonconventional energy technologies to a level of commercial competitiveness.

821. Robertson, Joe K. "An Empirical Analysis of a Peak Load Pricing Policy Applied to Residential Electricity Demand." The American University, 1980, 41:3204-A.

A central focus of the 1977 National Energy Plan is energy conservation. The plan's approach to conserving electric energy is based on the notion that non-differentiated electricity prices induce waste in electricity consumption and in fuel and capital inputs to electricity production.

822. Robins, Barbara J. "Protest and Public Policy: The Case of Airport Noise Controversies." Cornell University, 1979, 40:3583-A.

Examines the impact of protest on policies of public bureaucracies in American cities: specifically, the question of how bureaucratic policy outputs are affected by (1) protest activity, (2) the organizational and administrative characteristics of the policy-making unit, and (3) the policy maker's perceptions of protest.

823. Rothberg, Paul F. "The Relationship of Federal Policy to the Technological Innovation of Selected New Energy Technologies: An Exploratory Study." The American University, 1978, 39:6326-A.

Through the presentation of twelve case examples, the relationship between federal policy and the innovation of selected new energy technologies is studied.

824. Royer, Jack P. "An Analysis of an Open Land Policy for Flood Plain Management." Cornell University, 1980, 41:1249-A.

Critiques federal policy toward flood plain management, noting the absence of programs which encourage prescriptive zoning and acquisition of flood plains.

825. Rozelle, Martha A. "The Incorporation of Public Values into Public Policy." Arizona State University, 1982, 42:544-A.

Over one hundred interest groups with a stake in the outcome of the Central Arizona Water Control Study were invited to participate in a public values assessment. The participants rated fourteen attributes in terms of the relative importance of each attribute.

826. Ryan, Richard W. "Solar Energy Policy-Making in California." University of Southern California, 1978, 39:3134-A.

The roles of public organizations in the dissemination of solar energy technologies are assessed in the dissertation, which examines the involvement of public organizations in disseminating information for

citizen energy education, promoting consumer choices leading to energy
self-sufficiency, and assisting indigent people to provide for basic
energy needs.

827.   Schoene, Stephen W.   "The Economics of U.S. Public Land Policy Prior
to 1860."   The University of North Carolina at Chapel Hill, 1981, 42:
3696-A.

The subject is the market for land in the nineteenth century prior to
the Civil War, with the main thrust directed toward developing basic
data concerning the operation and structure of the land market.

828.   Schultz, Brian L.   "An Assessment of the Effects of Alternative
Policies on the U.S. Petroleum Market Using a Continuous System Model."
University of Notre Dame, 1980, 40:327-A.

Presents a framework for assessing alternative energy policy decisions
prior to their implementation into the U.S. economy.   Emphasis is
placed on one major energy source, petroleum.

829.   Shannon, Daniel W.   "A Cross National Comparison of Public Participation in Urban Shoreline Policy Development."   University of Washington,
1979, 40:3528-A.

Examines the utility of an alternative method for analyzing public
participation in the development of public policy.   Compares public
participation in urban shoreline policy development in two cases in
Canada and the U.S.

830.   Sharp, Basil.   "The Economics of Managing Water Quality: A Multi-
objective Analysis of Alternative Policies."   The University of Wisconsin-
Madison, 1978, 39:3073-A.

Develops a methodology which extends the dimensions of the problem of
water quality management to encompass not only efficiency but also
the concern for other objectives, such as distribution.   The methodology facilitates a more thorough appreciation of the pivotal position institutions occupy during the analysis, synthesis and implementation of policy alternatives.

831.   Srikar, Bellur N.   "Incentive Policy Analysis for Geopressured Resource Development."   The University of Texas at Austin, 1981, 42:1240-A.

Explores the use of economic incentives as an instrument to stimulate
the growth of geopressured resource development in the U.S. and identifies relationships between incentive policy options and the fundamental barriers to developing a U.S. geopressured gas capability.

832.   Stagliano, Richard A.   "Effect of the Energy Environment Simulator
and U.S. Energy Policy Game on Achievement, Attitudes, and Behavior Relative to Energy Education Concepts in a Community College."   The University
of Akron, 1981, 41:4351-A.

Determines the level of achievement in energy concepts attained by
(1) lecture-discussion simulation, (2) lecture-discussion game, and
(3) lecture-discussion methods of instruction.

833. Stoff, Michael B. "The Anglo-American Oil Agreement and the Development of National Policy for Foreign Oil, 1941-1947." Yale University, 1977, 39:2459-A.

During World War II, the U.S. government undertook to define and to carry out a coherent national policy for foreign oil development. Because of the rich stores of petroleum it held, the Middle East became the focus of American foreign oil policy, which ultimately sought to develop the region on a rational basis so that it might serve as a well head for Europe and so allow the Western Hemisphere to reduce the drain on its reserves after the war.

834. Stubbles, Russell L. "The History and Spatial Impact of the Texas Parks and Wildlife Department's Public Policy of Acquisition and Development: 1920-1975." Texas A&M University, 1979, 40:6420-A.

Investigates the influence of the Texas Parks and Wildlife Department's public policy of acquisition and development on the spatial distribution of state recreation parks.

835. Stumpp, Mark S. "Electric Utility Reliability, Pricing Policies, and Cost of Capital: Theories and Evidence." Brown University, 1981, 42: 503-A.

Most recent investigations into the area of power system,reliability levels have attempted to determine the optimal level of reliability through the use of tools such as cost-benefit analysis. The thesis is a departure from such empirical work in that it develops a theory which explains deviations from optimal reliability levels.

836. Summers, Michael R. "A Goal Programming Model for National Energy Policy." University of Illinois at Urbana-Champaign, 1978, 39:3040-A.

No current energy model adequately incorporates the variety and complexity of uncertainty regarding goals. Develops a model which is capable of considering several goals at once ranked by priority through the technique of goal programming.

837. Tashchian, Armen. "An Analysis of Consumer Preferences toward Governmental Policies Designed to Reduce Energy Consumption in the Private Transportation Sector." The University of Texas at Austin, 1980, 41: 4770-A.

Involves the psychometric development of a scale designed to measure consumer attitudes toward the energy problem, measuring public preferences toward four governmental policies designed to reduce the amount of energy consumed by the private transportation sector.

838. Thomas, Larry W. "Court-Agency Interaction in Environmental Policy-Making: The Cases of the Nuclear Regulatory Commission and the Environmental Protection Agency." The University of Tennessee, 1981, 42: 4930-A.

Examines the increasingly active participation of courts in the administrative process as well as agency responses to court-imposed policy shifts. Investigates the interaction between the federal courts, primarily the Supreme Court and the District of Columbia Court of Appeals, and two federal regulatory agencies, the Nuclear Regulatory Commission and the Environmental Protection Agency.

839. Toft, Graham S. "Land Use Guidance Strategies as Means of Achieving National Energy Goals: A Policy Analysis." Purdue University, 1978, 39:5765-A.

Reflects an awareness that the price and availability of energy will not only bring about adjustments in energy use but also in the way other factor substitutes are used. Recognizes at the outset that there are logical interrelationships between land and energy use.

840. Tolson, C. Frederick. "National Land Use Policy in the United States: An Historical Analysis." Illinois Institute of Technology, 1979, 40:4778-A.

Constitutes a historical analysis of the past policies of the U.S. federal government toward the use of land.

841. Weller, Steven. "Public Policy as Law in Action: The Implementation of the National Environmental Act of 1969 by the U.S. Army Corps of Engineers." Cornell University, 1979, 39:6949-A.

Investigates the implementation of the National Environmental Policy Act of 1969 by the U.S. Army Corps of Engineers, and attempts to assess the changes that took place in the Corps' decision making with regard to flood control and navigation projects and the reasons for the changes or lack of change.

842. Wiener, Don E. "Congress and Natural Gas Policy." The University of Wisconsin-Madison, 1978, 39:3812-A.

Analyzes the U.S. Congress' involvement in natural gas policy. The transportation of Alaskan gas is discussed through use of the case method approach, and regulation and pricing of natural gas is subjected to a congressional roll-call analysis.

843. Wilson, Donald E. "The History of President Truman's Air Policy Commission and Its Influence on Air Policy 1947-1949." University of Denver, 1978, 39:7488-A.

Begins with an analysis of major aviation issues in the U.S. from the end of World War II through mid-1947. Approached from the vantage point of President Truman's office, the study focuses on those areas of aviation interest that came to his attention.

844. Wood, Frederick E., Jr. "Public Opinion, Interest Groups and Environmental Policy: Incremental Change versus Speculative Augmentation." The Johns Hopkins University, 1980, 40:5182-A.

The dissertation is designed both to contribute to a better understanding of environmental policy and to shed some useful empirical light on general theories of public policy.

845. Yosie, Terry F. "Retrospective Analysis of Water Supply and Waste-

water Policies in Pittsburgh, 1800-1959." Carnegie-Mellon University, 1981, 42:2251-A.

The study is a retrospective technology assessment of wastewater and water quality decisions made by the city of Pittsburgh in the period from 1800 to 1959. It focuses upon the areas of technology development and implementation, impacts in the health, environmental, governmental, economic, and values areas, and the development of policies to deal with both implementation and regulation of water quality impacts.

846. Zimmermann, Charles F. "Uranium Resources on Federal Lands: An Evaluation of Policy Alternatives." Cornell University, 1978, 39:4388-A.

Attempts to accomplish three objectives: to identify deficiencies in the legal system regarding the disposal of uranium on federal lands, to assess major factors which influence uranium prices and production costs, and to analyze the relative merits of alternative lease bidding systems for uranium resources.

International Trade and Economics

847. Abbadi, Suleiman M. "Monetary Policy in LDCs with Special Reference to the Middle East." The University of Texas at Austin, 1981, 42:1243-A.

Attempts to shed light on monetary policy in developed countries and in LDCs, with emphasis on monetary policy in the Middle East. Also investigates the ability of the monetary authorities in the Middle East to control the money supply and to conduct monetary policy.

848. Abu-Shaikha, Ahmad. "A Theoretical Analysis of the Impact of Fiscal and Monetary Policies on Economic Activity in Closed and Open Economies." The George Washington University, 1979, 40:389-A.

Analyzes, in a very general framework, the impact of fiscal and monetary policies on the economy in the context of a macroeconomic model which includes both the demand for and supply of goods and services, indicating that both prices and employment are endogenous variables.

849. Accolla, Peter S. "The Maritime Policy of the Latin American Countries and World Public Order. A New International Law?" The Johns Hopkins University, 1979, 40:444-A.

Given the possibility for exploitation of living and mineral resources of the sea on a growing and profitable basis, coastal states of Latin America have extended their jurisdiction over parts of the sea and seabed adjacent to their coasts, traditionally considered part of the high seas.

850. Alam, Mohammad S. "Welfare Implications of Trade Policies: Three Essays." The University of Western Ontario (Canada), 1979, 40:5534-A.

Comprises three essays on specific trade policies and their welfare implications.

851. Bahry, Donna L. "Republic Politics and Federal Budget Policy in the USSR." University of Illinois at Urbana-Champaign, 1977, 38:6281-A.

The issue is the degree of political centralization in the Soviet Union. Do demands by some republic and local officials make a difference in the way resources are distributed? This study sets out to test their influence on policy by examining the federal budgetary system and its outputs.

852.   Bamakhramah, Ahmed S.   "Policies for Transfer of Technology to Developing Countries: The Case of Middle Eastern Oil-Exporting Countries." University of Miami, 1981, 42:5184-A.

Proposes policy measures for the Middle Eastern oil-exporting countries which would serve their national economic, social and political goals given the two main characteristics: (1) availability of financial resources to purchase needed technology, particularly for surplus countries; and (2) scarcity of labor, entrepeneurship and managerial skills.

853.   Bartholomew, Mark A.   "The Effect of International Interdependence on Foreign Policy Making: Canadian and United States Nuclear Technology Export." Miami University, 1980, 41:3249-A.

This is a study of Canadian and U.S. nuclear technology export policy.

854.   Bhaskaran, Sambandam.   "Decision-Making in American Foreign Policy with Special Reference to Economic Assistance to India." Northern Illinois University, 1978, 40:2867-A.

The central theme of the study is that whenever foreign policy issues involve the regulation of internal resources, foreign policy becomes a domestic issue. Its subject is the nature of domestic power relationships in a decision-making context.

855.   Brey, Gary B.   "Transnational Policy Analysis: Measuring Economic Policy Outputs." Syracuse University, 1977, 38:5029-A.

Uses an event data strategy to measure foreign policy outputs in the issue area of international trade and investment. The purpose of the research is to test the feasibility of generating event data that are specific to an issue area rather than gathering events that relate to all areas of foreign policy.

856.   Bruce, David C.   "The U.N. Economic Commission for Latin America and National Development Policies: A Study of Noncoercive Influence." The University of Michigan, 1977, 38:6918-A.

Since its inception in 1948, the United Nations Economic Commission for Latin America (ECLA) has been widely recognized both regionally and globally as a leader and innovator in the field of development economics. The dissertation is oriented specifically toward the study of the potential channels of ECLA influence such as research, advisory services, and training.

857.   Cha, Dong-Se.   "International Short-Term Capital Flows, Exchange Rate Expectations and Independence of Monetary Policy." Vanderbilt University, 1979, 40:2172-A.

Investigates two controversial problems related to floating exchange rates: how investors in international financial markets form their expectations on future exchange rates and how investors' expectations

affect the stability of the exchange market; and whether the independence of monetary policy has actually increased under the floating exchange rates, as theory claims.

858. Choo, Myung-Gun. "Economic Analysis of Public Policy with Respect
to International Trade: A Case Study of the U.S. Aerospace Industry."
University of Massachusetts, 1978, 39:354-A.

Critically examines the export pattern of the U.S. aerospace industry
in light of international trade theory, to show that the real driving
force of international trade is not comparative advantage but the will
of entrepreneurs and government to expand the market.

859. Clifton, Eric V. "International Capital Movements and Capital Accumulation in Less Developed Countries: Optimal Foreign Borrowing Policies." Indiana University, 1980, 41:5198-A.

Examines the effect of borrowing from abroad on the optimal growth and
capital accumulation of a less developed country. A series of theoretical models is built in order to show the effects of capital inflows
into that economy under various circumstances.

860. Cosgrove, Julia F. "United States Economic Foreign Policy toward
China, 1943-1946." Washington University, 1980, 41:3694-A.

Traces the development and pursuit of American economic foreign policy
toward China from 1943, when American extraterritorial privileges in
China were surrendered, to 1946, when the Sino-American Commercial
Treaty was signed.

861. Cunningham, John H. "The Influence of Maritime Policy on the Performance and Progress of the United States Merchant Marine." University
of Oregon, 1981, 42:3784-A.

Maritime policy of the U.S., first formally expressed in the Merchant
Marine Act of 1920, and reiterated in subsequent legislation, calls
for a U.S. flag merchant marine capable of substantial participation
in commerce and able to contribute to the requirements of national
defense.

862. Deering, Christopher J. "Arms Transfers and Congressional Policy
Making: Where Porkbarrel and Foreign Policy Meet." University of California, Santa Barbara, 1979, 41:1197-A.

Examines Congress's role in the control of conventional arms transfers
from the U.S. Focuses upon the events leading up to passage of the
International Security Assistance and Arms Export Control Act of 1976.

863. Dressner, Ira J. "Functionalism and Fair-Shares Industrial Policy
in International Organization: The European Space Research Organization."
Syracuse University, 1977, 39:1095-A.

The subject of the study is international integration examined within
the complex, changing environment of European nations involved in
space endeavors between 1959 and 1972. Details the development of
the European Space Research Organization with special emphasis on its

industrial policy formulation and implementation, goals and activities, and its relationship with, and ultimate impact on, industry.

864.   Drobnick, Richard L.   "Food Policy Choices in an Uncertain World: Policy Analysis with a Probabilistic World Food Model."   University of Southern California, 1979, 40:2184-A.

Demonstrates a method for evaluating alternative sets of North American food policies.   Interdependence among world regions and probabilistic regional weather patterns are fundamental parts of this analysis.   A single-sector, ten-region, probabilistic world food model is used to simulate alternative agricultural futures.

865.   Edress, Omar B.   "Attitudes of U.S. International Airlines toward the U.S. International Air Transport Policy as Reflected by the Various Bilateral Agreements, and the Possible Implications."   The University of Tennessee, 1980, 41:2324-A.

The Bermuda II event came at a time when American airlines were experiencing numerous problems, including anticompetitive practices abroad, restrictions of their scheduled operations by some foreign governments, and declining profits.   The purpose of this research is to test the hypothesis that such a situation was bound to create an air of dissatisfaction on the part of the airline industry toward the U.S. International Air Transport Policy and to show both how that policy affected the airlines and their reactions to it.

866.   Ellis, Doreen.   "Policy-Making, Regional Interdependence, and the International Technology and Investment System."   Northwestern University, 1980, 41:2756-A.

Examines two areas of present scholarly research on international political-economic development: (1) the development and maintenance of the present international system, in particular, the fundamental role of scientific and technological capacities and development and the prominent vehicle of economic exchange, the multinational corporation; and (2) the potential for government initiated change in the system resulting from industrial policy strategies chosen to use, regulate, and/or promote regional interdependence.

867.   Farrell, Victoria S.   "Optimal Pricing Policy for the OPEC Cartel, and the Effects of Non-OPEC Combative Tariff Policy and U.S. Price Controls Thereon."   The University of Wisconsin-Madison, 1979, 40:4164-A.

A dynamic model of discounted profit flow maximization for the Organization of Petroleum Exporting Countries (OPEC) is presented in this dissertation, one which facilitates analysis of a number of factors on optimal oil prices for the cartel.

868.   Feldman, Robert A.   "The Impact of Oil Import Price Shocks: The Interactive Effects of Domestic Price Controls, the Exchange Rate and Macro-Policy on Domestic Prices."   The University of Wisconsin-Madison, 1979, 40:5119-A.

Provides empirical estimates of the impact of the increase in the price of imported oil on the structure and level of domestic prices

using an input-output framework. In addition, the effects of two important policy responses to the oil price shock are analyzed.

869. Fonseca, Marcos G. "The General Equilibrium Effects of International Trade Policies." Yale University, 1978, 39:3045-A.

The first chapter to the dissertation is a survey of the theory of
protection. It also highlights the problems of measuring the impact
of protection in a general equilibrium framework, suggesting a general
equilibrium methodology to solve these problems.

870. Gavin, Joseph G., III. "The Political Economy of U.S. Agricultural
Export Policy, 1971-1975: Government Response to a Changing Economic Environment." Columbia University, 1980, 42:1681-A.

Examines the adjustment of U.S. commercial agricultural export policy
to changing global economic conditions in the period 1971-1975.

871. Gleizer, Guillermo A. "Effects of Economic Policies on the Foreign
Sectors of Argentina and Brazil, 1950-1974. A Reappraisal of the Struc-
turalist Approach to Latin American Economic Issues." New School for
Social Research, 1981, 42:2765-A.

Analyzes the effects of economic policies on the balance of payments
of Argentina and Brazil for the period 1950-1974.

872. Gowa, Joanne. "Explaining Large Scale Policy Change: Closing the
Gold Window, 1971." Princeton University, 1980, 41:1206-A.

The study is an analysis of the decision-making process that led the
Nixon Administration to suspend the convertibility of the dollar into
gold and other primary reserve assets on 15 August 1971.

873. Green, Philip E. "Conflict over Trade Ideologies during the Early
Cold War: A Study of American Foreign Economic Policy." Duke University,
1978, 39:7468-A.

In an effort to expand postwar American export markets, the Department
of State devised and sought international adherence to a world multilateral trade system. Such a system of nondiscriminatory trade was
to replace the restrictive and bilateral trade measures instituted in
the 1930's by all of the world's leading trading nations.

874. Harrison, Donald M. "Monetary Policy in an Open Country: The Case
of Belgium, 1951 to 1974." University of Virginia, 1977, 38:5631-A.

The conduct of monetary policy in Belgium during the period 1951 to
1974 is analyzed, employing the Brunner-Meltzer monetary framework.

875. Hartigan, James C. "Trade Policy and Income Distribution in the
United States and Canada." Duke University, 1979, 40:4685-A.

The dissertation is directed toward the determination of the effects
of the U.S. and foreign trade policy on the level and distribution of
real income within the U.S. It is argued that the simulation of a
general equilibrium model is necessary to consider both issues.

876.   Hawley, James P.   "U.S. Restriction of the Export of Capital, 1961-1971: State Policy and Long Term Economic Perspectives." McGill University (Canada), 1977, 38:4383-A.

Studies the various measures proposed and instituted by the government of the U.S. to restrict the export of capital between 1961-1971. The study seeks to examine the nature of the relation between multinational corporations and international banks and the U.S. state.

877.   Herzberg, James R.   "American Economic Policies towards Japan, 1931-1941." The University of Texas at Austin, 1977, 38:4327-A.

The study begins to correct the deficiency of the overall literature by taking a longer view of the entire decade and concentrating on more than diplomatic concerns. The point of view is not revisionist, although elements of a revisionist argument constitute portions of the main line of thought.

878.   Hodin, Michael W.   "A National Policy for Organized Free Trade, or, How to Cope with Protectionism: The Case of United States Foreign Trade Policy for Steel, 1976-1978." Columbia University, 1979, 40:5996-A.

Examines how the U.S. foreign trade policy is responding to two related problems of international trade: (1) structural changes in the global economy; and (2) the resultant trend toward protection among the industrial nations.

879.   Hussein, Aminu.   "The Group of 77, the United Nations and the Quest for a New International Technological Order: Political-Economic Analysis of Issues, Processes and Evolving Policies." Case Western Reserve University, 1981, 42:1304-A.

The focus is on the specific demands and political actions of the Group of 77, the responses of the industrialized countries, and the actions taken by the United Nations and its agencies. The influence exerted by nongovernmental transnational actors is examined also.

880.   Ivanovic, Mihailo S.   "A Model for Policy Analysis within the European Economic Community." Columbia University, 1977, 40:3420-A.

The process which should lead toward the European economic and monetary unification is enormously important since it entails adjustments in major macroeconomic policy targets and could also necessitate profound structural and institutional changes in most, if not all, of the EEC nations.

881.   Jarocha, Nancy M.   "The Foreign Labor Issue and Integration in Western Europe: A Case Study of Policy Determinants." University of South Carolina, 1980, 41:3251-A.

The primary focus is explanations for the success or failure of attempts to achieve some level of integration on the foreign labor issue within the EEC.

882.   Johannes, James M.   "Worldwide Inflation and U.S. Monetary Policy: Tests of the Structural Specification and Implications of a Monetary Bal-

ance of Payments Model." The University of Wisconsin-Madison, 1978, 39: 6234-A.

Investigates the empirical validity of several of the more salient hypotheses of the dominant country version of the monetary approach to the balance of payments regarding exogeneity and causal ordering.

883. Johnson-Freese, Joan S. "The Political Implications of U.S. Nuclear Export Policy Development." Kent State University, 1981, 42:4918-A.

The thesis is that a nuclear export policy which fails to consider its short-term ramifications, as the Nuclear Non-Proliferation Act of 1978 has been accused of, will be self-defeating. This work provides a comprehensive case study of U.S. nuclear export policy between the years 1976-80 in support of the thesis.

884. Jones, Chapman M. "Policymaking Efficiency and the International Monetary System." Yale University, 1979, 40:5957-A.

Attempts to define and to describe an optimal international monetary system. The conceptual framework is that of traditional welfare economics: agents pursue well-defined objectives by choosing an action from among those which are feasible according to the constraints on individual actions imposed by the form of social organization, and observed actions are supposed to be those which prevail in an equilibrium.

885. Kim, Hak Su. "Monetary Policy and Foreign Capital Inflows in a Dependent Economy: The Case of Korea." University of South Carolina, 1977, 38:5623-A.

Focuses attention on the problem of the relationship between foreign capital inflows and domestic money supply. Reviews and synthesizes three approaches in terms of an alternative money supply function appropriate for a dependent and developing economy. This alternative model is tested using the Korean data for the period 1965 I - 1975 IV.

886. Koehler, Wallace C., Jr. "Government Dominance and World Politics: Changing Canadian-American Relations in Energy Trade and Foreign Ownership Policies." Cornell University, 1977, 38:5696-A.

The role and power of government to intervene and modify international interdependencies have received relatively little attention in the international relations literature. The study seeks to determine what those powers are, how they can be effectively implemented and under what conditions they can be implemented successfully.

887. Kurihara, Shiro. "Imported Input and Macroeconomic Policy." The Johns Hopkins University, 1980, 41:1141-A.

Studies the macroeconomic effects of higher prices of imported input and policy reactions approached from both the theoretical and empirical aspects.

888. Kwon, O. Young. "Theory of Foreign Exchange and Economic Policy." New York University, 1980, 41:2716-A.

889. Lahera-Parada, Eugenio. "Public Policies and Foreign Investment in Latin America. The Cases of Argentina and Chile." Princeton University, 1979, 40:4216-A.

There is a basically positive correlation between shifts in host countries' public policies of foreign investment on the other. In order to test this hypothesis, two main indicators were selected, host-country public policies of foreign investment and their changes over time and the variations in the stock and flows of foreign direct investment, mainly U.S. direct investment.

890. Larrain, Mauricio R. "Policy Parameters, the Balance of Payments and Equations of Exchange Rate Equilibrium." Columbia University, 1978, 39:392-A.

Seeks to explain exchange rate behavior in a world where central banks intervene to manage the direction of exchange rate changes, as compared to a world where either fixed or freely floating rates exist.

891. Laskar, Daniel M. "Sterilization Behavior and Independence of Monetary Policy under a Pegged-Exchange-Rates System: An Econometric Approach." University of California, Los Angeles, 1981, 42:1721-A.

Tries to re-estimate the evidence on the short-run independence of monetary policy under a pegged-exchange-rates system.

892. Leung, Chi-Hung. "The Design of Stabilization Policies and the International Transmission of Economic Disturbances." The Johns Hopkins University, 1980, 41:1702-A.

The dissertation is a theoretical dynamic analysis of the effects of both external and internal shocks to an open economy. It emphasizes the economic interdependence of countries linked together through the trading of consumption goods and intermediate goods and the international flow of financial assets.

893. McIntyre, John R. "Interagency Policy Implementation: The Case of U.S. Export Licensing of Advanced Technology." University of Georgia, 1981, 42:849-A.

Using export licensing administration and the implementation of the conflicting policy goals contained in the Export Administration Act as a case study, the dissertation explores, at a micro-organizational level, the administrative dynamics of this complex and arcane decision process in which security, economics and politics are organizationally traded off in reading optimal decisions.

894. Mason, Robert E. "The Foreign Policy of Postindustrial Societies." The Ohio State University, 1981, 42:3292-A.

Studies a series of fundamental changes which are taking place in the relations between societies. These changes arise because a set of nations, the postindustrial societies, have entered a new stage in the process of modernization.

895. Mattos, Zilda. "The Effect of Free Trade Policy on Brazilian Agri-

culture: A Micro Approach."   The Ohio State University, 1979, 40:4680-A.

Analyzes the effect of a free trade policy upon farm enterprise mix,
resource use and farm income of large farms in the region of Ribeirao
Preto in Brazil.

896. Meeks, Philip J.   "The Crisis of Governance and Economic Policy in
Postindustrial States: The Politics of Corporatism and International Eco-
nomic Relations in the United Kingdom, West Germany and France 1958-1978."
The University of Texas at Austin, 1980, 41:1751-A.

It is the thesis of this study that the politicization of economic
policy has been fundamentally shaped by certain structural changes
in postindustrial societies. These changes have included the increasing use of automation technology in industrial production processes,
the decreasing use of skilled industrial labor, and increasing international competition for industrial trade and raw materials.

897. Meyer, Stephen A.   "Macroeconomic Policy in Large, Open Economies
with Floating Exchange Rates." Yale University, 1979, 40:3451-A.

What are the domestic and foreign effects of macroeconomic policy
undertaken by the large, industrialized countries in our interdepen-
dent world? Conclusions about the effects of policy actions may not
reflect the behavior of large, open economies, especially in the two-
or three-year medium run that seems to be of particular concern to
policy makers.

898. Miller, Gary E.   "Selected Aspects of Full Employment Policies in
France, West Germany and the United Kingdom, 1955-1969." University of
Southern California, 1977, 38:4942-A.

Attempts to ascertain the reasons for the maintenance of full employment in the period 1955 through 1969 in France, West Germany, and the
United Kingdom, as well as to assess the applicability of this for
the United States.

899. Monke, Eric A.   "Government Policy and International Trade in Rice."
Stanford University, 1980, 40:737-A.

The thesis contains an analysis of the role of government policy in
the international rice market during 1961-1977.

900. Muhalhal, Mutawakel A.   "Optimal Production and Pricing Policies
for the Organization of Petroleum Exporting Countries." University of
California, Riverside, 1980, 41:1155-A.

The objectives are to demonstrate analytically how the magnitude of
the joint gain to the OPEC countries can be measured and, by using
data on world demand and supply of oil, to obtain estimates of the
size of this gain under various assumed conditions.

901. Odjagov, Marianne.   "Foreign Ownership Policies of United States
Multinational Banks." Harvard University, 1978, 39:6221-A.

Examines the foreign ownership policies of American-based multinational banks by looking at the patterns of foreign holdings that various banking groups have come to display.

902. Poncet, Patrice J. "Monetary and Fiscal Policies in a Neoclassical Model: The French Case." Northwestern University, 1977, 38:6850-A.

Presents a theoretical model which emphasizes the importance of imperfect price and money wage perceptions, of the market for bank credit, and of the government financing constraint.

903. Ramsour, David L. "An Inquiry into the Meaning of and Policy Responses to Country Risk in Bank Credit." The University of Texas at Dallas, 1979, 40:5953-A.

The rapid rise in commercial lending by U.S. banks to foreign borrowers and to less developed countries in particular, has produced intensified public concern about new risks that this foreign exposure constitutes for banks. The distinct risk that banks are regarded as facing in lending abroad has come to be described as "country risk."

904. Rommel, Thierry J. "Monetary Policy Implementation under Open-Economy Conditions; The Case-Study: France." University of Illinois at Urbana-Champaign, 1977, 38:6239-A.

Focuses on the effectiveness of monetary policy in a small country, under fixed exchange rates and with international capital-mobility. Looks at the empirical validity of the theoretical proposition, which states that under such circumstances monetary policy is an uneffective demand-management tool. The case study applies to France.

905. Roy, Tapan K. "Export Diversification, Flexibility and Policy: A Study of Selected Underdeveloped Countries." Temple University, 1980, 42:787-A.

Focuses on a detailed analysis of the degree of diversification of exports, both commodity and geographic, of twenty-four underdeveloped countries during the period 1962-74.

906. Sampson, Martin W. "International Policy Coordination: A Game Theoretic Study of Necessary Conditions for the Formation of International Policy Coalitions." Indiana University, 1979, 40:5583-A.

Using OPEC (1973-1974) and the East African Common Market (1963-1967) as case studies, offers a definition of international policy coordination, uses cooperative game theory to ascertain necessary conditions for the formulation of international policy coalition, and concludes that there is substantial evidence supporting certain game theoretic solutions as necessary conditions for international policy coordination.

907. Slangor. "Economic Policies and Their Effects on the Performance of Some Major Export Commodities in Indonesia." The University of Wisconsin-Milwaukee, 1977, 38:6227-A.

Monetary, foreign exchange and selective credit policies of Indonesia are examined, and their effects on the individual export commodity estimated.

908. Soofi, Abdollah S. "Iranian Fiscal Policy, Foreign Trade, and Economic Development: 1930-1978." University of California, Riverside, 1981, 42:4080-A.

As a whole, the findings point out that despite an almost universal and common belief among economists, journalists and government officials about the degree of economic development in Iran in the decades of the 1960's and 1970's, the Iranian economy manifests classic characteristics of underdevelopment.

909. Spooner, Ward A. "United States Policy toward South Africa, 1919-1941, Political and Economic Aspects." St. Johns' University, 1979, 40:2817-A.

The U.S. is an important actor on the South African scene in terms of trade, investment and as a supplier of international credit. This study argues that during the interwar years, 1919-1941, the U.S. commenced its modern commercial and financial penetration of the country.

910. Stetson, Nancy H. "Congress and Foreign Policy: The 1972 U.S.-U.S.S.R. Trade Agreement and the Trade Reform Act." Columbia University, 1979, 40:2865-A.

Describes and analyzes the policy-making process which resulted in the formation in October 1972 of the East-West Trade and Fundamental Human Rights Amendment, commonly known as the Jackson Amendment and its enactment into law in 1974 as part of the Nixon Administration's general trade bill, the Trade Act of 1974.

911. Stocking, Thomas E. "The Political Objectives of American Foreign Trade Policy: 1948-1973." University of Minnesota, 1977, 38:6301-A.

Describes how trade is used to accomplish political objectives, determines how foreign policy objectives have influenced foreign trade policy making, and draws conclusions about the effectiveness of foreign trade as an instrument of foreign policy.

912. Tadie, Eugene P. "Modelling the Political Economy of East-West Trade: Legislative Development of United States Export Controls Policy, and Transfers of American Computer Technology to the Soviet Union." Northern Illinois University, 1981, 42:1782-A.

This is a study of congressional involvement in foreign policy decision making. Its objective is to examine the intrinsic conflict between the legislative and executive branches through their interactions over the proper scope and character of U.S. export controls policy since World War II.

913. Tamakloe, Emmanuel. "Social Welfare and Equity Considerations in Transportation Investment Policies toward Less Developed Regions." University of Pennsylvania, 1979, 40:3580-A.

The study is concerned with the development of a procedure to evaluate the equity of transportation investment policies toward less developed regions and is motivated by the hypothesis that equity is the primary goal which influences public policy toward less developed regions.

914. Wallerstein, Mitchel B. "The Politics of International Food Aid:
U.S. Policy Objectives in an Evolving Multilateral Context." Massachusetts Institute of Technology, 1978, 39:5713-A.

The study is concerned with how the process of giving and obtaining
food resources has been translated, in modern political terms, into
an international system of food assistance. It addresses the question of how the U.S., as the predominant food aid donor, has func-
tioned within this system, and it considers the resulting linkages
between food as an economic resource transfer and U.S. foreign policy.

915. Webb, Michael A. "Three Essays in International Trade Policy."
University of Illinois at Urbana-Champaign, 1980, 41:4785-A.

The thesis is divided into three essays which address policy issues
in the area of international trade.

916. Whitacre, Rick C. "An Evaluation of Japanese Agricultural Trade
Policies with a Multiregion-Multicommodity Model." University of Illinois
at Urbana-Champaign, 1979, 40:4684-A.

Concerns itself with the impact of the restrictive trade policies of
the Japanese government on intermediate and final output allocation,
patterns of consumption and trade, and the price structure of intermediate and final outputs in the grain-oilseed-livestock complex in
the U.S.A., Canada, Australia, as well as Japan.

917. Willman, Elliott S. "The Effectiveness of Monetary Policy in an
Open Economy under Fixed Exchange Rates: The Case of Germany and the
United Kingdom." Indiana University, 1977, 38:6853-A.

Develops a portfolio equilibrium model to determine the extent of
international capital mobility in an open economy under a fixed exchange regime. In particular, the study looks at international capital mobility in Germany and the United Kingdom during the 1960's and
early 1970's.

Judicial Policy Making

918. Angiello, Joseph L. "The Substantive Constitutional Rights of Students: Policies of Community Colleges in the Fifth Circuit Compared with Federal Court Decisions." The University of Texas at Austin, 1977, 38: 3894-A.

Analyzes the substantive constitutional rights of students in colleges in the Fifth Circuit of the U.S. Court of Appeals, examines the rules and regulations of the Fifth Circuit public community colleges that have a bearing on the above rights to determine the extent to which they recognize or protect those rights, and presents sample rules and regulations which reflect an adequate recognition of the rights of students.

919. Baughman, David L. "Reduction-in-Force in Higher Education: An Analysis of Court Decisions between 1970-1979 with Implications for Governing Board Policy." Northern Illinois University, 1981, 42:1503-A.

An analysis of court decisions was completed to determine decisions of the judiciary concerning the legal status of terminations of college and university personnel because of retrenchment.

920. Bloch, Frank S. "The Role of Litigation in the Development of Federal Welfare Policy: A Study of Legal Challenges to State Administration of Aid to Families with Dependent Children Programs as Politics of Redistributive Policy." Brandeis University, 1978, 38:7526-A.

Attempts to determine the role of the litigation made possible by the availability of free legal services for welfare recipients, in relation to the two federal welfare policy-making bodies, Congress and the Department of Health, Education and Welfare.

921. Buergenthal, Dorothy A. "Recent Court Decisions and Local School District Policies: Student Rights Issues." State University of New York at Buffalo, 1978, 39:5221-A.

Examines a variety of court decisions concerned with student rights issues. Three issues, student conduct, student activities and the suspension/expulsion of students are singled out for analysis and discussion.

922.   Caldeira, Greg A.   "Lower Court Judges and the American Supreme Court: Legitimacy, Judicial Power, and Public Policy." Princeton University, 1978, 39:7494-A.

Focuses on the judges of the lower courts and their relationships with the U.S. Supreme Court. As such, it is both an examination of trial judges--their backgrounds, recruitment, socialization, and political attitudes--and a consideration of the feelings of these judges--their perceptions and evaluations--about the Supreme Court and its public policies.

923.   Cann, Steve J.   "The Political Role of State Supreme Courts: Policy-Making Opportunities and Policy-Making." Purdue University, 1977, 38: 6283-A.

Constitutes a policy analysis of six state supreme courts, those of Illinois, Michigan, Nebraska, North Carolina, North Dakota, and South Carolina. The two-part analysis deals with opportunities for courts to make policy and analyzes the final court disposition of those opportunities.

924.   Carruthers, James R.   "A Comparison Study and Analysis of Policies and Procedures Pursuant to Separation of Faculty Members in Arizona Community Colleges in Relation to Procedural Due Process Safeguards." Northern Arizona University, 1981, 42:4216-A.

Compiles all the written policies, rules, and regulations promulgated by the nine Arizona community college districts relating to the separation (dismissal/nonrenewal of contract) of full-time teaching faculty, and analyzes these to measure the rate of compliance with essential (minimal as required by law) and recommended (optimal protection) procedural due process safeguards.

925.   Cohen, Larry J.   "Obedience and Sanctions: An Examination of Legal Social Control Policy." Syracuse University, 1977, 39:1074-A.

Adjustments in the level and types of sanctions employed in the criminal justice system are predicated on certain beliefs about the manner in which laws and their associated punishments influence behavior. One purpose of the study is to examine systematically these beliefs and their implications for punishment policy.

926.   Combs, Michael W.   "Courts, Minorities, and the Dominant Coalition: Racial Policies in Modern America." Washington University, 1978, 39: 1802-A.

Examines, over time since 1947, the participation of the Supreme Court in the formulation of national policies relating to racial problems in housing, voting, employment, and education.

927.   Crowley, Donald W.   "The Impact of *Serrano v. Priest*: A Study in Judicial Policy." University of California, Riverside, 1979, 40:2857-A.

Addresses the question of the capacity of courts to produce change consistent with their policy objectives by focusing on the California Supreme Court's attempts to alter the state's system of school financing in *Serrano v. Priest*.

928. Daniels, Stephen. "The Use of Social Science, the Constitution, and the Rule of Law: An Interpretation and Analysis of the Empirical Justification of Constitutional Policy." The University of Wisconsin-Madison, 1978, 39:5694-A.

Constitutes a case study analysis and evaluation of the use of social science and the empirical approach during the 1972 Supreme Court term.

929. Easton, Earnest L. "Licensing, Public Policy, and the Supreme Court." Cornell University, 1978, 38:7528-A.

Licensing is controlled by political officials on the local, state, and national levels. Politics and conflict are an integral part of the licensing process because there are often more individuals seeking licenses than there are available licenses.

930. Eubank, William L. "The First Five Years of the Burger Court: Policies and Attitudes." University of Oregon, 1978, 39:6322-A.

Two consequences of Richard Nixon's election to the Presidency and of his appointments to the United States Supreme Court are analyzed. The first issue, a comparison of the policies of the Warren and Burger Courts, is addressed with a time-series quasi-experiment. The second deals with the adequacy of one model of judicial decision making under conditions of change in Supreme Court membership.

931. Gibson, Harold D., Sr. "A Study of the Relationship of Selected Federal Court Cases to Student Control Policies Found in Virginia School Board Policy Manuals." The College of William and Mary in Virginia, 1981, 42:3824-A.

Investigates the relationship between the written student control policies established by Virginia school boards and the principles of law found in recent federal court decisions related to student conduct.

932. Jack, Elkin T. "Racial Policy and Judge J.P. Coleman: A Study in Political-Judicial Linkage." University of Southern Mississippi, 1979, 40:5574-A.

Attempts to determine if the negative attitudes toward race-related topics which some associated with J.P. Coleman's political life are reflected in his federal judicial career.

933. Kenty, Martha C. "Expert Testimony in the Pennhurst Case: A Critique of the Empirical and Theoretical Basis for Public Policy." The Medical College of Pennsylvania, 1979, 41:2789-A.

Challenges the adequacy of social scientific theory and empirical data, as presented by the expert witnesses in the Pennhurst Case, to justify the court-ordered policy of total deinstitutionalization of the mentally retarded residents of the Pennhurst State School and Hospital.

934. McIntyre, Geoffrey R. "A Comparative Analysis of Federal Port Policy in the United States and Canada." New York University, 1978, 39:3829-A.

The study is a comparative investigation of U.S. and Canadian federal government ocean port policies.

935. Munro, Robert J. "Grievance Arbitration Procedure: Legal and Policy Guidelines for Public Education." The University of Florida, 1981, 42:3829-A.

Analyzes the public jurisprudence of statutes, cases, and arbitration awards that determines grievance arbitration procedure in public education.

936. Murphy, John T. "An Examination and Analysis of Court Intervention into and Review of Academic Policies and Programs in the Student/University Relationship." State University of New York at Buffalo, 1980, 41:3449-A.

Through a content analysis of case data from local, state and federal, trial and appeals courts, investigates whether courts were intruding into academe--substituting their judgment for that of professional educators; and if so, the nature, type, extent, and whereabouts of such intrusion.

937. Puryear, Catherine W. "Policy Reform in Foster Care Administration: A Study of the Implementation of the 24-Month Court Review Law." New York University, 1977, 38:6310-A.

Studies the implementation of the court review law and its effect on the discharge of children from foster care in New York City. A measure of the effectiveness of the foster care system is its ability to return children to their families, or to place them in adoptive homes. Yet we find large numbers of children remaining in long-term foster care.

938. Roper, Robert T. "Measuring the Simulated Impact of Judicial Policy Making: The United States Supreme Court and the Jury's Operating Structure." University of Kentucky, 1978, 40:3513-A.

Tests the simulated impact of Supreme Court decisions which: allow for smaller than twelve-member juries and less than unanimous verdicts, and except as a last resort, prohibits the enforcement of Gag Orders. The primary objective is to evaluate how various operational structures affect the verdict's "correctness."

939. Rowland, Claude K. "Background and Environmental Effects on Federal District Court Policy Outputs." University of Houston, 1977, 38:7534-A.

Explores the relationship between federal district judges' backgrounds and their liberal or conservative policy propensities. The 21,142 federal district court opinions involving liberal/conservative questions issued from 1933-1972 serve as the data base.

940. Smith, Jordan M. "The Federal Courts and the Black Man in America, 1800-1883: A Study of Judicial Policy Making." The University of North Carolina at Chapel Hill, 1977, 39:430-A.

Our era's experience in the ongoing civil rights crusade has witnessed active judicial leadership from the outset. The purpose of the study is to provide insight into the origins of this special concern of the federal judiciary and to highlight the increasing determination on the judges' part to wrest the initiative from Congress in resolving the long and bitter controversy over the place of the black man in nineteenth-century American society.

941. Stefaniak, Gregory. "The Influence of the United States Courts of Appeals on Broadcast and Cable Regulation and Policy 1971-1980." Southern Illinois University at Carbondale, 1982, 42:1336-A.

Analyzes broadcast and cable regulations which were issued in each of the eleven U.S. Courts of Appeals.

942. Stephens, Ronald W. "A Study of U.S. Supreme Court Decisions from 1970 to 1977 as the Basis for Developing Policy for Censorship of Curriculum Materials by American Public Schools." The University of Nebraska-Lincoln, 1978, 39:5251-A.

This is a study of U.S. Supreme Court decisions from 1970 to 1977 as the basis for policy toward censorship of curriculum materials in American public schools. It is conducted as an historical study which seeks to embody principles of legal research in the study of an educational problem.

943. Stidham, Ronald. "An Exploration of Environmental Influences on Judicial Policy-Making by Federal District Judges." University of Houston, 1979, 40:5993-A.

The general assumption underlying this exploratory study is that federal district judges are influenced by the environment within which they operate. Both local and national environmental influences are explored.

944. Strope, John L. "The Impact of the United States Supreme Court on the Education Policies of the States with Particular Emphasis on *Goss v. Lopez* in Nebraska." The University of Nebraska-Lincoln, 1979, 40:1037-A.

Considers the impact *Goss v. Lopez* had on education policies in the United States and more particularly on the state of Nebraska.

945. Sullivan, Neil J. "Adjudication by Independent Agency: The Effects on Occupational Safety and Health Policy." Brandeis University, 1978, 38:7552-A.

The Occupational Safety and Health Act of 1970 established the Occupational Safety and Health Review Commission as an independent agency with adjudicative authority. The hypothesis of this project is that the establishment of a kind of administrative court for the purpose of promoting the due process guarantees of respondents would lead to an inefficient implementation of policy.

946. Wilkerson, Walter E. "The Implementation of School Board Policy to Legal Procedural Process." The University of Alabama, 1977, 38:63-A.

While most administrators and board members work with substantive
law, many courts find errors in the application of the law, i.e., the
processes designed to insure that procedural requirements are guaran-
teed. This paper develops processes which associate substantive requirements with procedural requirements.

947. Williams, Theodore R., Sr. "Educational Policy Implications (K-12)
of the U.S. Supreme Court Decision in the *Tinker v. Des Moines* Case." The
University of Iowa, 1978, 39:4651-A.

Investigates the influences on educational policy set in motion by
the U.S. Supreme Court decision in *Tinker v. Des Moines Independent
Community School District*, 393 U.S. 503 (1969). An effort is made
to analyze the scope of referent from the Supreme Court decision to
U.S. Circuit Court cases, to the state judiciary and to school policy.

Military Policy

948. Annesser, James W. "National Air Transportation System: Analysis of Defense Community Airlift Policy and Requirements." University of Miami, 1982, 42:1316-A.

National strategic airlift policy is examined in light of the increased importance of strategic military mobility and recent changes in the environment within which the Department of Defense and airline members of the Civil Reserve Air Fleet must operate.

949. Blanchard, Boyce W. "American Civil Defense 1945-1975: The Evolution of Programs and Policies." University of Virginia, 1980, 41:1746-A.

Traces the creation and evolution of American civil defense policy from 1945 to 1975.

950. Browning, Robert S., III. "Shielding the Republic: American Coastal Defense Policy in the Nineteenth Century." The University of Wisconsin-Madison, 1981, 42:1281-A.

American coastal defense policy is the least studied of all the major aspects of American military policy. Nevertheless, it was one of the consistent policies of the American military, and was a fundamental part of American military planning throughout the nineteenth century.

951. Clark, Asa A., IV. "U.S. Defense Policy-Making: Comparative Theories of Budgetary Politics." University of Denver, 1981, 42:1675-A.

Taking U.S. defense policy making as the dependent variable, the dissertation derives and empirically tests a variety of policy-making models within a budgetary framework in order to infer conclusions about the conceptual parameters of theories which best explain U.S. defense bdugeting.

952. Corbett, Patrick H. "Military Force Reductions and U.S. Policy in Europe." University of California, Santa Barbara, 1978, 39:7506-A.

Examines Mutual Force Reduction negotiations, concerning Central Europe, in the context of United States policy since World War II.

953. Doyle, Michael K. "The U.S. Navy: Strategy, Defense, and Foreign Policy, 1932-1941." University of Washington, 1977, 39:1058-A.

This study of the U.S. Navy's conception of strategy, defense, and foreign policy in the decade before Pearl Harbor is intended to cast new light on the inner workings of strategic planning and foreign policy in those crucial years.

954. Garrett, William B. "Arms Transfers, Congress, and Foreign Policy. The Case of Latin America, 1967-1976." The Johns Hopkins University, 1982, 42:1282-A.

Focuses on the conflict between the Congress and the executive branch for supremacy in the formulation of foreign policy for the U.S. Particular attention is centered on the effects this conflict had on U.S.-Latin American relations in view of the restrictions Congress developed and imposed on conventional arms transfers to Latin America.

955. Gormley, Daniel J. "From 'Arcadia' to Casablanca: The Formation of a Military-Political Policy: December 1941-January 1943." Georgetown University, 1978, 39:7482-A.

In the turmoil of those desperate days of Great Britain's lone struggle for survival, the seed of Anglo-American cooperation flourished. Comprehending the emergency aspects of the international situation, the United States-British leaders commenced formulating a combined strategic analysis.

956. Gray, Anthony W., Jr. "The Evolution of U.S. Naval Policy in Latin America." The American University, 1982, 42:1649-A.

Provides an understanding of the historical naval or maritime role in hemispheric defense by tracing the evolution of U.S. naval policy in Latin America through seven distinct although overlapping phases.

957. Hamilton, William A. "The Influence of the American Military upon United States Foreign Policy, 1965-1968." The University of Nebraska-Lincoln, 1978, 39:4422-A.

The failure of U.S. foreign policy in Southeast Asia was due, in large measure, to the ambiguity of U.S. policy aims and the inability or unwillingness of the Johnson Administration to formulate a clear-cut grand strategy capable of conversion into a coherent military strategy.

958. Hastedt, Glenn P. "The Impact of the Policy Making Process on Policy Outcomes: Military Unification in the United States, Canada, and Great Britain." Indiana University, 1979, 40:2249-A.

Attempts to determine the extent to which variations in policy outcomes may be attributed to the nature and workings of the policy-making process. The policy experiences of three similar systems are compared: the United States, Great Britain, and Canada.

959. Hughes, Peter C. "Essential Equivalence: The Objectives and Requirements of a Strategic Nuclear Policy: A Perspective on the Evolution

of U.S. Strategic Nuclear Policy, and an Assessment of Present and Emerging U.S. Strategic Policy and Force Structure Options." The Catholic University of America, 1979, 40:1672-A.

Provides a discussion of the origins and evolution of U.S. strategic nuclear policy, the objectives and requirements of U.S. nuclear forces, and an assessment of present and emerging U.S. strategic nuclear policy and force structure options.

960. Johnson, Robert G. "An Assessment of Perceptions of United States Army Provost Marshals Pertaining to Counterterrorism Policy and Programs on Army Installations." University of Georgia, 1981, 42:4578-A.

The study is based on a worldwide survey of U.S. Army provost marshals (senior military law enforcement officers) assessing their perceptions of: the numbers of past incidents of terrorism directed against Army installations; the availability and adequacy of intelligence concerning local terrorist activities; the degree of threat their local commands face from terrorists; the adequacy of measures of counterterrorism preparedness at their local commands; and the overall adequacy of protection currently provided likely terrorist targets within their areas of responsibility.

961. Nomura, Gail M. "The Allied Occupation of Japan: Reform of Japanese Government Labor Policy on Women." University of Hawaii, 1978, 39: 7475-A.

In the labor field the Allied Occupation acted as a catalyst which propelled a new labor policy on women which was based on the principle of women's equality with male workers. This study examines the formulation, implementation, and impact of the reform of government labor policy on women.

962. O'Brien, Larry D. "National Security and the New Warfare: Defense Policy, War Planning, and Nuclear Weapons, 1945-1950." The Ohio State University, 1981, 42:2263-A.

Not until 1948 was there any genuinely serious effort to analyze the relationship of foreign and defense policies. Even then there was no specific effort to analyze the usefulness of nuclear weapons for either deterrence or defense. Indeed, the administration deliberately avoided the issue.

963. Phillips, David W. "US National Security and Strategic Weapons: Measures for Policy Objective Evaluation and Force Effectiveness." University of Pittsburgh, 1979, 40:394-A.

Begins by asking the question why are additions to the U.S. strategic nuclear arsenal needed when both the U.S. and U.S.S.R. are capable of nuclear annihilation regardless of who strikes first. To answer this question, the study first looks to macro models of U.S.-Soviet interaction. Next, it looks at micro models dealing with U.S. weapons procurement.

964. Reynolds, Bradley M. "Guantanamo Bay, Cuba: The History of an American Naval Base and Its Relationship to the Formulation of United

States Foreign Policy and Military Strategy toward the Caribbean, 1895–
1910." University of Southern California, 1982, 42:1655-A.

The study of Guantanamo Bay's first decade under U.S. control is significant for delineating the relative importance of America's Caribbean policy to other foreign policy and domestic considerations, and
for evaluating the respective roles of military and civilian leaders
in determining United States actions abroad during the early twentieth century.

965. Sohlberg, Ragnhild. "Defense Manpower Policy Analysis: NATO Ground
Forces." The Rand Graduate Institute, 1980, 42:3302-A.

The dissertation: (1) investigates defense manpower policies in the
regular (peacetime) and reserve (mobilization) ground forces of seven
NATO countries; (2) explains possible differences in light of national
conditions; (3) develops a framework useful to individual nations for
assessing consequences of alternative manpower policies; and (4) uses
the Norwegian case for demonstrating the methodology.

966. Sorenson, David S. "A Multi-Method Analysis of Defense Policy-
Making: Military Construction Expenditures, 1963–1971." University of
Denver, 1977, 38:4360-A.

Examines and explains the size and change of military construction
expenditure practices over time. Three analytical models, the incremental model, the programmatic model and the political benefits
model are studied to explain the process.

967. Sorley, Lewis S., III. "Conventional Arms Transfers and the Nixon
Administration: A Policy Analysis." The Johns Hopkins University, 1979,
40:2875-A.

Analyzes the record of actual transfers of weapons and military equipment, including newly declassified materials, to determine the actual
scope, nature and direction of arms transfers, and compares the effects of these to the goals of the stated policy.

968. Stoffer, Howard. "Congressional Defense Policy-Making and the Arms
Control Community: The Case of the Anti-Ballistic Missile." Columbia
University, 1980, 41:1203-A.

Describes and analyzes the role of the nongovernmental arms control
community in the ABM debates and assesses how the participation of
the community in the ABM controversy may have contributed to producing a permanent change in Congressional defense policy-making procedures.

969. Waugh, William L., Jr. "International Terrorism: Theories of Response and National Policies." The University of Mississippi, 1980, 41:
3258-A.

The psychological impact of international terrorism's violence has not
only affected the perceptions of its purposes by popular audiences,
but has also affected the responses to its events by the governments
involved. This study focuses on the perspectives of the governments

most directly involved in the violent events and their selection of response policies.

970. Yost, David S. "Strategic Policy Implications of British Views on the Defense of Western Europe, 1945-1976." University of Southern California, 1976, 38:6302-A.

The focus of the study is on alternative policies applicable to deterrence and defense in Western Europe, and specifically, in the central European region. It begins by detailing the development of official British policy since 1945; this policy is virtually identical to that held by the North Atlantic Treaty Organization.

971. Yurechko, John J. "From Containment to Counteroffensive: Soviet Vulnerabilities and American Policy Planning, 1946-1953." University of California, Berkeley, 1980, 41:3687-A.

Analyzes aspects of American policy planning during the period 1946 to 1953 which aimed at weakening the power of the Soviet Union.

Social, Health, and
Welfare Policy

972. Adams, James P. "Federal and State Policies on Aging: Implementing Comprehensive Health Care and Support Services." University of Colorado at Boulder, 1981, 42:3734-A.

   Studies government policies on medical care, nursing homes and support of social services for older Americans generally and older Coloradoans specifically.

973. Allen, Joyce E. "An Analysis of the Food Stamp Program: Policy Decisions and Household Food Expenditure Patterns." University of Illinois at Urbana-Champaign, 1980, 40:741-A.

   Data from the second year of the 1972-73 Consumer Expenditure Survey were used to determine food expenditures of food stamp households and other low-income households eligible but not participating in the Food Stamp Program.

974. Andreassen, Eric D. "Judgmental Policy Analysis of the Educationally Handicapped Category." University of California, Riverside, 1980, 41:4646-A.

   Collects and analyzes the judgments of four groups of professionals who evaluated hypothetical case histories with respect to values placed upon cue variables, diagnosed levels of severity, and recommended placements. These judgments were analyzed to determine whether differences would be found among groups, where differences would be found, and whether the decision-making processes could be modelled.

975. Auten, Nancy L. "Systems Analysis of School Responsibility in Child Abuse and Neglect: Five Case Studies in Policy Formation and Implementation." The University of Nebraska-Lincoln, 1979, 40:3639-A.

   Analyzes the formation and implementation of existing school policies and procedures on child abuse and neglect in order to identify the components of existing policies and procedures and the processes by which they were formed.

976. Balasalle, Nicholas M. "A History of Public Policy for the Education of Handicapped Children in Massachusetts." Harvard University,

1980, 41:3982-A.

 Traces the historical development of public policy for the education
 of handicapped children in Massachusetts.

977. Bass, Gary D. "Socio-Psychological Perspectives on Social Policy
Implementation: Explorations of a Paradigm." The University of Michigan,
1980, 40:589-A.

 The specific objective is to develop a theoretically practicable model
 on the implementation process to help in the delivery of human services.

978. Beck, Rochelle. "The Child Care Policy Stalemate: An Analysis of
Federal Policies and an Examination of Options for the 1980's." Harvard
University, 1981, 42:2482-A.

 The stalemate is analyzed, with a series of recommendations presented
 to break it, including public clarification of national child care
 policies; collection and reporting of adequate data to address need
 and other policy questions; creation of political unity among outside
 interest groups and within government agencies; recognition of the
 necessary diversity of publicly supported child care services; and
 nurturance of political leadership.

979. Becker, Babette. "The Nursing Home Scoring System: Analysis of
Implementation of Policy to Appropriately Place Patients in Residential
Health Care Facilities." Adelphi University, 1980, 42:383-A.

 The purpose of this quantitative-descriptive study is to determine
 whether the implementation of a policy fulfilled its intents, by
 examining the effect of the DMS-1 scoring system used for assessment
 and placement of long-term care patients in residential health care
 facilities.

980. Berkeley, Terry R. "Children in Transition: The Effect of Policy
on Early Intervention Programs in the Commonwealth of Massachusetts."
Harvard University, 1981, 42:2605-A.

 An analysis of the policy which constitutes the foundations of the
 early intervention programs in Massachusetts is performed.

981. Blakslee, Sylvia F. "High School Diplomas for Educationally Handicapped Students: Information for Policymakers." George Peabody College
for Teachers, 1980, 42:652-A.

 Provides information to policy makers who are developing high school
 graduation requirements and diploma policies.

982. Borowski, Allan. "The Adequacy of Social Security Retirement Benefits in 1982: Policy Exploration through Microanalytic Computer Simulation." Brandeis University, 1980, 40:6443-A.

 Examines the adequacy of the retirement income provided under the Social Security legislation (i.e. the 1977 Amendments) for workers re-
 tiring between 1979 and 1982 without private pensions.

983. Borzilleri, Thomas C. "A Microsimulated Model of Retirement and Social Security Policy." University of Maryland, 1979, 41:1136-A.

This is a study of retirement and its impacts on the outlays of the social security system. A microsimulation model has been constructed to integrate a variety of research findings pertaining to the economics of aging.

984. Brown, Philip M. "From Back Wards to Boarding Homes: US Mental Health Policy since WWII." Brandeis University, 1979, 40:2903-A.

According to its proponents within the psychiatric establishment, deinstitutionalization in mental health policy has been motivated by a humanistic critique of custodialism, by the beneficial new technology of psychoactive drugs, and by deep concern for patients' rights. This dissertation explores those reasons to see if they are the actual ones, and explores the network of state hospitals, community mental health centers, and nursing homes to see if they are doing the promised job.

985. Browning, Robert X. "Political and Economic Predictors of Policy Outcomes: U.S. Social Welfare Expenditures, 1947-1977." The University of Wisconsin-Madison, 1981, 42:5230-A.

Addresses the problem of measuring policy and analyzing determinants of U.S. federal social welfare policy by testing hypotheses drawn from the American political institutions literature and from studies of social welfare policy.

986. Butler, Erik P. "Youth Employment in the United States: A Review of Problems, Programs and Policies." Harvard University, 1980, 41:3287-A.

While some progress may have been made in reducing inequities in American society, there remains substantial, even worsening, inequality in youth joblessness.

987. Byrd, Jackie L. "Design and Delivery of Human Services: A New Theory and Model with Proposed Policy Intervention Strategies." University of Minnesota, 1980, 41:2321-A.

The problem addressed by this study is: to provide persons involved in the design, management and delivery of human services with an understanding of the structure of human service systems.

988. Cain, Lillian P. "The Rehabilitation of Kidney Transplant Patients: Implications for Social Policy." Brandeis University, 1978, 39:3142-A.

The prolongation of life through kidney transplantation raises many social policy issues. The study raises three major research questions concerning the relationship between rehabilitation and occupational role, type of donor, and social welfare dependency.

989. Calavita, Kitty C. "A Sociological Analysis of U.S. Immigration Policy, 1820-1924." University of Delaware, 1980, 41:1223-A.

Examines U.S. immigration policy from 1820-1924 and relates it to conflicts and contradictions within the context of emerging American capitalism.

990.   Calmain, Kenneth E.   "The Relationship between Ideology and Social Policy."   University of Toronto (Canada), 1979, 40:6426-A.

The dissertation has its general rationale in the social work profession's value base and its knowledge base.   The principal claim is that certain overarching ideological factors are embodied in the knowledge base and that these weaken the profession's capacity to realize the intentions implicit in the value base.

991.   Cassetty, Judith H.   "Child Support and Public Policy."   The University of Wisconsin-Madison, 1977, 38:5714-A.

Eight years of data from a panel study, originally involving five thousand American families, and data from several state child support enforcement programs are analyzed for the purposes of: (1) designing and testing a predictive model for levels of child support payment; (2) making comparisons between current payment levels and absent fathers' ability-to-pay; and (3) getting an estimate for the marginal rate of return on the public investment in child support enforcement programs.

992.   Cole, Charles B.   "Social Technology, Social Policy and the Severely Disabled: Issues Posed by the Blind, the Deaf, and Those Unable to Walk." University of California, Berkeley, 1979, 41:3296-A.

Explores policies, programs and social technologies designed to help persons with severe physical disabilities attain increased levels of socioeconomic participation.

993.   Collins, Raymond C.   "Children and Society: Child Development and Public Policy."   Princeton University, 1981, 42:996-A.

Explores the role of science in the formulation of public policy for children.

994.   Coughlin, Richard M.   "Ideology and Social Policy: A Comparative Study of the Structure of Public Opinion in Eight Rich Nations."   University of California, Berkeley, 1977, 38:5078-A.

Examines the structure of public opinion on a range of issues central to welfare-state development in eight rich nations, and conducts exploratory tests of "convergence" theory.

995.   Davis, Deborah.   "The Delivery of Child Development Services in California: A Case Study in the Politics of Policy Change."   Claremont Graduate School, 1979, 40:1855-A.

Describes some policy issues and points of decision making in the reorganization of child development services in the state of California. First is described and organized some of the information available and some definitions relevant to the policy-making process posited.   Then the available data is applied to a model for policy analysis which could be useful for child development advocates confronting the political system.

996. Dennison, Laura B. "The Policy and Politics of Juvenile Diversion
and Delinquency Prevention." Claremont Graduate School, 1979, 39:6935-A.

Studies some policy and political problems of juvenile diversion, and
deals with some juvenile diversion projects in Southern California,
based on the published literature, personal observation and many interviews.

997. Duncan, Carolyn W. "Center Based Child Care: A Descriptive Analysis of Policies for the Soviet Kindergarten and New Jersey Title XX Funded
Programs." Rutgers University, 1981, 42:129-A.

Provides a descriptive analysis of policy for the Soviet Kindergarten
and the Title XX funded centers in New Jersey. Analyzes policies
governing purpose of service, funding, eligibility, and program implementation.

998. Eisler, Susan L. "Community-Based Services for the Developmentally
Disabled: A Study of Public Policy Innovation." New York University,
1981, 42:3295-A.

Examines, within the context of current organizational theory, the
processes and variables involved in implementing the community-based
services approach to service delivery. The study reviews theoretical
constructs and research findings and identifies a number of factors
considered to influence implementation.

999. Emling, Diane. "Aging: Long-Term Care and the Fiscal State. A
Sociological Study of the Public Policy Process." Michigan State University, 1981, 42:2888-A.

Using a case study of long-term care of the elderly in Michigan, the
dissertation examines the explanatory power of theories of political
economy in accounting for events in the public sector.

1000. Enochs, David H. "The Development and Implementation of Federal
Policy Concerning Health Maintenance Organizations." North Texas State
University, 1980, 41:3244-A.

The major question is whether or not the HMO policy of the federal
government has been a success. The primary focus is upon the development and evolution of the federal HMO program.

1001. Entwisle, Barbara D. "Education, Pension Programs, and Fertility:
A Cross-National Investigation, with Special Reference to the Potential
Held by Education and Pension Programs as Fertility Reduction Policies."
Brown University, 1980, 41:5252-A.

Uses least-squares procedures to assess the impact of education and
pension programs upon levels of, and rates of change in fertility in
120 nations from around the world.

1002. Fournier-Negroni, Yvonne. "A Framework for Policy Analysis: An
Application to Mainstreaming Handicapped Children." Memphis State University, 1978, 39:1411-A.

Attempts to propose a framework for policy analysis, its deductive
component providing for analysis of the language by which the policy
will be communicated to its potential implementors.

1003.   Francis, Ethanie. "The History of Social Welfare and Foreign Labor
in the United States Virgin Islands: A Policy Analysis." Columbia University, 1979, 40:2897-A.

Examines the foreign-worker crisis in the United States Virgin Islands
during the twenty-year period from its inception to 1976. The role of
social workers in policy formulation is discussed in terms of the development and role of the Virgin Islands Department of Social Welfare,
specifically this agency's response to the needs of the foreign workers and to the community in general.

1004.   Goggin, Malcolm L. "Implementing Public Policy: Outputs--Process--
Outcomes Linkages and the Politics of Health and Welfare." Stanford University, 1981, 42:3748-A.

The conventional wisdom is that policy implementation is bound to
fail, regardless of the circumstances. This dissertation demonstrates
that there is considerable variation in the way policy is implemented,
from a process which is primarily political to one which is mainly
administrative.

1005.   Grant, Jane A. "National Policy, Citizen Participation, and Health
System Reform: The Case of Three Health Systems Agencies in the San Francisco Bay Area." University of California, Berkeley, 1981, 42:5269-A.

Examines the organizational, political, and structural consequences
of implementing a national health planning program in three San Francisco Bay Area communities during the years 1976-1980, the National
Health Planning and Resources Development Act of 1974.

1006.   Hamilton, Kenneth L. "An Application of Socioeconomic Accounting
to Analysis of Nursing Home Regulatory Policy." Georgia Institute of
Technology, 1979, 40:5946-A.

A conceptual framework for the analysis of complex issues in health
care is developed in the context of socioeconomic accounting. The
approach is then applied to an empirical analysis of a specific nursing home regulatory problem in the state of Georgia.

1007.   Harris, Charles M. "Justice and Value in Health Policy." University of Missouri-Columbia, 1980, 41:4738-A.

Leading theories of justice and dominant values present in recent
health legislation are articulated and clarified. Methods are developed for identifying theories of justice and leading values in
health legislation to determine the coherence of health policy.

1008.   Hartson, Richard M. "An Exploratory and Descriptive Study of the
Implementation of Air Force Policy Regarding Child Abuse/Neglect." University of Utah, 1978, 39:2549-A.

The purpose of the study is twofold: (1) to describe to what extent the Child Advocacy Program as defined in USAF Regulation 160-38 is being implemented at USAF bases throughout the continental U.S.; and (2) to describe what factors may be associated with the differential implementation of the Child Advocacy Program at these USAF bases.

1009. Heimovics, Catherine A. "Impact of Values on Social Policy: A Reexamination of the Economic Opportunity Program." University of Missouri-Kansas City, 1977, 38:6928-A.

The study is concerned with the programs funded under the Economic Opportunity Act of 1964, and focuses on the reasons for the failure of the poverty program to achieve stated goals.

1010. Ingraham, Patricia W. "Patterns of Social Welfare Policies in Western Societies." State University of New York at Binghamton, 1979, 40:2881-A.

Utilizes a comprehensive model of the policy process which is posited to be applicable across time, across nations, and across social welfare programs. Within the model, the impacts of socioeconomic development, social change, conventional and unconventional participation, and national bureaucratic institutions are considered.

1011. Jackson, Susan J. "Definitional Flux: Ambiguity, Uncertainty and Inconsistency in Programs and Policy for the Developmentally Disabled." University of California, San Francisco, 1980, 41:3747-A.

Sensitized by the grounded theory methodology this study is a qualitative field evaluation of the implementation of the California program for the developmentally disabled derived from the federal Developmentally Disabled Assistance and Bill of Rights Act of 1975 (P.L. 94-103) and the complementary California Lanterman Amendments of 1976.

1012. Jacobowitz, Steven. "Determinants of Variation in Infant Mortality Rates among Counties of the United States: The Roles of Social Policies and Programs." City University of New York, 1981, 42:1247-A.

From 1964 to 1977, the infant mortality rate in the U.S. declined at an anually compounded rate of 4.4 percent per year. This was an extremely rapid rate of decline compared to the figure of 0.6 percent per year from 1955 to 1964. The purpose of this dissertation is to shed light on the causes of the reduction for the period between 1964 and 1977.

1013. Jacobs, Claude F. "Strategies of Neighborhood Health-Care among New Orleans Blacks: From Voluntary Association to Public Policy." Tulane University, 1980, 41:4757-A.

An analysis of the health status of blacks and their health-care behavior can provide significant information for the social scientist and can assist those who are involved in making improvements in systems of health-care delivery.

1014. Jeffe, Sherry B. "Citizen Participation in Health Care Policy and Administration: The Case of HSA/LA." Claremont Graduate School,

1980, 41:3715-A.

A survey of the leadership and of selected members of the Health Systems Agency for Los Angeles County (HSA/LA) was conducted to evaluate attitudes toward and effectiveness of citizen participation in health care policy and administration. The purpose is to determine who participates and whether the mandate of P.L. 93-641 to achieve citizen participation in health care planning was achieved within HSA/LA.

1015.   Jones, Charlie A.   "An Analysis of the Effects of Policy Resources, Economic, and Political Conditions on the Implementation of the Comprehensive Employment and Training Act of 1973."   The Ohio State University, 1979, 40:4210-A.

Looks at the impact of CETA implementing agencies' policy resources and selected economic and political environmental variables of implementing jurisdictions on the local implementation of Title I of the Comprehensive Employment and Training Act (CETA) of 1973.

1016.   Karls, James M.   "Community Mental Health Care of the Elderly: A Study of Policy Making and Implementation."   University of Southern California, 1978, 38:7564-A.

Explores factors that might shed light on the question as to why elders were generally underserved in the community mental health system.   Seeks to determine if certain characteristics of those who develop policy and implement community mental health services might be related to the rate of service delivered to the aged.

1017.   Katz, Arnold.   "The One Parent Male Headed Family: Exploration of Changing Family Policy."   University of California, Berkeley, 1980, 42: 386-A.

This descriptive, exploratory investigation examines some of the life experiences of 409 single male parents and their children.

1018.   Kincaid, Steven R.   "The Dynamics of American Welfare Policy: Testing Models of Growth for Aid to Families with Dependent Children."   University of Illinois at Urbana-Champaign, 1980, 41:4824-A.

Examines the causes of growth in the Aid to Families with Dependent Children program over the years 1946 through 1977 in Illinois.

1019.   Kinsinger, Billie A.   "A Study of Policies, Procedures and Forms for Child Abuse Referral and Follow-Up in Selected California and Kern County School Districts."   Brigham Young University, 1981, 42:2407-A.

The purpose of the study is to determine the status of policy adoption procedures and forms for referral and follow-up of child abuse in selected California and Kern County school districts.   The purpose then was to recommend necessary components for policies, procedures and forms.

1020.   Kirchheimer, Donna W.   "Implementation of Federal Social Policy." Columbia University, 1979, 40:5574-A.

A model of implementation of federal social policy is formulated from research by the Oakland Project. Three initial conditions and twelve implementation factors are tested for their contribution to policy achievement in three federal social policy areas, preventive health care, nutrition, and due process rights in public benefits.

1021. Krushelnicki, Bruce W. "Planning for Human Development: An Application of the Concept of the Life Cycle to Planning and Policy-Making." University of Waterloo (Canada), 1980, 41:1248-A.

Extends the application of the life cycle to the arena of public policy and the evaluation by means of social indicators of the performance of various social institutions.

1022. Levy, Baruch. "A Comparative Study of Attempts to Formulate Social Policy at the National Level in the USA, United Kingdom and Israel." Brandeis University, 1980, 41:2296-A.

Examines the extent to which new organizational mechanisms designed to bring coherence to the policy-making process and coordination in domestic and social programs have fulfilled their own missions and what factors have accounted for the degree of success and influence achieved.

1023. Lo, Joan. "The Labor Supply of the Elderly--Its Reaction to the Earnings Test and Compulsory Retirement Policy." State University of New York at Albany, 1980, 40:751-A.

Focuses on the labor supply of the elderly and its reaction to compulsory retirement and the earnings test of eligibility for Social Security benefits.

1024. Louis, Debbie. "Public Policy and the American Family." Rutgers University, 1980, 41:4153-A.

Reviews major public policy influences on the internal and social dynamics of the family unit in the U.S. in order to consider these from an historical and integrated perspective.

1025. McCarthy, Patrick T. "Child Welfare Workers and the Dilemma of Adolescent Noncriminal Behavioral Problems: Practice Decisions as Public Policy." Bryn Mawr College, 1981, 42:4152-A.

This exploratory case study of the decision-making process in a child welfare agency attempts to identify the consequences of a recent Pennsylvania law which transfers responsibility for status offenders from the juvenile justice system to the child welfare system.

1026. McCawley, William J. "An Exploratory Study of the Acceptance of Current Federal Health Care Policy by Hospital Administrators, Trustees, and Physicians." Adelphi University, 1980, 41:2769-A.

The research assumes that hospitals' acceptance of P.L. 93-641 goals can be determined by surveying the opinions of hospital trustees, administrators, and physicians of the thirty-three hospitals in the Health Systems Agency of Northeastern Pennsylvania.

1027. Madson, Patricia O. "Social Equality and Public Policy: Conceptual and Evaluative Problems." Colorado State University, 1977, 38:6351-A.

   Analyzes the concept of equality, particularly as it may be used in the formulation and evaluation of public policy. Two dimensions of equality are identified: equality of opportunity and equality of outcome. The juxtaposition of these dimensions results in four conceptions of equality.

1028. Malson, Michelene R. "Child Care Decision Making: Families, Child-rearing Support Networks and Social Policy." Harvard University, 1979, 40:6438-A.

   Looks at fifteen families and how their decisions about child care are influenced by: (1) supply variables; (2) demand variables; and (3) the presence and utilization of social networks.

1029. Martin, Frances E. "The Impact of Child Care Policy: An Evaluation and Analysis of Madison, Wisconsin." The University of Oklahoma, 1977, 38:5685-A.

   The study is concerned with the effectiveness of national, state and local government policy in meeting the substitute child care needs of working parents in the U.S.

1030. Mattingly, John B. "The Management of Change: Juvenile Justice and Social Policy Innovations." The Pennsylvania State University, 1979, 40:496-A.

   The dissertation is an effort to go beyond most recent studies of social policy implementation, to analyze in more detail why many social programs fail to achieve their stated objectives and to point out policy issues often unrecognized in current critiques of governmental action.

1031. Meyering, Mary V. "Political Structure Centralization and Social Policy: A Cross-National Study." Michigan State University, 1979, 40:6407-A.

   Tests hypotheses concerning the impact of political and economic variables on social policy, and investigates the role of political structure centralization and economic development in affecting health, education and social welfare policies.

1032. Mokwa, Michael P. "Strategic Marketing Evaluation for the Social Action Organization: A Formulative Policy Study." University of Houston, 1979, 40:5161-A.

   Focuses on the operational formulation of an evaluative policy framework for facilitating the development and adoption of strategic marketing in social action organizations.

1033. Murillo, Louis C. "The Detroit Mexican *Colonia* from 1920 to 1932: Implications for Social and Educational Policy." Michigan State University, 1981, 42:3546-A.

Focuses on the development of the Mexican *colonia* in Detroit and the primary influences of its growth during the decade of the 1920's. Also outlines its dramatic decline in the 1930's as a result of the depression and particularly in response to the Mexican Repatriation Campaign of 1932.

1034. Murphy, Karen E. "Overcoming Resistance of Local Mental Health Administrators to Compliance with State Community Mental Health Policy: The Case of Rhode Island, 1963-1973." University of Southern California, 1977, 38:6309-A.

Investigates a problem associated with the decentralization of mental health service delivery systems in Rhode Island, and examines the difficulties of permitting local program autonomy and ensuring compliance with state mental health policy.

1035. Odynocki, Boris. "Planning the National Health Insurance Policy: An Application of the Analytic Hierarchy Process in Health Policy Evaluation and Planning." University of Pennsylvania, 1979, 41:1249-A.

Attempts to establish which of the three national health insurance proposals is more likely to improve the health care system, and which proposal is likely to emerge as the adopted NHI policy.

1036. Oppermann, Theo A. "California's Child Health Disability Prevention Program: A Public Policy Implementation Study." Stanford University, 1980, 41:2462-A.

The study is a policy analysis of a relatively obscure child health program, the Child Health and Disability Prevention Program.

1037. Peroff, Kathleen A. "A Time-Series Analysis of Health and Social Welfare Expenditure Policy in Canada, the United Kingdom and the United States." The University of Wisconsin-Madison, 1977, 38:5689-A.

Presents and tests hypotheses about the determinants and behavioral properties of health and social welfare expenditure policy over the last fifty years in three modern, industrialized states: Canada, the United Kingdom and the U.S. The purpose is to contribute to the refinement of a theory of public expenditure, and to a theory of the welfare state.

1038. Pierce, Avery D. "Adoption Policy and the 'Unwed Father': An Exploratory Study of Social Worker Response to Changing Conceptions of Fatherhood." University of California, Berkeley, 1980, 42:387-A.

Explores the implications for adoption policy and practice growing out of the 1972 United States Supreme Court decision in *Stanley v. Illinois*. This decision granted to the unwed father certain rights in adoption/custody proceedings involving his child(ren).

1039. Porter, Donna V. "Nutrition Policy Making in the United States Congress." The Ohio State University, 1980, 41:1764-A.

Examines the effect of the organizational structure and process of decision making on nutrition legislation in the U.S. Senate.

1040. Price, Stephen C. "The Effect of Federal Anti-Poverty Programs and Policies on the Hasidic and Puerto Rican Communities of Williamsburg." Brandeis University, 1979, 40:2299-A.

Examines two communities, the Hasidic Jews and Puerto Ricans of the Williamsburg section of Brooklyn, with regard to their perception and use of federal anti-poverty programs. Explores how the political culture of each group conditioned its behavior and how, in turn, its political culture changed as the result of participation in the programs.

1041. Pyle, Kathryn S. "Institutional Peonage: A Study in Mental Health Policy." University of Pennsylvania, 1978, 40:1687-A.

Describes the policies adopted as a result of a 1973 class action which was brought in Pennsylvania on behalf of five thousand patient workers at state mental hospitals.

1042. Raiford, Gilbert L. "Community Mental Health Policy and the Training of Mental Health Professionals: A Study of Training Needs as Reflected by Funded Applications to the National Institute of Mental Health." Brandeis University, 1981, 42:388-A.

Explores the extent to which educational institutions proposing to train personnel in five disciplines actually related to community mental health policy guidelines in their applications for federal funding.

1043. Rein, Mildred. "Dilemmas of Welfare Policy: Work Strategies in AFDC." Brandeis University, 1982, 42:1713-A.

Documents and examines the rise in welfare (AFDC) costs and caseloads in the late 1960's and 1970's and the theories that were advanced to explain the rise. Looks then at government policies to contain the AFDC program's expansion--specifically in the area of work for AFDC family heads.

1044. Rhodes, Terrel L. "Bury My Heart on the Lone Freeway: An Evaluation of Federal Employment Assistance Policy toward Urban Native Americans." The University of North Carolina at Chapel Hill, 1980, 41:1754-A.

The one area in which the federal government has had a formulated policy and an established program directed toward urban Indians is in the area of employment assistance. The immediate focus is on the federal CETA program for Indians.

1045. Robinson, Gail K. "Models for Change: Community Mental Health Centers and State Policy." Brandeis University, 1979, 40:825-A.

The objectives of this evaluation of the CMHC program are to develop an index with which to measure the integration of CMHC's into a state's deinstitutionalization process and determine if a state's stance on integration is influenced by its previous commitment to community mental health or its natural ability to support this program.

1046. Rosenberry, Sara A. "The Role of Ideology in Policy Development:
A Comparison of British and American Old Age Income Security Efforts."
Rutgers University, 1980, 41:4196-A.

   Consists of a comparison of the organization and financing of and
   the coverage and benefits provided by the programs currently used in
   Britain and the U.S. to provide old age income security, and a comparative analysis of the development of those programs.

1047. Rounds, James H. "Social Theory, Public Policy and Social Order."
University of California, Los Angeles, 1979, 40:3390-A.

   In this thesis policy responses to the "problem of crime" are treated
   as a cultural construct through analysis of the developmemt of the
   American prison system during the nineteenth century.

1048. Roysher, Martin K. "Policy and Bureaucracy: The Case of Children's
Health." University of California, Berkeley, 1977, 39:1145-A.

   This is a case study of politics, policy, and bureaucracy in children's health, focusing on the context and operation of school health
   and the Federal Early and Periodic Screening, Diagnosis and Treatment
   (EPSDT) programs in the state of Massachusetts.

1049. Scanlon, William J. "The Market for Nursing Home Care: A Case of
an Equilibrium with Excess Demand as a Result of Public Policy." The
University of Wisconsin-Madison, 1980, 41:4451-A.

   Investigates the role of government in the market for nursing home
   care and estimates its impact on utilization by private pay and Medi-
   caid residents and changes in the supply of beds.

1050. Seck, Essie T. "Political Decision Making on Full Employment Policy: Implications for Social Work Political Intervention." University of
Southern California, 1981, 42:3760-A.

   Develops a theoretical model of influences on decision and explores
   the validity of the model by applying it to a case example--the political decision-making process on the Humphrey-Hawkins Act.

1051. Sedgwick, Jeffrey L. "Welfare Economics and Criminal Justice
Policy." University of Virginia, 1978, 40:1070-A.

   It is the argument of the dissertation that to the extent public officials responsible for law enforcement planning have relied on a sociological understanding of criminology, they have been less successful
   in dealing with crime and law enforcement than they would have been
   if they utilized a welfare economic approach.

1052. Sellitti, Steven L. "A Study of Program Evaluation Procedures and
Policies of Handicapped Programs and Services in California Community Colleges." United States International University, 1982, 42:4678-A.

   There are currently 104 California community colleges providing programs and services for the disabled. Studies program evaluation procedures and policies for handicapped programs and services in the
   California community colleges.

1053. Silverman, Marsha A. "Factors Associated with Effective Implementation of Policy Goals of the Community Mental Health Centers Act of 1963." Northern Illinois University, 1978, 39:7515-A.

   Ascertains the extent to which the federal Community Mental Health Centers Act has been implemented and determines factors associated with effective implementation.

1054. Skelley, Ben D. "Implementing Federal Health Manpower Distribution Policy: The Performance of the National Health Service Corps Program." University of Georgia, 1980, 41:2763-A.

   The dissertation is a case study of the implementation of the National Health Service Corps program.

1055. Smith, Barbara J. "Policies and Procedures for the Implementation of the Education for All Handicapped Children Act of 1975 within the North Carolina Division of Youth Services Schools." The University of North Carolina at Chapel Hill, 1978, 39:6703-A.

   Attempts to document the incidence of handicapping conditions in a sample of children residing in the North Carolina Division of Youth Services institutions and to propose administrative policies to govern the development of special education services which would comply with those that are now federally mandated.

1056. Soroka, Mordachai B. "Optometric and Ophthalmological Care for the Elderly under Medicare: Implications for National Health Policy." New York University, 1979, 40:6005-A.

   The main thrust of the study is an investigation of Medicare reimbursement policies on the use and the cost of eye care services.

1057. Spector, Alan J. "The Deinstitutionalization of Child Welfare Services in Illinois: Social Change and Policy Change." Northwestern University, 1980, 41:4188-A.

   Examines the development and implementation of the deinstitutionalization policy as an expression both of local idiosyncratic factors and of broader social, economic, political, and cultural forces.

1058. Stenzel, Merry. "Deinstitutionalization: A Policy in Pursuit of a Program." University of Pittsburgh, 1979, 40:5182-A.

   Examines the policy of deinstitutionalization in Pennsylvania's Mental Health System. The central question addressed is the feasibility of this policy.

1059. Stoner, Madeleine R. "Public Policy Implementation through the Promulgation of Administrative Regulations: A Case Study of the Regulations for the Health Maintenance Organization Act of 1973 (Public Law 93-222)." Bryn Mawr College, 1979, 40:6010-A.

   Addresses itself to the matter of social policy implementation in the U.S. through the process of promulgating federal regulations for legislation and tests a conceptual framework for social policy implementation.

1060. Striar, Sharna L. "Relating Staff Attitudes to the Development of a Comprehensive Sexual Policy for the Institutionalized Residents with Mental Retardation." The University of Michigan, 1981, 42:2585-A.

Examines, through the use of a survey, staff attitudes and opinions toward the sexual behavior of persons with mental retardation.

1061. Styles, Gwenelle M. "Leadership Orientation and Policy Implementation in Community Mental Health Centers." Columbia University, 1981, 42:3761-A.

The question addressed is whether the leadership orientation of community mental health center executive directors affects the implementation of community mental health policy.

1062. Tenhula, John D. "United States Refugee Resettlement Policy as Seen in the Indochinese Refugee Movement." Columbia University, 1981, 42:4135-A.

For the U.S., refugee admissions are a part of its immigration experience. The recent and large influx of admissions—especially people from non-white, non-Western backgrounds—poses serious policy concerns for their integration as well as for the local communities in which they choose to live.

1063. Thompson, Joel A. "Workmen's Compensation and Public Policy in the American States." University of Kentucky, 1979, 40:792-A.

Assesses the relative influence of socioeconomic factors (primarily economic structure) and political factors (primarily the involvement of organized interests) on state compliance with the recommendations of the National Commission on State Workmen's Compensation Laws.

1064. Ueber, Mary S. "The Health Policy Process, If You Want to Win, You Have to Play the Game." The Johns Hopkins University, 1977, 38: 7537-A.

Analyzes the ecology of health policy making and resource allocation at the national level, and addresses two gaps in health policy and planning: (1) the lack of a theoretical framework for the analysis of health resource allocation at the national level; and (2) the lack of past and present political support for technically optimal health programs as advocated by health professionals and technicians.

1065. Underhill, Patricia A. "Policy Implications of a Comparison between the Predictors of a Life Satisfaction Model and a Problem Indicator Model for Service Delivery to Persons 63 Years of Age and Older in Independent Living Situations." University of Colorado at Boulder, 1981, 42: 1803-A.

Creates a recursive causal-analytical model of the major predictors of life satisfaction culled from life satisfaction studies made over the past thirty years, and expands the traditional theoretical frameworks that have used life satisfaction as a dependent variable to a causal model in which the more transitory sociophysical needs or problems of older persons become the dependent variable with life satisfaction as an intervening, independent variable.

1066. Williams, Carol W. "Guardianship: A Minimally Used Resource for California's Dependent Children: A Study in Policy: 1850-1978." University of Southern California, 1980, 41:1779-A.

Documents developments in California's public policy governing guardianship of the person of children between 1850-1978 in the context of a changing social environment which affects dependent children.

1067. Williams, Peyton, Jr. "A Survey of Admission Policies and Practices of State Operated Residential Schools for the Deaf in the United States." Georgia State University, 1982, 42:623-A.

Investigates the influence of governance, admission policy, admission procedures, denied-admission procedures, the individualized education plan and the placement of deaf students in state-operated residential schools for the deaf in the U.S.

1068. Wilson, Beclee N. "The Role of Symbols in Forming the Public Policy of the War on Poverty." University of Minnesota, 1979, 40:3517-A.

The study is concerned with the sources of persuasive energy within language symbols. The focus is upon the power of symbols to create and direct human cooperative action, most specifically, political action.

1069. Wintfeld, Neil S. "Aid to Families with Dependent Children: Politics and Welfare Policymaking." The University of Rochester, 1981, 42: 3751-A.

The question underlying this research is how the character of state decision making—politics—affects the characteristics of public welfare policy in the states. The issue is explored through consideration of the largest public assistance program—Aid to Families with Dependent Children.

1070. Wolfson, Elaine M. "The President and the Poor: The Interface of Fiscal and Social Policy-Making during the Johnson Presidency." New York University, 1977, 38:6298-A.

Examines Johnson's "active force" position (with secondary references to the other post-World War II presidential administrations) using as its focus the interface of general economic policy and poverty policy formulation.

1071. Zebich, Michele L. "The Politics of Nutrition: Issue Definition, Agenda-Setting, and Policy Formulation in the United States." The University of New Mexico, 1979, 40:4735-A.

Examines the determinants of policy change in the area of nutrition. The purpose is to explain the change from a selective, or low-income orientation, to a comprehensive orientation in nutrition policy.

Author Index

Subject Index

Capital formation:
  and tax policy, 424
Capital policy, 378
  expansion, of a monopoly, 382
  optimal, of a regulated firm,
    391
  structure, and corporate
    strategy, 334
Capitalism:
  black, 385
  plantation, 226
Caribbean Common Market, 344
Casino credit policy, 729
Child abuse and neglect:
  Air Force policy regarding, 1008
  policies, procedures and forms
    for, 1019
  school responsibility in, 975
Child care policy, 1028
  impact of, 1029
  national, 978, 997
Child development policy, 993, 995
Child support, 991
City councils:
  policy activity in, 75
  and public policy, 77
City manager, role of, 95, 119
Civil Aeronautics Board, perform-
    ance analysis of, 937
Civil Rights, Office for, 284
Civil rights policy, and income
    equality, 269
Climate analysis, 108
Coalition(s):
  congressional, 151, 183
  governments, European, 12
  policy: legislative, 181
    international, formation of,
      906
Coleman Report, 559
Collective bargaining:
  of public employees, 117
  and university workload policies,
    468
Columbia Basin Irrigation Project,
    207
Committees:
  congressional, policy role
    orientations of, 191
  school: decision making in, 494
    in policy making, 505
Commodity policy, 614
  and the farm firm, 244
Communication:
  broadcasting, and U.S. Courts of
    Appeals, 941

Communication:
  mass, in foreign policy, 636
  social, and the mass policy
    agenda, 163
  urban, and public policy imple-
    mentation, 107
Confidentiality, and social
    science research, 16
Conglomerates, 142
Congress, U.S.:
  campaign expenditures of, and
    voting behavior, 150
  the conservative coalition in,
    183
  and critical realignment effects,
    172
  foreign policy behavior of, 145
  and legislative policy coali-
    tions, 181
  and the National Commission on
    Water Quality, 814
  and natural gas policy, 842
  and the Northeast-Midwest coali-
    tion, 151
  oversight and impoundment policy,
    166
  patterns of change in, 172
  policy making of, 30
    for arms transfers, 862
    for nutrition policy, 1039
  response of, to special revenue
    sharing, 149
  Senate voting alignments in, 186
Congressional Budget Act of 1974,
    373
Conservation:
  energy, 780, 789, 819
  soil, 234
Conservation policy:
  energy, 780, 789
  and gasoline consumption, 805
Consumer protection policy:
  consumer rights, 369
  implementation of, 431
Consumerism, student, 11
Consumption policy, 319
Cost control policy, 797
Court review law, implementation
    of, 937
Courts, federal district:
  outputs of, 939
  policy making of, 943
Crime control policy, 143
Criminal justice:
  Criminal Justice Act of 1964,
    275

About the Compiler

JOHN S. ROBEY is Associate Professor of Political Science at the University of Texas and has contributed articles to journals such as *Social Science Quarterly, PS,* and the *Policy Studies Journal.*